PHILOSOPHERS AND THE JEWISH BIBLE

PHILOSOPHERS
AND
THE JEWISH BIBLE

edited by
Charles H. Manekin
and
Robert Eisen

University Press of Maryland
Bethesda, Maryland
2008

LIBRARY OF CONGRESS CATALOGING-IN-PUBLICATION DATA

Philosophers and the Jewish Bible / edited by Charles H. Manekin and Robert Eisen.
   p. cm. -- (Studies and texts in Jewish history and culture ; no. 17)
   ISBN 978-1-934309-20-9
   1. Bible. O.T.--Philosophy. 2. Bible. O.T.--Criticism, interpretation, etc. 3. Philosophy,
   Jewish. 4. Jewish philosophers. I. Manekin, Charles Harry, 1953- II. Eisen, Robert,
   1960-
   BS645.P56 2008
   221.601—dc22   2008033429

Cover Art: Govert Blinck, 1638: Isaac Blessing Jacob (housed in the Rijksmuseum,
      Amsterdam)

ISBN 978-1934309-209

STUDIES AND TEXTS
IN
JEWISH HISTORY AND CULTURE

The Joseph and Rebecca Meyerhoff Center
for Jewish Studies
University of Maryland

XVII

General Editor: Bernard D. Cooperman

UNIVERSITY PRESS OF MARYLAND

CONTENTS

ACKNOWLEDGMENTS

WE WOULD LIKE to thank the Joseph and Rebecca Meyerhoff Center for Jewish Studies at the University of Maryland for underwriting the publication of this volume, as well as sponsoring one of the conferences in which earlier versions of its chapters were presented. The other conference was organized by Professor Menachem Kellner and sponsored by the Sir Isaac and Lady Wolfson Chair of the University of Haifa. We are greatly in Professor Kellner's debt.

We also would like to acknowledge the Publication Committee of the Studies and Text in Jewish History and Culture, which accepted this volume into its series, and our colleague, Bernard D. Cooperman, who serves as its general editor. We are especially grateful to Michele Alperin, who labored long and hard on copyediting the book.

INTRODUCTION

THE PRESENT VOLUME consists mostly of essays based on presentations given at two conferences held in the fall of 2003, one at the University of Maryland at College Park and the other at the University of Haifa in Israel, focusing on the theme of philosophers and the Hebrew Bible. Since the advent of Jewish studies as an academic discipline two centuries ago, the fields of Jewish philosophy and biblical exegesis have been mostly separate from each other, in line with the rigid categorization of fields already in place in nineteenth-century European universities when Jewish Studies began to develop.

In recent years, the view in Jewish scholarship that philosophy and biblical interpretation are separate areas has begun to change. Scholars in the field of Jewish philosophy have increasingly recognized that Jewish philosophy has always been intertwined with biblical interpretation and that an awareness of that relationship is essential to a full understanding of Jewish philosophy. The first Jewish philosopher, Philo, expressed his philosophical views through the medium of exegesis. In the medieval period, particularly after Maimonides, Jewish philosophers including Saadia Gaon, Samuel ibn Tibbon, Gersonides, Joseph ibn Kaspi, and Isaac 'Arama produced a large body of commentaries on various parts of the Bible. Moreover, one finds a great deal of biblical exegesis even in the systematic treatises of medieval Jewish philosophers. Thus, Maimonides explicitly introduces his *Guide of the Perplexed* as an exegetical work concerned with anthropomorphisms and philosophical parables found in the biblical text. In such works as Saadia's *Book of Beliefs and Opinions* and Gersonides' *Wars of the Lord*, interpretations of the biblical text are frequently interspersed with philosophical argumentation.

In the modern period, interest in the Bible among Jewish philosophers has continued. In his *Theological-Political Treatise*, Spinoza subjects medieval Jewish philosophers like Maimonides to withering criticism for, among other things, their philosophical readings of the biblical text. Yet, in the final analysis, Spinoza was himself a philosopher grappling with the biblical text, if only to replace the antiquated philosophical method of the medievals with his own innovative approach. Moreover, much of the Jewish philosophy that comes after Spinoza responds to his many challenges—including his views of the Bible and its philosophical value—and thus modern Jewish philosophers, though chastened by Spinoza's diatribes, continued to engage in philosophical exegesis. Of course, the terms of the enterprise had changed, becoming far more complicated. First, account had to be taken of the biblical scholarship pioneered by Spinoza that challenged the whole notion that the Bible was a revealed text. Second, philosophy itself had accepted new models of the relationship between scripture and science. Modern philosophers gradually moved away from the medieval notion that philosophy and science were continuous with one another. Also, as the modern period wore on, a bewildering variety of competing philosophical systems developed, none of which could claim supremacy and each of which had a different set of premises. Thus there was no monolithic "system" such as medieval Aristotelianism that all could agree upon and that formed the background against which the biblical text had to be interpreted.

Still, Jewish philosophers confronted these difficulties and forged ahead with new readings of the Bible. In response to biblical criticism, some Jewish philosophers, for instance, replaced "divine authorship" with "divine inspiration" as the operative paradigm, a move that enabled these philosophers to accept the human authorship of the Bible while retaining a belief that it had a divine element in it. As for the proliferation of new philosophical paradigms, Jewish philosophers tended to settle comfortably into one or another school of thought, and sometimes even combined them. As postmodernism has come into vogue in some circles, scholars are recognizing that not only is this instability acceptable but even desirable. In order for the biblical text and Judaism in general to remain relevant, the Bible must be reinterpreted in each generation according to new paradigms that may yield a multiplicity of readings.

Few Jewish philosophers in the modern period produced the kind of independent commentaries on the Bible of the sort composed by medieval Jewish thinkers, such as Gersonides or 'Arama. The *Bi'ur* of Moses Mendelssohn and his young colleagues was the first Jewish commentary produced in the modern period that had philosophers associated with it, but while it was an original combination of classical exegesis and Enlightenment sensibilities, it did not contain much in the way of philosophy. Perhaps the closest modern analogue to the philosophical commentaries of the medievals is the work of Martin Buber on various books of the Bible, which combined academic scholarship with insights drawn from his religious-existential thought. One might also cite Samson Raphael Hirsch's biblical commentaries as examples of exegetical works that had a great deal of philosophy in them, in this case drawn primarily from his Kantian and Hegelian background. Another example that may fit into this category is Simon David Luzzatto's biblical commentaries, which also contain a good deal of philosophical reflection.

Yet, even if they did not write full-length commentaries, biblical exegesis is hardly unimportant to modern Jewish philosophers. Hermann Cohen presents a philosophy of Judaism in his posthumous work, *Religion of Reason Out of the Sources of Judaism*, which relies consistently on a form of exegesis that is a peculiar combination of biblical scholarship and neo-Kantian philosophy. In Franz Rosenzweig's *Star of Redemption* and his other Jewish works, exegesis is a constant presence as Rosenzweig attempts to read his existential thinking into the biblical text. Mention should also be made here of Rosenzweig's collaboration with Buber on a German translation of the Bible. All translations are interpretations, and this translation—begun by the two thinkers but finished by Buber long after Rosenzweig's death—is no exception. It constitutes, in effect, an existential commentary on the Bible in its own right. Finally, Abraham Joshua Heschel places the Bible front and center in his works as a source of insight for his depth theology as exemplified in his two-volume work, *The Prophets*, and his many other writings. In fact, one is hard pressed to think of any Jewish philosopher who does not engage in some way in philosophical exegesis of scripture.

The first section of this volume presents scholarly analyses of a variety of issues in such exegesis. Diana Lobel's "Speaking about God: Bahya as Biblical Exegete" focuses on Bahya ibn Pakuda, the eleventh-century Spanish thinker and author of the celebrated pietistic work, *Duties of the Heart*. Lobel examines Bahya's treatment of an issue that has been of great interest to scholars of Jewish philosophy: divine attributes. In the biblical text, God is depicted as possessing many characteristics that appear to be anthropomorphic, and medieval Jewish philosophers had to find a way to understand those attributes so as not to compromise the philosophical notion that God could in no way resemble his creatures. According to Lobel, Bahya's approach to this problem is heavily indebted to Saadia Gaon, but Bahya also departs from his predecessor in several ways. For example, Saadia understands the biblical depictions of God as positive attributes, and he takes this approach because he sees it as the only way to ensure that human beings can have a relationship with God. Bahya is similarly concerned with how we relate to God but goes in a different direction by adopting a negative theology of divine attributes and by arguing that human beings can establish a relationship with God in a direct, experiential manner through philosophical contemplation of those attributes.

Hannah Kasher's essay, "The Dual Nature of the Biblical Angel in the Philosophy of Maimonides," grapples with a key problem in the exegesis of the most important thinker and biblical interpreter in medieval Jewish philosophy. Kasher shows how Maimonides attempts to deal with the biblical term "angel." For medieval Jewish philosophers, the notion of angels was particularly problematic because in its traditional understanding it signified the existence of a group of animate beings mediating between God and the world for which there was no empirical evidence—at least according to Aristotelian science. Kasher shows how Maimonides met this challenge by effectively demythologizing the term and coming up with a series of referents for it in Aristotelian natural science and metaphysics. Thus, according to Maimonides' philosophical understanding of the biblical text, angels can refer to the separate intellects. Alternatively, in its literal meaning of "messenger," angel can refer to any natural cause that mediates between God and his activities in the world.

Charles H. Manekin takes us into post-Maimonidean territory in his essay, "The Ambiguities of Philosophical Exegesis: Joseph ibn Kaspi on God's Foreknowledge." Kaspi was a fourteenth-century French philosophical exegete in the school of Maimonides who produced a large body of biblical commentaries that are often colorful and provocative though insufficiently studied. Manekin focuses on a passage in Kaspi's *Tam ha-kesef* dealing with the issue of divine foreknowledge and examines it against the background of passages in Kaspi's other works and Jewish and Islamic philosophy in general. Manekin entertains seven interpretations of the passage in *Tam ha-kesef* and ranks them according to their probability of correctness, but without being able to come to a definitive conclusion as to which one is Kaspi's true view. Manekin's paper thus highlights the difficulties of interpreting Kaspi's philosophical views. Kaspi is one of the most elusive philosophers in medieval Jewish philosophy, a fact that may be explained in part by his adoption of Maimonidean esotericism. But Manekin's analysis also highlights the difficulty of examining the exegetical writings of medieval Jewish philosophers in general. Some of these thinkers, such as Kaspi, composed no systematic philosophical treatise and expressed their philosophical views *only* in the form of biblical commentaries, and it is often difficult to construct their philosophical views on a particular issue given the unsystematic nature of these works.

Robert Eisen's essay, "The Hermeneutics of Order in Medieval Jewish Philosophical Exegesis," deals with a dimension of philosophical exegesis in Judaism that has also been much neglected, and that is its hermeneutics. Here he examines how several medieval Jewish philosophers—Maimonides, Samuel ibn Tibbon, Joseph ibn Kaspi, and Gersonides—dealt with the question of order in the biblical text. He attempts to demonstrate that the positions adopted by these philosophers regarding the issue of order were tied to their approaches to philosophical writing in general. Maimonides laid the groundwork for this connection, which is later developed by the other three thinkers. Much of Eisen's essay focuses on Kaspi, who provides the most comprehensive treatment of the issue of order in the biblical text in several of his works. Kaspi makes intriguing use of the principle that there is no chronological order in the biblical text (*ein muqdam u-me'uḥar ba-torah*), which was used widely by the major medieval Jewish exegetes who were not philosophers. Kaspi gives this principle an innovative philosophical spin. This paper therefore highlights the fact that the distinction between the fields of medieval Jewish philosophy and medieval Jewish exegesis is not always clear.

The final paper of the historical section is Michael Rosenthal's "Spinoza, History, and Jewish Modernity." Rosenthal analyzes Spinoza's views on history, messianism, and divine providence by looking at how he deals with those themes in the Bible. Rosenthal shows that Spinoza tried to point the way to a naturalistic understanding of these matters but without denying their value as religious concepts. From this, Rosenthal concludes that Spinoza's views may have relevance for Jewish modernity in that he provides a modern philosophical framework within which to grapple with God's role in history. Rosenthal's analysis thus shows that despite Spinoza's diatribes against Judaism and medieval Jewish philosophy, Spinoza's reading of the Bible is potentially of great value to modern Jewish theology.

The second section of this volume offers a series of essays that present another dimension of the relationship between philosophy and the Hebrew Bible. In recent years, philosophers have engaged the biblical text for constructive and creative philosophical purposes. While the contemporary project of philosophical exegesis differs greatly from the medieval project, both share a fascination with the Bible and a desire to make sense of it in philosophical terms. The rise of analytical philosophy of religion in Anglo-American philosophical circles and the small but significant presence of religiously-committed analytic philosophers have set contemporary philosophical exegesis on a par with literary, psychological, anthropological, and sociological approaches. (Who would have thought fifty years ago that analytical philosophy would provide a congenial context for biblical exegesis!)

Charlotte Katzoff's essay, "Jacob and Isaac—A Tale of Deception and Self-Deception" presents a sophisticated interpretation of Isaac's motivations and mental state in blessing Jacob rather than Esau. The story in Genesis is problematic, not only because of the dubious moral behavior of the protagonists, but because of the questions it raises for divine providence; is it really God's will, Katzoff asks, that the patriarchal succession be determined by trickery and deceit? The gist of her interpretation is that Isaac deceives himself into believing that the person he is blessing is Esau and that Esau is worthy of the blessing, despite his strong suspicion that in fact the person is Jacob and his belief that Jacob should receive the blessing. Drawing on recent philosophical and psychological literature on self-deception, and appealing to textual and literary considerations for support, she not only argues for and analyzes Isaac's self-deception in detail, but also finds ways to justify it, despite the fact that self-deception is ordinarily considered an epistemic vice. The essay even provides an ingenious interpretation of God's indirect providential role in ensuring that the succession goes to the worthier of the sons.

Eleonore Stump's essay on "Samson and Self-Destroying Evil" concerns itself not so much with the suffering of the righteous but rather with that of the wicked. Does such suffering serve any deeper purpose besides retributive justice? Suffering for moderate deeds of wickedness may serve as a wake-up call to the perpetrator to mend her ways; from such evil may come good. But what about the suffering for the crimes perpetrated by a war criminal who has finally come to grips with the enormity of his actions? Or, on a less dramatic scale, what about the lifelong anguish of a driver who, in a moment of recklessness, inadvertently kills a pedestrian? Why would a benevolent, omnipotent, and omniscient God allow the crime to take place, and the suffering to occur, if he could have somehow prevented it?

The story of Samson, on Stump's reading, provides us with an answer to these questions. According to Stump, Samson loses his strength because he takes God's protection for granted and belittles his Nazirite obligation. For these sins he is abandoned by God and then captured, tormented, and blinded by the Philistines. On Stump's reading, Samson's humiliating suffering is not so much divine retribution for his hubris, but the means by which he is able to draw closer to God. What is distinctly philosophical about Stump's treatment is her sophisticated interpretation of the Samson story in light of the philosophical problem of evil. Both her and Katzoff's essays are examples of how contemporary philosophers can approach the Bible without accepting the doctrinal and hermeneutical assumptions of their predecessors.

Jerome Segal's essay, "God's Project," looks at some key incidents in the early books of the Torah to figure out God's motivations and goals in his encounters with humans in general and the Israelites and their prophets in particular. Attempts of this sort are not new, of course; Harold Bloom and Jack Miles are only two of the many writers who have turned to literary analysis in an attempt to flesh out the personality of God. But because Segal approaches the Bible not merely as a literary critic but as a philosopher, he is open to making connections that are "out of the box." Thus take, for example, God's cryptic response to Moses's request for a name by which God can be identified to the Israelites, i.e., "I am who I am" or simply "I am." These "names" seem to say nothing more about God than that he exists. Perhaps the Bible wishes to imply thereby that God lacks attributes or predicates by which he can be comprehended, and that he is totally self-sufficient. This is an interpretation of God's response with which a philosophical exegete like Maimonides could agree. The problem is that the behavior of God in the early Bible does not appear to be particularly incomprehensible, and, in any event, what purpose would he have in declaring his incomprehensibility or self-sufficiency at this point in the story? Appealing to the Sartrean idea of "bad faith," Segal sees God's response to Moses as a case of posturing, of playing the role of a self-sufficient existent. God wants to project the image of an independent deity that is not concerned with how he is seen. But in fact how he is seen by humankind, and especially by Israel, is vitally important for him. For God to fully exist, argues Segal, he must be recognized, which means that he must create an Other who is capable of recognizing him, an Other who is sufficiently like him to enter into a meaningful relationship with him—but not so much like him as to be God. Weaving into the story past cases of God's relations with humans, Segal portrays a God who is not only complex but has complexes. He is also a God whose personality develops and matures over time.

The volume ends with two differing conceptions of the relationship between Bible and philosophy. In "What Maimonides Can Teach Us about Reading the Bible" Kenneth M. Seeskin argues against Spinoza's claim that the Bible should be interpreted without regard to the question of its truth or of its larger significance for us. Seeskin does not suggest that we return to the earlier project of projecting within the text a meaning that conforms to our philosophical or scientific worldview, a procedure that would assume a view of the Bible and science that does not jive with contemporary sensibilities. Yet to treat the Bible merely as secular literature or historical narrative or even poetry is not only to fail to read it on its own terms—the biblical authors did not see themselves as secular historians or novelists or poets—but to lose its significance as a religious document.

Those who wish to retain that significance should not be intellectually embarrassed about interpreting it in ways that would have been beyond the ken of its original audience. Philosophers need not be defensive about offering philosophically motivated readings of scripture, even readings that are neo-Maimonidean, such as the ones Seeskin himself has offered.

Like Seeksin, Howard Wettstein doesn't wish for a return to the medieval philosophical project of recasting the Bible in philosophical terms, certainly not a return to medieval philosophical theology. But Wettstein, in "Against Theology," seems more disturbed than Seeskin about the underlying premise of the Maimonidean project, which he sees as "thinking about one culture (traditional Jewish) from the point of another, to the point of denying relevant differences." It seems that for Wettstein, Maimonides' philosophical worldview is essentially Greek, at best a harmonization of Athens and Jerusalem that appears not only puzzling today but foreign to the spirit of rabbinic Judaism. Maimonides' emphasis on theology and religious dogma, his view of religious practices as instrumental to intellectual contemplation, indeed, the overemphasis on intellect, etc., seem to be hard to square with traditional Jewish faith and practice. In reading Wettstein's essay one hears not only the criticism of Spinoza against the philosophical-exegetical project of the medievals, or that of Wittgenstein against the pretensions of Western philosophy, but also that of a twenty-first-century traditional Jew against a philosophical-religious sensibility that seems so foreign to his experience of Judaism.[1]

Wettstein ends his essay by suggesting that it is legitimate to explore the "uncrystallized" theological ideas of Judaism in the light of one's favored philosophical outlook, but that such an exploration should face the question: "how much and in what way one's favored way of thinking maps on to that of the rabbis." This shows the gap between his project and that of the medieval philosophical exegetes. Their goal was not to present a "philosophy of Judaism" that would accord with classical sources (and whose "authenticity" would be tested in its light), but to uncover the eternal truths that had been revealed to the prophets, contained within the sayings of the rabbis, and discovered by the philosophers. If the search for the truth in scripture has abated, the search for meaning has not, and there is no reason why philosophers should not be part of that search.

---

1. Yet one should be wary of projecting European, largely Eastern-European, constructions of Jewish religiosity onto a consciousness of the past. We wonder whether the late Yemenite-Israeli scholar of Maimonides, Rabbi Joseph Kafih, for whom medieval Jewish philosophy was part of a living intellectual and religious tradition handed down from generation to generation, would view Maimonides' religious sensibility as foreign to traditional Judaism.

PART I

HISTORICAL PERSPECTIVES

SPEAKING ABOUT GOD
BAHYA AS BIBLICAL EXEGETE

Diana Lobel
Boston University

THE HEBREW BIBLE does not hesitate to speak about God; God is a main character in its text. In the book of Genesis alone, God creates the world by speaking; God speaks to Abraham, Sarah, and their family in an intimate way. God acts, regrets, responds, gets angry, interacts with human beings like the gods of Greek and Roman mythology. The Bible betrays no discomfort or self-consciousness when describing God's intimate role in human life.

Such interaction becomes problematic for medieval thinkers influenced by the legacy of Greek philosophy. They are troubled by the human qualities ascribed to God in Scripture, which conflict with the abstract, demythologized God of Plato, Aristotle, and the Aristotelian and Neoplatonist Arabic philosophers. Their solution: we must read the biblical text through the eyes of reason and demythologize the way God is portrayed in the Bible.

In this paper, I will examine the work of two medieval Jewish thinkers: Saadia Gaon and Bahya Ibn Paqūda. I will demonstrate the way Saadia Gaon carries out his project of philosophical exegesis of the Bible. Saadia is as unself-conscious about his philosophical exegesis as the Bible itself is straightforward about its frankly human God. Saadia thoroughly integrates philosophy, theology, and the exegesis of Scripture.

Bahya Ibn Paqūda follows in his footsteps. I will show that Bahya also innovates in four ways:

1. Whereas Saadia as a theologian is comfortable making positive assertions about God's nature, Bahya ultimately takes a philosophical turn, asserting that we can speak about God only by negation.

11

2. Bahya makes an argument that Scripture itself gives us a model for philosophical demonstration and offers a philosophical proof for the existence of God.

3. Bahya offers us a twofold process of interpreting Scripture: first, by accepting anthropomorphic images, and second, by gradually refining these images to reveal philosophical truth.

4. Bahya's rationalism is of a contemplative type. The exercise of reason is for Bahya a duty of the heart; reason ultimately brings us to an experience of God. Philosophical exegesis of the Bible does more than give us correct information about God; it brings us into communion with the Divine.

Bahya Ibn Paqūda

Bahya Ibn Paqūda lived and worked in the second half of the eleventh century, circa 1080, in Saragossa, in Muslim Spain. We have from him just one book and several religious poems. However this book, *Guidebook to the Duties of the Heart (Al-hidāya ilā farā'iḍ al-qulūb; Torat ḥovot ha-levavot)* has been influential to this day as a manual for Jewish piety. It is sometimes called a book of ethics, but is actually a guidebook for inner devotion. Written in Judeo-Arabic—Arabic in Hebrew letters—the book quotes extensively from Islamic texts, especially sources from Sufi mysticism.[1]

What makes Bahya's book unique among Sufi manuals is that it contains a strong philosophical component. Whereas other Sufi thinkers include philosophical and theological elements, Bahya engages in full demonstrative proof. Thus the work is not only a devotional manual akin to Sufi compendia; it is also a philosophical work in the tradition of Saadia Gaon's *Book of Doctrines and Beliefs (Kitāb al-amānāt wa'l-i'tiqōdāt; Sefer emunot ve-de'ot)* in the ninth century and Maimonides' *Guide of the Perplexed (Dalālat al-ḥā'irīn)* in the twelfth.

In the study of Jewish philosophy, Bahya is often classified as a Neoplatonist. But this is only one dimension of Bahya's thought. Bahya draws

---

1. See A. S. Yahuda, *Al-hidāja 'ilā farā'id al-qulūb des Bachja Ibn Josef ibn Paqūda* (Leiden, 1912), 53–113; Georges Vajda, *La théologie ascétique de Bahya ibn Paqūda* (Paris, 1947); Amos Goldreich, "Possible Arabic Sources for the Distinction between 'Duties of the Heart' and 'Duties of the Limbs'" [in Hebrew], *Te'udah* 6 (1988): 179–208. Bahya wrote his work in Muslim Spain by 1080 at the latest; it was translated into Hebrew by Judah Ibn Tibbon in 1161 under the title *Ḥovot ha-levavot*, and in Hebrew translation has enjoyed immense popularity down to the present day. For the dating of Bahya's work, see P. K. Kokovtzov, "The Date of the Life of Bahya Ibn Paquda," *Livre d'hommage à la mémoire du Dr. Samuel Poznanski* (Warsaw, 1927), 13ff.

equally from the school known as *kalām* or Islamic theology. He praises and closely follows the approach of Saadia Gaon, often referred to as the first Jewish philosopher, but equally associated with rationalist *kalām* of the Mu'tazilite school.[2] Thus, to make clear Bahya's philosophical project, it will be important to begin by outlining Saadia's approach to biblical interpretation. I will then demonstrate how Bahya follows Saadia, but diverges by inserting a Neoplatonic turn in his exegesis. I will focus particularly on the problem of language about God, the central problem for philosophical interpretation of Scripture, to illustrate Bahya's unique approach to God's essential nature.

Saadia's Approach to Biblical Interpretation: The Problem of Anthropomorphism

Saadia translated the entire Hebrew Bible into Arabic. As both a translator and commentator, he approaches the Bible as a medieval rationalist. Whereas in discussions of modern philosophy we speak of rationalism in relation to empiricism, in discussions of medieval philosophy the term rationalist is most often used to describe a stance on the relationship between faith and reason. In this sense, there are two ways in which one can be a rationalist. The stronger sense of rationalism is the claim that we can come to a complete understanding of the universe solely by the exercise of reason, independent of revelation. A weaker rationalism claims that certain truths are accessible to human beings through reason alone, prior to or independent of revelation.[3] Although Bahya and Saadia are probably not rationalists in the stronger sense, they are certainly rationalists in the weaker sense.

Saadia and Bahya hold that there are two sources of knowledge, reason and revelation, which ultimately teach the same truth and do not con-

---

2. However, Sarah Stroumsa points out that these characterizations are erroneous in two ways. Saadia was not the first Jewish philosopher; he inherits the beginnings of a Jewish philosophical tradition from the ninth-century figure Dawūd al-Muqammiṣ and the tenth-century philosopher Isaac Israeli (d. circa 932). Second, while Saadia does use the term "philosophers," he uses the term in a generic sense. He does not belong to the school of the *falāsafa*, the Arabic Aristotelians including Al-Fārābī, Ibn Sīna, Ibn Bājja, Maimonides, and Ibn Rushd, nor does he refer to himself as a *mutakallim*. Stroumsa shows that while his work shows similarities to the work of the *mutakallimūn*, it also presents distinct differences. See Sarah Stroumsa, "Saadia and Jewish *Kalam*," in *The Cambridge Companion to Medieval Jewish Philosophy*, ed. D. Frank and O. Leaman (Cambridge, 2003), 77ff.; idem, *Sa'adya Ga'on: hogeh yehudi be-ḥevrah yam-tikhonit* (Tel Aviv, 2003), 9ff.

3. See Daniel Gimaret, "*Mu'tazila*," *EI* 2:91.

tradict.[4] Saadia asserts that Scripture gives us a head start on the truth; reason is left at leisure to verify the teachings of Scripture.[5] Bahya's claim is even stronger: we have a religious duty to verify for ourselves the teaching we have received by tradition.[6]

While at first glance these positions appear very similar, at close inspection they represent two different kinds of rationalism. Saadia is an optimistic, "enlightenment" thinker.[7] He assumes we can know the truth without Scripture, and is bothered by the opposite problem: If we can discover truth with unaided reason, why do we need revelation at all? His answer is that Scripture gives us a head start on the truth. It takes time to discover truths by reason, and not all human beings are equally capable of the search.[8] Scripture is a democratizing factor. However, reason can only teach us the outlines of ethical behavior; we need positive law to apply these ethical principles in specific cases. Revelation supplies us with positive law of the highest order, that from the divine lawgiver.[9]

Bahya's rationalism is of a different type. For Bahya, knowledge itself is of value; the discovery of truth is a religious experience. It is a duty of the heart to verify the teachings of Scripture for oneself, to discover religious truth through the exercise of one's own reason. For Saadia, reason is

4. See Harry Wolfson, "What Is New in Philo?" in *Philo: Foundations of Religious Philosophy in Judaism* (Cambridge, Mass., 1947), 2:439–60; Herbert Davidson, "The Study of Philosophy as a Religious Obligation," in *Religion in a Religious Age*, ed. S. D. Goitein (Cambridge, Mass., 1974), 53–68.

5. Saadia, *Kitāb al-mukhtār fī'l-'amānāt wa'l-i'tiqādāt*, trans. J. Qafih (Jerusalem, 1972–73), Introduction: 6; *Book of Doctrines and Beliefs*, trans. A. Altmann, in *Three Jewish Philosophers* (New York, 1982), 45–47; *The Book of Beliefs and Opinions*, trans. S. Rosenblatt (New Haven, 1976), 31–33.

6. Bahya Ibn Paqūda, *Torat ḥovot ha-levavot*, ed. J. Qafih (Jerusalem, 1973), Introduction; Qafih, 25–26; *Book of Direction to the Duties of the Heart*, trans. M. Mansoor (London, 1973), 94.

7. See Alexander Altmann, "Saadia's Conception of the Law," *Bulletin of the John Rylands Library* 28 (1944): 320–39, reprinted in *Saadiah Gaon*, ed. S. T. Katz (New York, 1980), 3–22; idem, *Ḥaluqat ha-mitzvot le-Rasag* in *Rav Sa'adya Gaon: kovetz torani mada'i*, ed. J. Fishman (Jerusalem, 1943), 658–73.

8. *Amānāt*, Introduction; Qafih, 7; Altmann, 31; Rosenblatt, 9.

9. *Amānāt*, 3:3; Qafih, 122; Altmann, 103; Rosenblatt, 145. Altmann, "Saadia's Conception of the Law," 12–15. Altmann points out that Saadia accepts Aristotle's distinction between natural justice and legal justice, the universal law of nature and the particular law of each country. His innovation is to suggest that divine revelation plays the role of establishing positive law. Ibid., 12–13; Aristotle, *Nicomachean Ethics* 5, 1134b; *Rhetoric* 1.13.2.

of purely instrumental value; for Bahya, reason is of intrinsic value. Bahya himself may not notice this difference; he takes Saadia as a mentor in both the interpretation of Scripture and in the rational demonstration of truth.

Saadia's principle of exegesis is simple. The biblical text is to be understood according to its plain sense unless its plain sense is contradicted by (1) sense perception, (2) reason, (3) a clear biblical text, or (4) a reliable tradition. In the case of any of these contradictions, we must reinterpret the text.[10]

Let us examine Saadia's examples in the first two categories. As an illustration of texts that contradict sense perception, Saadia brings Genesis 3:20, where Eve is called Ḥava—related to the Hebrew verb *ḥayah*, "to live"—because she is the mother of all living. Since Eve is not the mother of the ox and the lion, Saadia argues, we should understand the mother of all living as the mother of all human beings.[11] And indeed, in Saadia's Arabic translation of the Bible, known as the *Tafsīr*, Saadia translates the phrase as "the mother of all rational or speaking living beings who are mortal" (Arabic: *umm kull ḥayy nāṭiq māʾit*; Hebrew: *em kol ḥay medaber shesofo lamut*).[12] The evidence of our senses is to be trusted. Since we perceive that a human being cannot be the mother of all living creatures, we know the text is speaking metaphorically.

As an illustration of texts that contradict reason, Saadia's offers "the Lord your God is a devouring fire, a jealous God" (Deut. 4:24). Saadia argues that since fire is created, dependent on matter, and extinguishable, reason cannot accept that God can be likened to it. He therefore argues that we must understand the statement in an elliptical sense, namely that God's *punishment* is like a devouring fire, just as we read in Zeph 3:8: "For all the earth shall be devoured with the fire of my jealousy."[13]

Saadia here argues on exegetical grounds that the biblical text is genuinely elliptical; the text leaves out a word that should be understood. But his grounds for arguing thus are rational, philosophical grounds: fire is created and destructible, whereas God is uncreated and indestructible. God can be compared to his creatures only metaphorically. In reality, the creator of all bodies is not of the genus of created things, and cannot be described by their qualities.[14]

---

10. *Amānāt*, 7:1; Qafih, 219–20; Altmann, 157–58; Rosenblatt, 7:2, 265–67. The text of Book 7 differs widely between the Oxford and Leningrad manuscripts.

11. Ibid.; Qafih, 219; Altmann, 157; Rosenblatt, 265.

12. Rational mortal being is the common medieval Aristotelian definition of human being, "mortal" to distinguish humans from the angels.

13. Ibid.

14. *Amānāt*, 1:1, 2:8; Qafih, 84, 96–97; Altmann, 81, 85; Rosenblatt, 96, 111–12. 2:8:

This is a radical principle; it cuts to the heart of biblical speech about God. All human language speaks about created being. If God cannot be spoken of in the categories of any created thing, we are reduced to silence when it comes to the Divine. Yet the Bible does not hesitate to speak about God; the Torah must, therefore, be speaking metaphorically. The alternative to silence is poetry and metaphor. What we need is an interpretive key that unlocks the metaphorical meaning of the text. Saadia's rational canon of exegesis provides such a key.

Saadia and Bahya argue that the Bible does not teach anything that contradicts reason. What precisely does it mean to say that a passage contradicts reason? Are biblical miracles excluded, such as God's intervention at the Sea of Reeds (Exod 15) or Elisha's reviving a boy from death? Judah Halevi, often characterized as an antirationalist, can help us clarify this issue, for even he accepts the rationalist principle of exegesis. The Jewish sage in Halevi's dialogue, the *Kuzari*, exclaims, "God forbid that the Torah should teach anything that contradicts reason or what is manifest!"[15] However, in contrast to the typical medieval philosopher, Halevi radically restricts the sovereignty of reason. He argues that reason cannot explain everything experience attests to be empirically true, such as the parting of the sea, the giving of manna in the wilderness, and the revelation at Mount Sinai.[16] However, this does not mean that to accept these events as facts is unreasonable. Like modern scientists, Halevi is an empiricist. He argues that although the events in question may not be comprehensible by reason—at least, not yet—they do not necessarily contradict reason, as would, for example, the attempt to square a circle. In the same way, for the medieval rationalists Saadia and Bahya it is not irrational to hold that the Creator can communicate with human beings or perform miracles. What is irrational is the claim that the Creator partakes in the qualities of the created world.

"There is left nothing, be it substance or accident, or any of their attributes, that could be applied to him, it being recognized and clearly established that he, the creator, has made anything." Cf. Bahya, 1:7: "the Creator of substance and attribute cannot be touched in his essence by their qualities." Qafih, 65; Mansoor, 126.

15. Judah Halevi, *Kitāb al-radd wa'l-dalīl fī'l-dīn al-ḏalīl (al-kitāb al-Khazari)*, ed. D. Z. Baneth and H. Ben-Shammai (Jerusalem, 1977), 1:67, p. 18; cf. 1:89, p. 25.

16. Ibid., 1:37–91. Halevi also critiques philosophical teachings he believes are simply scholastic dogmas, such as the theory of the four elements, or the belief in an Active Intellect that is an intermediary between God and human beings. Ibid., 4:25; 5:14.

Saadia bases his argument for this principle upon reason, Scripture, and tradition. His argument from reason is that since God is creator of all categories of being, there is no category that could be applied to God, who is uncreated. All created categories, including those of substance and attribute, arise with creation. Since they do not preexist creation, they cannot characterize the one being that does clearly precede creation, both logically and temporally, i.e., the Creator.[17] Scientists today make a similar argument with respect to the category of time. Since time is a feature of the created universe, we cannot intelligibly speak about time before the universe came into existence. It is meaningless to ask what took place before the Big Bang; the very categories of before and after arose with the Big Bang.[18] Similarly, there are no qualities of created beings before creation; all such qualities arise with the created world. Therefore, we cannot attribute any qualities of our universe to God.

Thus proceeds Saadia's argument from reason, which lays the foundation for a similar argument offered by Bahya. From Scripture, Saadia brings passages that deny God's likeness to each of five categories of created being: God is unlike minerals, plants, animals, stars, and even angels.[19] From tradition, Saadia brings the evidence of the Targums, the Aramaic translations of Scripture.[20] Saadia argues that if the Aramaic translators thought descriptions of God had an anthropomorphic meaning, they would have translated them in their literal sense. But they knew

---

17. *Amānāt*, 2:8; Qafih, 96–97; Altmann, 85; Rosenblatt, 111–12. "There is left nothing, be it substance or accident, or any of their attributes, which could be applied to him, it being recognized and clearly established that he, the Creator, has made everything." Cf. Bahya, 1:7: "the Creator of substance and attribute cannot be touched in his essence by their qualities." Qafih, 65; Mansoor, 126.

18. See, e.g., Paul Davies, *The Mind of God: The Scientific Basis for a Rational World* (New York, 1992), 57; cf. Saint Augustine, *Confessions*, trans. R. S. Pine-Coffin (London, 1951), 11:13, p. 263.

19. God is not like minerals, even the most precious, gold and silver, he argues, citing Isaiah: "Whom will you liken to me and make my equal and compare me to that we may be like? You that lavish gold out of the bag and weigh silver in the balance?" (Isa 46:5–6). As a master of the Bible, he is able to skillfully adduce similar passages showing that God is not like animals, nor stars, nor the angels. As for stars, he quotes Isaiah: "To whom will you liken me that I should be equal? Lift up your eyes on high, and see: who has created these?" showing that God cannot be compared to the stars. As for the angels, he quotes Psalms, "who in the skies can be compared to the Lord, who among the divine beings can be likened to the Lord?" (Ps 89:7). Qafih, 98; Rosenblatt, 113–14.

20. Both Saadia and Bahya use the term "the sages" when they are clearly referring to the Aramaic translators of Scripture. They include these traditional

both from their own reason and the authority of the prophets that anthropomorphic expressions were intended to convey certain sublime ideas, so they translated them according to what they knew was the true, non-anthropomorphic meaning.[21]

Following the approach of these Aramaic Targums, Saadia deciphers the biblical metaphors.[22] He includes not only such statements as "God wanted," "God was pleased," or "God was angry," but even "God was," which implies that God is encompassed by time.[23] Saadia travels through the ten Aristotelian categories—the categories of all created being—to show that all scriptural language that describes God through these categories must be interpreted metaphorically.

First he shows the tendency of language to broaden the meaning of words regarding ordinary topics. For example, the phrase "the heavens declare the glory of God" (Ps 19:2) is clearly a metaphor; the heavens do not literally speak. Rather this phrase is a poetic way of saying that when we look at the heavens, we see the glory of God.[24]

Similarly, "by the mouth of Aaron and his sons" (Num 4:27) refers to Aaron's teaching and command, not the physical organ on his face. If this language is metaphorical with respect to human beings, all the more so is it metaphorical regarding the nonphysical Creator.[25] Saadia draws up a list of ten anthropomorphic expressions he interprets metaphorically.[26] Face, for example, signifies favor or anger; ear signifies acceptance; heart points to wisdom. The bowels signify amiability, as in "your Law is in my bowels (*me'ai*)" (Ps 40:9). Foot denotes coercion, as in the phrase, "Until I make your enemies your footstool" (Ps 110:1).

Now as Saadia suggests, we might well ask: How does language help us by using words so loosely that they are likely to be misunderstood? Why does Scripture not limit itself to precise usage and save us the trouble of seeking out the correct meaning? Saadia's answer is that if language

---

translators as authentic transmitters of rabbinic tradition. *Amānāt*, 2:9; Qafih, 99–100; Altmann, 87–88; Rosenblatt 115–16; *Hidaya*, 1:10; Qafih, 77; Mansoor, 135–36. Bahya here uses the term *awwalūnā*, lit. our early ones, one of the terms Saadia uses as well for the sages. Saadia here uses *'ulama' ummatinā*, the sages of our nation.

21. Ibid.
22. *Amānāt*, 2:8; Qafih, 96–97; Altmann, 85–86; Rosenblatt, 111–12.
23. Ibid.; Qafih, 97; Altmann, 85; Rosenblatt, 112.
24. *Amānāt*, 2:10; Qafih, 100; Altmann, 88; Rosenblatt, 117.
25. Ibid.; Qafih, 101; Altmann, 89–90; Rosenblatt, 118–19.
26. These include head, eye, ear, mouth, lip, face, hand, heart, bowels, and foot.

were limited to a single, precise word for each idea, it would be a poor instrument of expression and would not convey even a fraction of what we think. If the Torah were to speak of God in exact language, it would have to refrain from describing God as hearing, seeing, being merciful, and willing; the only activity we could ascribe to God would be existence alone (*al-anniyya faqat*).[27] While a philosopher might be content with this, the poetic soul would be impoverished. Precise, nonmetaphorical language is too prosaic to describe God's interaction with the world. Therefore, the Torah speaks in poetry and metaphor, relying upon human beings to use reason, Scripture, and tradition to decipher its true intent.

In a piece on philosophy and exegesis, Josef Stern has used a distinction from literary theory between the meaning of a literary work and a reading of a work. The *meaning* of a work intends to get at the intent of the author, that conveyed by language in the context of the author and the author's intended audience. In contrast, a *reading* of a work conveys an understanding that makes sense to the interpreter; it strikes the interpreter as somehow true. [28]

I would argue that Saadia believes that the nonanthropomorphic rendering of Scripture is its true meaning, and not just a philosophical reading. He sees his work as exegesis, not eisegesis—as uncovering the true intent of Scripture, not as a reading in, derived from foreign, rationalistic canons of understanding. To the contrary, he believes that reason and revelation support rather than contradict one another. Saadia argues that it would be a misunderstanding of poetic language to read Scripture with the rigid eye of the literalist. Scripture uses anthropomorphic images for a

---

27. *Amānāt*, 2:10; Qafih, 101; Altmann, 89; Rosenblatt, 117–18. See also Simon Rawidowicz, "Saadia's Purification of the Idea of God," in *Israel, the Ever-Dying People, and Other Essays*, ed. Benjamin Ravid (Rutherford, N.J., 1986) 142–43. On the term *'anniyya* or *'inniyya* see Alfred Ivry, *Al-Kindi's Metaphysics* (Albany, N.Y., 1974) 120–21 and sources cited there; Warren Zev Harvey and Steven Harvey, "A Note on the Arabic Term *'Anniyyah/'aniyyah/'inniyyah*" [in Hebrew], *Iyyun* 38 (April 1989): 167–71. On this term in Maimonides, see *Guide*, 1:58; Ed. Issachar Joel (Jerusalem, 1931), 92; Trans. Shlomo Pines (Chicago, 1963), 135; Josef Stern, "Maimonides' Demonstrations: Principles and Practice," *Medieval Philosophy and Theology* 10 (2001): 47–87, 71–72; Diana Lobel, "'Silence Is Praise to You': Maimonides on Negative Theology, Looseness of Expression, and Religious Experience," *ACPQ* 76, no. 1 (2002) 25–49, esp. 26, 26n4, 45–46, and 45n82.

28. Josef Stern, "Philosophy or Exegesis: Some Critical Comments," in *Judaeo-Arabic Studies: Proceedings of the Founding Conference of the Society for Judaeo-Arabic Studies*, ed. N. Golb (Amsterdam, 1997), 213–28, esp. 217–18.

purpose: to describe God's interaction with the world through the rich and textured language of metaphor. But poetic language should not mislead us in our rational understanding of the Creator. Poetry is not metaphysics.

Philosophical and Theological Approaches to Language about God

Saadia argues that Scripture deliberately employs metaphor so we can assert more about God than the mere fact of his existence. But is it philosophically accurate to do so? How does one adjudicate between the theological need to speak about God and the philosophical claim that this is impossible?

Here we come to the heart of the matter. Rationalist theologians, both Islamic and Jewish, point out that Scripture asserts that God is incomparable, unlike anything in the created world. In the Bible we read, "To what can you compare me, says the Lord?" (Isa 40:25). In the Qur'ān we read, "there is no thing like him" (*laysa ka-mithlihi shay'*) (Qur'ān 42:11). Scripture itself thus acknowledges a philosophical claim, a demand of reason. How then can we use human language to speak of God and God's relationship to human beings, when both reason and Scripture deny this is possible?

Islamic theologians acknowledge we must steer a delicate course between two equally dangerous poles: those of *tashbīh*, likening God to anything created, and *ta'ṭīl*, divesting God of all qualities. The Mu'tazilites—the most radically rationalist among the *kalām* theologians—avoid the danger of likening God to the created world by rejecting all positive descriptions of God. In response, the orthodox accuse Mu'tazilites of rendering God purely abstract, a something I know not what.[29] They ask: How can one have a relationship with a nameless, faceless God, about whom we know nothing beyond the fact of mere existence? Don't we then lose any sense that this God is a real presence in human life?

Saadia seems genuinely torn between these two poles—between the philosophical impossibility of using human language to talk about God and the religious necessity to do so. It is precisely this tension that Bahya addresses.

---

29. The Mu'tazilites, who rejected all positive attributes of God, were called by their opponents Mu'taṭīlites, those who empty God of all qualities. Majid Fakhry, *A History of Islamic Philosophy* (New York, 1982), 57; idem, *A Short Introduction to Islamic Philosophy, Theology, and Mysticism* (Oxford, 1997), 18–19. The term for emptying God of all qualities is *ta'ṭīl*.

BAHYA AND SAADIA ON DIVINE ATTRIBUTES

Bahya's Distinction between Essential and Active Attributes

Bahya tackles the problem of language about God in the tenth and final section of the Gate on Divine Unity. If God is essentially unknowable and all we can reasonably say is that God exists, what sense can we make of the descriptions of the deity we find in the Bible?

This is related to another central *kalām* problem. We hear in Scripture not only that God is one, but also that God is merciful and gracious, slow to anger. If God is truly one, how can God have many attributes? For the philosophical mind, oneness does not signify numerical unity. Number is a quality of created beings, of bodies. One is the root of all numbers; it is logically prior to multiplicity. Before there can arise a complex world, there must exist a being who is absolutely One, pure unity. Moreover, for the philosophical mind unity must be internal as well. God must be internally simple, free from all complexity and composition. If God has many different qualities—mercy, justice, compassion—these would seem to compromise God's absolute unity.

Bahya chooses the Mu'tazilite solution to these problems: he makes a distinction between essential and active attributes.[30] The multiple qualities of God we hear about in the Torah are attributes of action; they describe God's many actions with respect to creation.[31] Bahya defines essential attributes, in contrast, as those that belong to God independent of creation; they were God's before the world came into being and will remain God's eternally.[32] God has three essential attributes: God is existent, eternal, and one. These are distinct in name alone. While human

---

30. The Mu'tazilites, seeking to preserve God's unity, did not want to ascribe to God any qualities that would introduce multiplicity into God's essence. Thus they held that eternity alone belongs to God's essence, and that it is only by virtue of God's essence that God has knowledge, power, and life—not because knowledge, power, and life are real qualities that inhere in God. Bahya is therefore in keeping with the Mu'tazilite stark ideal by confining God's essential qualities to oneness, eternity, and existence. See Muḥammad al-Shahrastānī, *Kitāb al-milal wa-l-nihal*, ed. William Cureton (London, 1846), 1, p. 30; A. J. Wensinck, *The Muslim Creed* (Cambridge, 1932), 75. Some even went as far as to deny eternity as an attribute of God. Al-'Ash'arī, *Maqālāt al-islāmiyyīn al-muṣallīn*, ed. H. Ritter (Istanbul, 1929-33), 180; Fakhry, *History*, 60. Cf. *Amānāt*, 2:12; Qafih, 110; Rosenblatt, 129; Haggai Ben Shammai, "*Kalām* in Jewish Philosophy" in *History of Jewish Philosophy*, ed. D. Frank and O. Leamann (London, 1995), 115–48, esp. 118, 131–32.

31. Bahya, *Hidāya*, ed. Qafih, 1:10, p. 77.

32. 1:10, p. 73.

beings can only conceive of them as three separate notions, they point to one unified essence of the Divine. The attributes are conceptually but not ontologically distinct; the three attributes are only a human way of describing a God whose essence is one.[33]

Saadia on Essential and Active Attributes

Bahya bases his presentation on that of Saadia, who also argues that God has three essential attributes. For Saadia, God is living, powerful, and knowing; each of these derives from the fact that God is creator.[34] We learn these three qualities first from the Bible; reason then confirms them. The three come to us in a single flash of intuition as one reality. A being who creates must be alive and powerful, capable of action. A well-ordered creation such as this demands a Creator who can know the projected results of creative action.

Now, although the three aspects of God occur to our mind in combination, they cannot be expressed in a single word in human language. This is what misled Christian theologians, says Saadia. Recognizing that a Creator must also be living and knowing, they thought God's vitality and knowledge were two real entities distinct from God's essence, which gave them a Trinity. Saadia offers the analogy of fire. A person might claim, "I don't worship fire but that thing that burns, gives light, and rises upward." This, of course, is nothing other than fire.[35] One can use many words to describe one entity. Similarly, it is not that God has many attributes, but that the human mind can only describe God's unique nature from varying angles.

Saadia insists that these three attributes do not imply diversity or change within God. Diversity and change are characteristic of bodies and their accidents, whereas the Creator of physical beings is above all change. What gave rise to the idea of essential attributes? In his refutation of the Trinity, Saadia explains that the reason we believe the life of a human being is distinct from the human essence is because we sometimes see a

---

33. Ibid., 76. Bahya borrows this formulation from Saadia, who made substantially the same claim about the three essential attributes living, powerful, and knowing. Saadia's three essential attributes, which he asserts are three in name alone, are the standard *kalām* triad. See Saadia, *Amānāt,* 2:4, pp. 98–99. Bahya's proof that the three are mutually entailing is more detailed and logically complex than that of Saadia.

34. At the end of Book 2, Saadia does assert that God is eternal and one, as well as living, capable, knowing, and the original creator of all. *Amānāt,* 2:12; Qafih, 114; Rosenblatt, 134–35.

35. *Amānāt,* 2:5; Qafih, 90–91; Rosenblatt, 103–4.

person alive and sometimes dead. Thus, we infer that there is something
in the person by virtue of which he or she lives and that, if removed, causes the person to die.[36]

It is clear, however, that there is never a time at which the Creator is
not living or lacks knowledge. God is intrinsically alive and knowing; God
knows and is alive by virtue of his essence. The three attributes of life,
power, and knowledge are actually identical to God's essence, and not—
as Saadia interprets the Christian doctrine of the Trinity—three distinct
entities or persons.[37]

However, in the end it is not clear whether Saadia actually identifies
God's attributes with God's essence, as he goes on to qualify his position.
He argues that when we call God "Creator" we add nothing to God's
essence; we merely inform that there is a world created by him. Likewise,
to say God is living, powerful, and knowing is merely to say that there is a
world that came into being as a result of God's action.[38] Saadia's allusion

---

36. Ibid.; Qafih, 91; Rosenblatt 104.

37. Ibid.; Qafih, 90; Rosenblatt, 103. Altmann argues that Saadia is here following
the Mu'tazilite school of Abū l-Hudhayl, who hold that the three attributes of
life, knowledge, and power are identical to God's essence. Abū Hudhayl
adopts this approach because he is uncomfortable with the orthodox claim
that the essential attributes (ṣifāt dhātiyya) are real entities within God; the
essential attributes then come too close to hypostases, like the persons of the
Christian Trinity, which to the Mu'tazilite mind mar divine unity. Israel Efros
denies that Saadia identifies God's attributes with his essence. Efros, *Studies in
Medieval Jewish Philosophy* (New York, 1974), 53.

38. *Amānāt*, 2:12; Qafih, 110; Rosenblatt, 129. This position would seem to collapse
the distinction between attributes of essence and attributes of action. Saadia
here describes the essential attributes in terms usually reserved for attributes
of action, i.e., in terms of the creation, the recipients of God's creative activity.
Saadia mentions the distinction between essential and active attributes in 2:12,
where he gives several examples of what he means by attributes of action.
When Scripture tells us that God remembered Noah after the flood, we are
really being informed that the world was delivered from disaster. Similarly,
when Scripture asserts that God is merciful and gracious, we are really being
told about God's creatures, the beneficiaries of God's acts of kindness.

In another context (5:7) Saadia explains that although the Torah speaks of
mercy in connection to God, it is not possible that mercy subsists in or applies
to the Creator, for God has no accidental qualities. God is not suddenly struck
by the accidental quality of mercy. Rather, mercy applies to his creatures.
When the Torah tells us that God is *ḥanun ve-raḥum*, merciful and gracious, we
should really translate the passive participle into an active participle: God is
ḥonen and *meraḥem*, which means merely that human beings are the recipients
of God's merciful and gracious actions.

to the concept of attributes of action thus introduces complexities and tensions into his approach that he does not resolve. These tensions are left for Bahya to systematically work out and refine.

Saadia shows a degree of comfort in speaking of God in positive terms. On a theoretical level, he acknowledges the philosophical problem of positive statements about God; he admits that if we wanted to speak of God in exact language, the only thing we could assert of God would be his existence. However, Saadia believes this position is religiously untenable. Therefore, he does not take the Neoplatonic stance that God's essence is unknowable and, therefore, we can say nothing about the Divine. Language expresses in three words the unity that is God's essence; God's essence is not, for Saadia, unknowable and beyond all qualification.

Bahya on Essential Attributes

While Saadia's essential attributes all relate to God's status as Creator, Bahya's rendering of God as existent, eternal, and one specifically relate to God's status independent of creation. They are purely ontological; they belong to God by virtue of God's existence alone.

Bahya thus introduces a new twist: he shifts our focus to divinity prior to and independent of creation. While opening within a clear *kalām* framework based on Saadia, Bahya takes a Neoplatonic philosophical turn. Bahya focuses on the essential nature of the unmanifest God.

Bahya's demonstration of the validity of his three philosophical attributes—echoes of his earlier discussion in Book One—nevertheless owes much to the *kalām*. I will focus on his proof that God must be existent, which reveals a great deal about his approach to biblical exegesis. Bahya asserts we can prove God is existent by observing God's traces in the world. Bahya here follows the *kalām* method of proof, which begins with that which can be perceived by the senses (the *shāhid*, or that which is seen) and from it points to that which cannot be perceived (the *ghayb*, that

---

How is this different from the essential attributes, as Saadia has described them? Saadia suggests that God is intrinsically living, powerful, and knowing, independent of whether creatures are affected by these qualities. The three attributes are just terms parsing the meaning of God's status as Creator. Saadia's attributes of essence all relate to the fact that an eternal, unchanging God must exist as the cause of this changing, created world. In contrast, attributes of action speak of the ways created beings are affected by God's actions; these can be many and changing as God interacts with the created world. But these are refinements I am introducing to resolve tensions in Saadia's presentation. Saadia himself does not systematically work out these tensions. The refinement and systematization of his position is worked out by Bahya.

which is unseen or absent).[39] The standard example, which Saadia gives, is that when we smell smoke, we can infer there is a fire; or if we hear a human voice, we can infer the presence of a person behind a wall.[40] This approach is based on the trustworthiness of the senses as well as rational inference. We look up into the night sky, see the stars, and know that they must have a cause, as nothing can come into existence from nothing.[41] The *kalām* approach of looking up into the night sky for proof of God's existence is precisely what a verse from Isaiah teaches us, according to Bahya, who quotes the following text: "Lift high your eyes and see who created these? He who brought forth their host by number, who calls them each by name. Because of his great might and vast power, not one is absent" (Isa 40:26).[42]

This chapter in Isaiah was a favorite among both philosophers and *mutakallimūn* as it articulates a key principle of monotheism: God is indescribable and incomparable. "To whom, then, can you liken God, what form compare to him?" asks the prophet. "The idol? A woodworker shaped it, and a smith overlaid it with gold." And then God declares in his own name: "To whom, then, can you liken me, to whom can I be compared," says the Holy One. "Lift high your eyes and see: who created these? He who brings out their host by number, calling them each by

---

39. The procedure is known as an analogy from that which is perceivable to that which is imperceptible (*qiyās al-shāhid 'alā'l-ghayb*). The indirect method of proof, from the *dalīl* to the *madlūl*, is typical of *kalām* thought. See Joseph Van Ess, "The Logical Structure of Islamic Theology," in *Logic in Classical Islamic Culture* (Wiesbaden, 1970), 26–27.

40. *Amānāt*, Introduction; Qafih, 18–19; Altmann, 39; Rosenblatt, 21.

41. As Josef Stern has pointed out in relation to Maimonides, this is what medieval scholastics termed proof *quia*: proving that God exists through observation of God's effects. We see here a major division between the school of Aristotelian philosophy—those in Islamic culture known as *falāsifa*, the school of which Maimonides was a proud adherent—and that of Islamic theology or *kalām*, the approach of Saadia and Bahya. From the perspective of the Arabic Aristotelian philosophers, this form of demonstration is an indication (*dalīl*), not a demonstrative proof; demonstrative proof indicates why a thing is so, which one can only do by knowing a being's causes, not its effects. See Josef Stern, "Maimonides' Demonstrations: Principles and Practice," *Medieval Philosophy and Theology* 10 (2001): 47–84, esp. 56. However, proving God's existence from God's effects is the standard method of the school of *kalām*. The practitioners of *kalām* (the *mutakallimūn*) argue that we can indeed infer the cause (e.g., fire) from observation of its effects (smoke).

42. Bahya, 1:10; Qafih, 74; Mansoor, 132.

name: Because of his great might and vast power, not one is absent." That is, I am the incomparable Creator of all.

To the theological mind, this verse is a proof of the existence of God.[43] If we look at the created world, we cannot fail to realize there is a Creator. The evidence of our senses is clear testimony. Our first indication is the world we see around us. The intellect tells us that something cannot come forth from nothing; from an absence or void nothing can appear. Since we see a world of effects, we can infer that they must come forth from something that exists. The Creator must exist, for we perceive his traces in the world.[44] The source of these traces must be characterized as existent (literally, "found"; Arabic: *mawjūd*; Hebrew: *nimẓa*) rather than nonexistent (literally, "missing" or "absent"; Arabic: *ma'dūm*; Hebrew: *ne'edar*).

Note that Bahya quotes the entire verse, which is often not done in medieval texts. Perhaps he wants to call attention to the end of the verse, which expresses the idea of absence. God brings forth all creatures into existence; not one is absent (*ne'edar*). Likewise, God himself, who has the power to bring forth these creatures, must himself be existent rather than absent. [45]

---

43. A *quia* proof; see note 34 above.

44. Necessity (*darūra*) compels us to describe the Creator as existent; God's traces force themselves upon us because they are manifest when we look at the sky. *Darūra* is a key category in *kalām* thought. See David Sklare, *Samuel ben Hofni Gaon and His Cultural World: Texts and Studies* (Leiden, 1996), 146.

45. Bahya's use of this prooftext from Isaiah is not found in Saadia. Saadia does quote the verse in his philosophical work, but for a slightly different purpose. In the *Kitāb al-amānāt*, Saadia uses the verse in its larger context of the passage in Isaiah to argue that nothing resembles the Creator, that God does not fall under the category of substance or accident. He expands on this idea in his commentary on the biblical book of Isaiah. "Lift up your eyes on high," Saadia writes, "Look at the stars and meditate upon them, in order to know that they are created and guided, as the pious one said, 'When I look at your heavens, the work of your hands [what is man that you are mindful of him?]' (Ps 8:4). In this verse, he mentions four things that are repeated about God. The first is that he created the stars. His saying, 'Who created these?' testifies to the fact that they are created; he refutes those who claim they are eternal. The second is that he shows that he brought them out by number at the time he determined for them to rise and set according to their various courses. The language of 'who brings forth' testifies that they do not go out of their own volition; rather, it is God who brings them forth." Saadia asserts here that Scripture testifies to the fact that the stars are created; according to Saadia, the verse is revelation's assertion that the heavens are created rather than eternal. It is Bahya who makes explicit the notion that Scripture is teaching us to deduce God's existence from his effects. *Amānāt*, 2:9; Qafih, 98; Rosenblatt, 113–14; Yehuda

Bahya argues that something that is nonexistent cannot accomplish anything and, therefore, we must describe God as existent. How does Bahya use his biblical proof text? It is not that the verse gives us information that we do not have independent of revelation. Rather, the verse teaches us correct philosophical procedure: to use the evidence of our senses and from their testimony deduce rationally that God exists.

Bahya's Neoplatonic Turn

For the attributes of eternal and one, Bahya summarizes proofs he gave earlier in his work.[46] He then asserts, like Saadia, that the three attributes do not entail plurality in God's essence.[47] He gives two reasons for this.

The first is that the attributes are three in name alone. It is only due to a deficiency of human language that we cannot express in one word three aspects of God's essence. This is precisely the argument we find in Saadia.

Bahya's second argument brings us into the realm of negative theology. The reason these attributes do not entail plurality is that they only serve to deny their opposites. While essential attributes look like positive statements about God's essence, they are, in fact, negations; these terms are simply meant to deny that their opposites are applicable to God. Regarding the nature of the Creator, we should understand that "there is nothing like him" (*laysa ka-mithlihi shay'*), a Qur'ānic phrase often invoked

---

Razhabi, ed., *Tafsīr Yesha'ya le-Rav Saadia* (*Kitāb al-istiṣlāḥ*), (Kiryat Ono, 1993), Arabic, 206; Hebrew, 314–15.

46. Bahya's argument for the second essential attribute, God's eternity, is found in 1:5 and 1:6. Here he presents a concise restatement of its logic. Logical indicators point to the fact that the world must have an unprecedented beginning; there cannot be an infinite regress of causes. Bahya's proof of the third essential attribute, God's oneness, is found in 1:7–9. In 1:7 he demonstrates that God cannot be multiple; in 1:8–9 that every other kind of oneness is only metaphorical, while God is the only true one. Here again his thinking takes a philosophical turn. To assert that God is one is really to deny of God's essence every form of multiplicity: change, transformation, accidents, coming to be and passing away, composition and dissolution, resemblance, association, and diversity. Each of these is a form of multiplicity: to say God is one is not to make a positive assertion, but to insist that God's essence is not touched by any of these accidental properties of bodies. Bahya, 1:10; Qafih, 74; Mansoor, 132–33.

47. This is a principle Saadia asserts with respect to his own three essential attributes. However, whereas Saadia proves that the three attributes are mutually entailing in a concise manner, Bahya undertakes a much more rigorous and comprehensive proof. *Amānāt*, 2:4; Qafih, 89; Altmann, 83; Rosenblatt, 102; *Hidāya*, I:10; Qafih, 76; Mansoor, 134.

by *mutakallimūn* in asserting the uniqueness of the Creator and his absolute unlikeness to anything created. [48] To say God is one, existent, and
eternal is really to say that God is neither multiple, nonexistent, nor created. We should not think that by describing God with three terms we mean
to imply that God possesses a plurality of attributes. It is only the deficiency of language that compels us to describe God with three different
words, since there is no word in human language that can describe these
three aspects at once. As Saadia has argued, it would not be advisable to
create a new term for this conception, as the new term would convey no
meaning in itself. It would still be necessary to explain that term—this
would lead us back to a plurality of words in place of one term. [49]

Philosophical and Theological Approaches to Attributes

How can we characterize the difference between the theological
approach of Saadia and the philosophical approach of Bahya? The
Mu'tazilites were disturbed by the approach of negative theology. They
were troubled by the possibility that if one negates all attributes, one
strips God of any real existence, leaving a purely abstract notion of God.
As theologians, they do not want to lose the personal, active God of Scripture. Thus, they choose as essential attributes qualities that describe God
as a living, knowing presence who interacts with human beings. To the
theological mind, these qualities are so essential to God's nature that they
cannot be negated. What must be negated is any sign of multiplicity,
change, or being created.

Thus, while the *kalām* theologians do make use of negation—they
negate the notion that God could be nonliving, ignorant, or created—their
ultimate goal is to achieve a positive conception of God as a vital, knowing, eternal presence. The function of negation is more radical for philosophers. Philosophers fear that any positive assertion defines and thus
delimits that which is indefinable. To use concrete human language is to
set limits, borders, and finitude upon the infinite. The Absolute cannot
ultimately be known—at best, we can approach it as an asymptote by

---

48. Qur'ān 42:10. See for example, Māturīdī, *Kitāb al-tawḥīd*, ed. F. Kholeif (Beirut,
    1970), 126, cited by Stroumsa, 172n62. On God's unlikeness to anything else,
    see also al-Ash'arī, *Maqālāt al-islamiyyīn wa-ikhtilāf al-muṣallīn*, ed. H. Ritter
    (Istanbul, 1929–33) 1: 148, 156;. Stroumsa, 159n29; 166n46. Stroumsa (172n6)
    notes that Christian *mutakallimūn* were not comfortable denying the dissimi-
    larity between God and everything in the world, for obvious reasons. See
    Yaḥyā b. 'Adi, *Maqāla fī'l-tawḥīd*, ed. Samīr Khalīd (Juniah-Rome, 1980), 161,
    168–78. Bahya repeats this phrase in the same chapter; Qafih, 85; Mansoor, 143.

49. *Amānāt*, 2:4; Qafih, 88–89; Altmann, 82–83; Rosenblatt, 101–2.

negating all that is relative. Philosophers insist that to say God is living is only to negate that God is nonliving. Their ultimate mode of approach to the Divine is indirect: to strip away all traces of the created, material world.[50]

Likewise for Bahya, the function of the three essential attributes is to negate their opposites, not to make positive statements about the divine. Bahya insists that negative attributes are more accurate than the positive.[51] This is because whatever quality we ascribe to God cannot avoid the properties of substance and accident, whereas the creator of substance and accident cannot be described by their properties. If we say, for example, that God is one, this implies there is a substance God, who bears the attribute of oneness. On the other hand, negation of attributes is appropriate because God transcends any quality of the created world.

We have seen that Saadia expresses ideas quite similar. Saadia too has said that God cannot be described through the categories of substance and accident.[52] Moreover, Saadia asserts that to say that God is a Creator is ultimately only to say there is here something created.[53] Likewise, to say God is living, powerful, and knowing—which explain what it is to be a

---

50. If there is a synthesis that is achieved from these two notions—that God is living in a superessential way, and that God has nothing in common with our form of life—it is not articulated in this positive form by those influenced by Neoplatonism (Bahya, Maimonides), although certain Christian theologians do move to the positive affirmation (Pseudo-Dionysus, St. Thomas Aquinas). Among Jewish philosophers, the fourteenth-century Provençal philosopher Gersonides follows this path as well.

51. "Negative attributes are more accurate than positive," he cites as a statement attributed to Aristotle, which he learned from the first Jewish *mutakallim*, Dawūd al-Muqammiṣ's. It is instructive to compare Muqammiṣ's use of the quote to that of Bahya. Muqammiṣ writes that "when we say about God that he is eternal, living, and knowing, these are affirmations. The philosophers claimed that they do not say that 'he is' (or 'he exists') in the affirmative because this would be a statement that he is such." In other words, to make an affirmative statement is to define, restrict, and limit the unlimited. He continues: "We, however, say that affirmative propositions may be as correct as negative ones, provided (it is understood that) God has neither diversity nor variety. The attributes vary and differ in the linguistic expression, but not in meaning." Bahya, in contrast, sides with the philosophers rather than with the theologians, with the quote from pseudo-Aristotle rather than with Muqammiṣ and Saadia. See Muqammiṣ 9:20; Stroumsa, 201.

52. *Amānāt*, 2:8; Qafih, 96–97; Altmann, 84–85; Rosenblatt, 111–12.

53. Literally: to say that God is a Maker (*ṣāni'*) is ultimately to say only there is here something made (*maṣnū'*).

Creator—is merely to call attention to that which God has created. This introduces the approach of attributes of action, suggesting we can say nothing positive about God's essence; we can speak only about events in the created world.[54] But Saadia does not take the ultimate turn to the negative. We can sense Saadia struggling between his comfort as a theologian with the positive descriptions of Scripture and the inkling that such attributions are problematic—if only because they veer close to the Christian Trinity.

Bahya resolves the problem by deciding in favor of negation; he takes Saadia's thinking to its ultimate conclusion. The essence of God is ultimately unknowable; all we can know are God's traces in creation. Negation is the fundamental path for the Neoplatonic philosopher. Bahya here reveals his ultimate philosophical loyalty.

Attributes of Action

Bahya's approach to Scripture is most clearly articulated in his analysis of God's attributes of action, since the entire category is built upon interpretation of biblical terms. The categories of essential attributes and attributes of action developed as the Mu'tazilite resolution to the problem of describing God. The Mu'tazilites argue that we can know nothing about the essence of God other than his eternity. All the epithets Scripture uses to describe God thus represent attributes of action, terms that describe God's actions with respect to creation. Bahya asserts that although God is ultimately incomparable and indescribable, when speaking of God's actions, we can borrow terms from the created world.[55]

What allows Bahya to do this? How does he navigate the theological dilemma regarding language about God? We have seen that, on the one hand, there is a danger of lowering God to the level of something created of tashbīh, making God similar to creatures. On the other hand, there is the danger of making God so inaccessible that there is no being to worship, of

---

54. *Amānāt*, 2:4; Qafih, 89; Altmann, 83–84; Rosenblatt, 102.

55. We recall that Saadia, with the Mu'tazilites, insisted on the ultimate dissimilarity between God and all creation; Bahya, too, insists that "there is nothing like him." Bahya must thus explain how we are able to describe God with qualities he shares with creation. He argues that it is admissible to describe God by means of these attributes because of the necessity of making God known and establishing his existence so that human beings will take on obedience to God. Bahya asserts twice that "there is nothing like him" (*laysa ka-mithlihi shay'*: Qur'ān 42:10). 1:10; Qafih 76, 85; Mansoor, 134, 143. Two of Saadia's six essential attributes are that "there is nothing like him" and "there is nothing like his actions." 2:1; Qafih, 82; Altmann, 80.

dissolving God into a void—of *ta'ṭīl*, stripping God of all qualities. Bahya's argument is that we cannot worship a being we don't know. There is a religious duty to know the creator; it is a duty of the heart. Thus, although from a philosophical point of view it is impossible to make positive statements about God, we must endow God with human qualities to establish God's existence in people's minds. While from a philosophical perspective, Bahya follows the strategy of negation, from a theological perspective, he recognizes that we must describe God in order that we have a divinity to love and serve.

Attributes of Action: Theory of Language

In describing God by means of his actions with respect to creation, Bahya divides these attributes into two categories. The first includes attributes that refer to an image or bodily form. He cites several examples: "God created humanity in his image" (Gen 1:27); "I, my hand, stretched out the heavens" (Isa 45:12); "under his legs" (Exod 24:10); "in the eyes of the Lord" (Gen 6:8); "God spoke to his heart" (Gen 8:21). All these verses describe God in terms of bodily limbs and organs. Here it is easy to see, in accordance with Saadia's methodology, that these verses are to be understood metaphorically.

The second category is more subtle; these attributes describe movements and bodily acts. For example, "And God saw the light" (Gen 1:4); "And the Lord regretted that he had made man on the earth, and it grieved him in his heart" (Gen 6:6); "God smelled" (Gen 6:21); "God remembered" (Gen 8:1); "the Lord woke as one out of sleep" (Ps 78:65). Note that Bahya includes under the category of movements and physical actions *inner* activities we would consider perceptual, mental, or emotional: seeing, regretting, grieving, smelling, remembering. He is using the term movements (*ḥarakāt*) to signify any kind of movement within the human entity, whether mental or physical.

We find this usage in Saadia as well. Saadia suggests that mental states, including thinking, are like any other human activity or action. In his journey through the ten Aristotelian categories, Saadia first shows that biblical literature at times ascribes physical organs to human beings in a figurative sense, then, that organs are ascribed figuratively to nonhuman and even inanimate beings in such phrases such as, "the face of the earth" (Num 11:31); "the earth opened her mouth" (Num 11:31); "the belly of the netherworld" (Jon 2:3). All the more so, therefore, must these attributes be understood metaphorically when applied to the Creator, who is nonmaterial and possesses no physical organs.

Saadia's second step is to demonstrate that just as these organs are attributed to God metaphorically, so are the acts associated with these organs. When the Torah asserts that God hears, sees, speaks, and thinks, each must be understood in a nonliteral sense. Bahya displays the same attitude here: smelling and remembering are human activities; in God they are attributes of action. Bahya's division of attributes of action into the two categories of physical limbs and their activities can thus be traced back to Saadia, as can his classifying of mental activity together with acts of the human organs and senses.

This way of looking at the human being is typical of *kalām* thought. Neoplatonism upholds a body-mind dualism, in which remembering, grieving, or regretting would not be thought of as actions in the same sense as physical movements. Bahya shows here his immersion in the *kalām* perspective he inherits from Saadia, despite his strong mind-body dualism in other contexts.[56]

---

56. Bahya further follows Saadia in relying on the approach of the Aramaic translations of the Bible known as Targums. Bahya asserts that our predecessors (*awwālunā*)—a term both he and Saadia use to refer to the sages, in which category he includes the Aramaic translators of the Bible—translated or rendered these kinds of divine attributes in a manner that is most refined, subtle, delicate, or appropriate (*altaf*). That is, the Aramaic translators softened the gross materiality of anthropomorphic expressions by attributing them to the Glory of God. They translated expressions such as "And the Lord stood over him" as "The Glory of the Lord stood over them" (Gen 28: 13, and Targum Onqelos); "God went up from him" as "the Glory went up from him" (Gen 35:13, and Onqelos); "The Lord descended" as "the Glory of God was revealed" (Gen 11:5, and Onqelos).

Bahya follows Saadia's terminology by referring to the sages as the early ones (*awā'il*), our early ones (*awwalūnā*), or the predecessors (*qudamā'*; Hebrew, *qadmonim*). In this context it is clear that he is speaking about Onqelos, including the Targums under the rubric of rabbinic literature. Even certain Karaites use the term "the early ones" (*al-awwalūn*) in reference to the rabbis. See Haggai Ben Shammai, "Yeshu'a b. Judah—A Characterization of a Karaite Scholar of Jerusalem in the Eleventh Century," *Pe'amim* 32 (1987): 3–20.

Bahya, like Saadia, relies for his rationalistic interpretation of anthropomorphism on the procedure of Targum Onqelos. Bahya thus couches his rationalism in the name of tradition; Onqelos has already justified this procedure. Targum Onqelos was regarded by tradition as an inspired translation. Bahya endorses his approach by characterizing this rendering as appropriate, beautiful, or respectful (*makhrajan hazanan*). Qafih translates here "they interpreted them well" (*be'urum be'ur na'eh*); however, Haggai Ben Shammai suggested to me it is unlikely that *ahraja* here means "to interpret." Saadia uses this form— the verbal noun of the fourth form—to indicate translation specifically. For instance, at the beginning of both Isaiah and Daniel, he describes himself in the third person as "the one who has undertaken to translate (*ihrāj*) the meanings of this book into Arabic" (*qāla al-mutawallī ikhrāj ma'ānīhi ilā al-lugha al-'Ara-*

Scripture is thus not being careless when it uses language in an extended sense. We are embodied beings; our concepts reflect our physical nature. The first step of Scripture is to use words that create an anthropomorphic image or concept in the mind of the listener. The second step is to assert that the time has come to refine or abandon the image.

Why is this two-step procedure necessary according to Bahya? This is especially puzzling since Bahya ultimately asserts that anything that exists in the imagination is other than God. Bahya's critique is nevertheless subtle. What is the alternative to describing God through images and the language of personhood? We can use abstract terms such as "ground of being" or "necessary existent" without any idea what they mean. If we use an anthropomorphic image, at least we know that we will create a genuine image or concept within the listener's mind: the word strikes a conceptual chord with the listener. If Scripture used purely abstract language such as "ground of being," the mental concept or image (ma'na) would be a void;[57] the spiritual words would have no meaning for them and would simply draw a mental blank.[58] The prophets thus speak about a divine king or parent; listeners can relate to the being whose image these words evoke. In the second stage, the image is purified and demythologized.[59]

---

biyya). We should, thus, understand Bahya's praise as "they rendered it in a very appropriate rendition/rendering."

Bahya asserts that the predecessors denied these attributes to the Creator in order not to attribute to the Creator any bodily trait or accident. He explains that Saadia has already expounded this approach thoroughly; Bahya fully accepts and relies on Saadia's defense of the rationalistic method of exegesis.

57. The ma'na is the concept existing in the mind. It is not a concept in the abstract sense; it is not a Platonic idea of the good, of justice, or of God. The ma'na is the idea as it exists in an individual's mind, a bit of mental data.

58. See Hilary Putnam, "On Negative Theology," Faith and Philosophy 14, no. 4 (October 1997): 407–22; Ehud Ben Or, "Meaning and Reference in Maimonides' Negative Theology," Harvard Theological Review 88, no. 3 (1995): 339–60.

59. Bahya, 1:10; Qafih, 78; Mansoor, 136. The rendering of the Arabic passage in which Bahya makes this assertion needs some clarification. Bahya writes that it is necessary that the terms and concepts (ma'ānī) be in accordance with the understanding of the listener, so that the concept (ma'na) at first be present in his thought in accordance with the corporeal meaning understood from the corporeal term. Then it (the concept) can be purified (yulaṭṭaf bihi) (Or: he can be gently guided) and he can be made to understand that this is an expression that is accessible, an approximation (taqrīb) and a figure of speech (ta'bīr) on the part of Scripture, and that God's true nature (or the true meaning of the text) is far too subtle (alṭāf) and exalted for us to understand in its full sublimity.

Although Bahya is a philosopher, his pietistic sensibility overrides concern for philosophical precision. Maimonides argues that if we conceive of God as having a body we do not actually apprehend God; we worship a false imagining we call God.[60] In contrast, for Bahya it is acceptable for the average person to worship a God conceived in bodily terms. Anthropomorphic descriptions at least convince people of God's existence. God, the referent whom we want to describe in language, is a purely spiritual being. However, most people cannot comprehend that which transcends the physical. If the Torah had spoken of a purely abstract being who is one, eternal, and existent, most people would not be convinced that such a being exists, much less commands our worship. However, when Scripture speaks of a magnificent king of all the earth, who rescues people with a mighty hand and an outstretched arm, such powerful images can reach the ordinary person. And there is no harm in Scripture's speaking this way, because the wise can then strip the image of its physical accretions and understand the purely spiritual God these mask.[61]

Qafih asserts that the subject of *yulaṭṭaf* is the listener. Haggai Ben-Shammai suggested to me that it can be read also in the passive, in which case the subject is the listener. It will be explained to the listener in a subtle way; the listener will be handled subtly and will be informed that this (the anthropomorphizing term) is only an approximation (*taqrīr*) and interpretation or explication (*taʾbīr*).

Bahya uses the root *l-ṭ-f* in three ways: (1) to describe the process of refining words or of gently guiding the hearer to a correct understanding; (2) to describe God's essence, which is more subtle and refined than the physical; and (3) to describe abstract matters such as the world-to-come. The basic premise with respect to God is that it is impossible to understand God in the full subtlety of his essence, so we have to find ways to bring the matter as close as possible (*taqrīb*) to our understanding. This is similar to Saadia's idea that human language is not adequate to express the essence of God; we must find various parables and metaphors in order to circumvent this difficulty. On figurative speech (*majāz*), see Wolfhart Heinrichs, "Contacts between Scriptural Hermeneutics and Literary Theory in Islām: The Case of *Majāz*," *Zeitschrift für Geschichte der Arabisch-Islamischen Wissenschaften* 7 (1991–92): 253–84, esp. 255–57.

60. *Guide* 1.60; Joel 99–100; Pines 145–47.

61. Bahya has adopted Saadia's view of Scripture: the anthropomorphic husks do not express the true meaning of Scripture. However, he has added a contemplative dimension, a ladder of ascent. One must engage in the process of stripping away the anthropomorphic accretions until one has an accurate conception of God. Bahya expresses this process with regard to God's unity as well. Here Bahya reiterates that part of the process of coming to a true understanding of God is knowing that we cannot know God in his essence; even the

Scripture thus reaches two audiences at once.[62]

Bahya derives this view of Scriptural language from Saadia's views in both the *Kitāb al-amānāt* and the *Commentary to "Sefer yeẓirah."* We have seen his view in the *Kitāb al-amānāt*. In the *Commentary to "Sefer yeẓirah"* Saadia asserts that when the prophets came to teach people about divine matters, they failed to find in conventional language expressions through which they could convey divine concepts. They thus had two options: either to invent words, or to extend meanings from existing words. If they had chosen to invent words to express divine concepts, the new words would have been incomprehensible. The prophets chose rather to borrow words that humanity had coined to describe noble matters, extending them to express concepts that pertain to the Deity. The familiar words would be known and comprehended, but the prophets emphasized that these are just metaphorical expressions, whereas in reality, nothing resembles God or his actions.[63] Saadia and Bahya agree that in order to express that which transcends ordinary human experience, we must borrow language from ordinary experience and extend its meaning. If we coin new terminology, we do not help a person understand the spiritual reality to which we are pointing. By borrowing meanings from ordinary terms, we communicate to others with that which is familiar and comprehensible, extending the realm of listeners' experience by emphasizing that the words are metaphorical.[64] Ultimately, however, Bahya quotes a Sufi dictum: Anything that exists in the imagination is other than God.

Bahya's Negative Theology

It is thus that Bahya genuinely moves in the direction of Neoplatonic negative theology. Bahya informs us that the correct approach is to seek to know the reality of God through God's traces or effects (*āthār*), not through God himself. For God is exceedingly close from the perspective of his traces, but just as remote when one tries to conceptualize God's

---

abstract, ontological attributes of existence, eternity, and oneness are intended only to deny their opposites: that God is nonexistent, created, multiple, or composite.

62. Today we might argue the opposite: biblical anthropomorphism impedes the believability of the biblical God. Cf. Warren Zev Harvey, "Maimonides and Aquinas on Interpreting the Bible," *Proceedings of the American Academy for Jewish Research* (1988): 59–77.

63. Saadia, *Kitāb al-mabādī'*, Introduction; Qafih, 25–26; Mayer Lambert, *Commentaire sur le Séfer Yeṣira, ou Livre de la création* (Paris, 1891), 21–22 (French); 6–7 (Arabic).

64. On this passage, see note 58 above.

essence or self. If we can arrive at a point where we efface God from the senses and imagination as if he doesn't exist, and find him from the perspective of his traces as if he is inseparable from us, this is the utmost of human knowledge of God, as the prophet encouraged in saying, "And you shall know this day and lay it upon your heart, that the Lord is God" (Deut 4:39). Bahya leaves out the conclusion of the verse: "the Lord is God in heaven above and in the earth below, there is none else." We can see God in the earth below through God's traces in creation.[65]

God cannot be defined or grasped through discursive knowledge. We find God not through concept, but through contemplation. The person most knowing of God is the one most perplexed by him, who knows he or she does not know. [66] On the other hand, one should be continually on the lookout for traces of God that fill heaven and earth. The greatest of knowledge is to admit that we are utterly ignorant about the true nature of God's essence. If we find ourselves conceiving of God with a form or likeness in the imagination—if our concept of God has become reified in an image—we should use the method of investigation until we efface the image from our imagination and realize God indirectly by the method of inference (istidlāl). Then the fact of God's existence will become certain for us through proof, while reified images will disappear.

Limitations of Human Knowledge

Bahya appears to espouse a cautious, indirect approach to God, one that respects the limits of human knowledge and does not seek to overstep its bounds. At the same time, where logic respectfully hesitates, Bahya hints at a form of illumination or religious experience.[67]

In expressing the limitations of human knowledge, Bahya draws an analogy to the physical senses. Eyesight alone can perceive objects of vision; if we try to see with our ears, we will not find the object of perception and conclude it does not exist. Each of the senses can grasp its appropriate sense object, but is strained if it tries to go beyond it, like the eye when it looks into the sun.

---

65. Ibid.; Qafih, 84; Mansoor, 142.

66. This Sufi dictum, cited in the name of the ninth-century Sufi Dhū'l-Nūn al-Miṣrī by the tenth-century Sufi Qushayrī, is quoted word for word by Bahya. Bahya here may have influenced Maimonides' notion of perplexity.

67. I argue in my book on Bahya that in the First Gate, qua philosopher, Bahya upholds a negative theology, while in the Eighth Gate, as a teacher of practical piety, Bahya suggests that the gap between human beings and God can be overcome. Here we discern that movement within the First Gate itself.

We know the sun indirectly, through its rays of light and the fact that it takes away the darkness. Suppose someone were to find this insufficient and say, I want to know the sun directly, by looking intently at the sun itself. The person would be blinded. Such a person does not realize that he or she already possesses the most a human being can achieve: knowing the sun by experiencing its effects.[68] When we seek knowledge of God through God's traces, the intellect is illumined, and we perceive all that is in human power. In contrast, when we seek to grasp God's essence, we lose our apprehension, like someone who looks too closely at the sun.[69]

In the beginning of Book Two of the *Kitāb al-amānāt*, Saadia warns about the person who is disappointed that we cannot discover God in the way we achieve the gross knowledge of the senses.[70] Such a person would come to believe God does not exist, because God is not as apparent as the presence of the mountains and the trees. Bahya makes a similar argument here. If we cease trying to find God directly and find God instead through evidence of God's traces in creation, we will find God manifest and inseparable from us. God can be shown to exist just as we know a tree exists because we touch its trunk and smell the scent of its leaves.[71] However, we should not think that once we have inferred the fact of God's existence, we

---

68. This is an interesting reversal of the Platonic image of the cave. In the Platonic story certain cave dwellers say and do just that; realizing that all they see are effects, traces, shadows of real things, they want to see the things themselves, as well as the source of light that makes all seeing possible. And yes, at first they are blinded by the sun, but slowly adjust and become able to look at the sun directly, and upon return to the cave learn to make out the shadow world as well. It is difficult to know whether Bahya knew of this image and deliberately inverted it, or is simply unaware of it.

69. *Hidāya* I:10; Qafih, 89–90; Mansoor, 145–46. Bahya quotes Isa 48:17: "I am the Lord your God who teaches you in order to benefit you, who guides you in the way for you to walk." Bahya's intention in quoting the verse is that just as we know the sun and its purpose best by benefiting from its rays, not by looking at its rays directly, so we know God best by benefiting from his guidance. Note that whereas until now Bahya has been adamant that we cannot know God through reason or understand God's essence (*ma'na*), here he reverses himself and says there is much we can apprehend—as long as we seek to understand in the way that God can be known, through God's traces.

70. *Amānāt*, 2, introduction; Qafih, 76–82; Altmann, 75–80; Rosenblatt, 87–94.

71. We know the tree must have come from some source. Causes cannot go back indefinitely, so there must have been a first cause of the tree's existence. The Creator is as present to us as the tree, if we use our senses and mind well to discover his existence. It is thus that for Bahya there is a religious duty to use one's mind to achieve knowledge of God.

should continue in our search and try to discover the true nature of God's essence through conception, image, or definition. By doing so, we may lose the reality of God altogether, for "anything that exists in our imagination is other than God."[72] Bahya thus urges respectful caution, quoting a verse from Proverbs: "Have you found honey? Eat as much as is sufficient for you, lest you be filled with it and vomit it" (Prov 25:16).[73] Maimonides cites the verse for the same purpose: to show that the mind has limits beyond which it cannot reach. We should be satisfied with those limits, lest we lose the knowledge we have.

The Experiential Turn

Bahya takes a critical, skeptical stance regarding the limitations of knowledge. But he has also added that if one approaches knowledge of God in the proper, indirect way, one's mind will be illumined by wisdom. He continues this turn in a final admonition to the reader. When we have arrived at this level of acknowledging God's unity (*tawḥīd*) through reason, we should devote ourselves wholeheartedly[74] to the Creator and strive to grasp God's existence by way of his wisdom, compassion, and care for creation—that is, through attributes of action. We should make this our way of drawing near to God so that we may be among the "seekers of the Lord" (*mevakshei Hashem*). Then we will obtain from God help and assistance (*awn wa-ta'yīd*) to understand God and grasp his true nature, as we find in Psalms: "The secret of the Lord is with those who fear him (*sod Hashem li-yre'av*); to them he makes known his covenant" (Ps 25:14). Bahya twice quotes this verse. In the first instance, he speaks about the importance of circumspection, of not speaking too much about the essence of the Creator; it is the "glory of God" to hide the secret of the Creator from the masses.[75] Here he turns to the select and promises that if they seek to know the Lord in the correct way—through God's traces— God will, in fact, assist them to know of God all that it is in their power to comprehend.

---

72. *Hidāya* I:10; Qafih, 88; Mansoor, 145. Bahya is clearly aware of Sufi use of *kalām* discourse, and very much in the spirit of Qushayrī's integration of Sufism and *kalām*. However, whereas Qushayrī and most Sufis are Ash'arites and thus their position could be tolerated by Orthodox Muslims, Bahya's *kalām* is Mu'tazilite. Orthodox Muslims looked askance at the rationalism of the Mu'tazilite approach.

73. *Hidāya*, I:10; Qafih, 88; Mansoor, 145. Maimonides, *Guide*, 1:32; Joel, 46, Pines, 69.

74. *Ikhlās nafsaka.*

75. *Hidāya* I:10; Qafih, 86; Mansoor, 144.

Thus, although Bahya denies we can cognize God's essence, in several passages he does suggest a Neoplatonic illumination or religious experience. In the Gate on Contemplation he offers a meditation whose goal is to perceive God's wisdom through the beauty of our elegant universe. God's wisdom is like one light reflecting on various colored window panes. Scientific study of the universe shows that each detail of creation reveals another facet of God's wisdom. For Bahya, this is an authentic way to know the Divine: through contemplation of God's wisdom in the world, and through the ensuing experience of gratitude, awe, and love for the source of all being.

CONCLUSIONS

We have seen that from a strictly philosophical point of view, the Bible should not speak about God at all. Human language applies only to that which is created, while God, as Creator of all, is not of the genus of created things. From the perspective of philosophy, we cannot attribute any qualities of our universe to God. However, there is a tension between the claim of philosophy that it is impossible to speak about God and the theological need to do so.

Saadia as exegete chooses the theological approach. He teaches that the Torah asserts three essential attributes of God: God is living, knowing, and powerful. Bahya follows Saadia's lead, but endows God with the purely abstract attributes of oneness, eternity, and existence, which describe God independent of creation. Moreover, he asserts that even these attributes are meant only to negate their opposites. The qualities we hear about in the Torah—those of the personal God who is compassionate and gracious—are attributes of God's actions. We cannot describe God's essence, except by negation.

Bahya uses a *kalām* method of proof to demonstrate the existence of God by pointing to God's traces in creation. However, Bahya innovates by asserting that the Bible itself—specifically the prophet Isaiah—models this method of philosophical demonstration. Isaiah teaches us to use our senses and deduce rationally that God exists.

Bahya also offers us a process of interpreting Scripture. The reason Scripture describes God in anthropomorphic terms is to make God accessible to the ordinary person. Human beings need the God of poetry and metaphor; the Torah endows God with human qualities so that people will be able to love and serve the divine. Bahya thus suggests a twofold process of interpreting the biblical text. First, we should accept the Bible's testimony that there is a God intimately involved with our lives; second, we should strip from our description of God its anthropomorphic shells. The Torah describes God in familiar, comprehensible language; it is for the philosophical reader to refine the image of God depicted in the plain sense of Scripture.

Bahya's philosophical exegesis of the Bible is also a method of contemplation. We should look in the text and in our world for traces of the Divine. These traces do not give us knowledge of God's essence; they leave us in a state of wonderment and perplexity. However, although we cannot cognize God's essence, we can experience God's presence. Bahya's God is ultimately the intimate, personal God of both rabbinic Judaism and Sufi mysticism.

Saadia and Bahya thoroughly integrate biblical exegesis and philosophical argument. Both believe that reason and revelation teach one truth; reason can teach us independent of revelation, and reason ultimately confirms that which we know from the Bible. When these thinkers use reason as a canon for interpreting Scripture, they do not believe they are importing something foreign, but rather revealing Scripture's genuine spiritual intent. Human beings have been granted the gift of intellect to know the Creator. This is a religious duty, a duty of the heart. Thus, if we do not verify through reason what we have learned through Scripture, we have failed in our duty to the Creator. Moreover, the Bible teaches the correct philosophical approach: to find God's presence by investigating the world.

Saadia, a translator sensitive to language, argues that poetry conveys a richer sense of God than does prose. Bahya's sensibility is that of the pietist, not the poet. His first concern is that we have a God with whom we can relate. Human metaphors make God accessible to us, so that human beings can love and serve the divine. By gradually stripping away these anthropomorphic images, we can ascend through philosophical contemplation to achieve the genuine purpose of Scripture: the duties of the heart.

THE DUAL NATURE OF
THE BIBLICAL ANGEL
IN THE PHILOSOPHY OF MAIMONIDES

Hannah Kasher
Bar-Ilan University

ONE OF THE ROLES that the naturalist philosophers took upon themselves in their interpretation of the Bible was demythologization, or emptying these texts of their mythical components. They did so by interpreting certain biblical stories as allegories, for example, the story of the talking serpent in the Garden of Eden and the heavenly drama in the book of Job, in which the major actors are Satan and the divine beings. One such mythical motif in the Bible that the Jewish philosophers of the Middle Ages worked to demythologize is the angel.

The Hebrew word *mal'akh* (based on the root *l-'-kh*)[1] means "messenger." In the Bible, this word can mean a messenger sent by one person to another, or a messenger of God. The discussion below will relate only to those figures called "messengers of God" or "messengers of the Lord," what we call in English "angels."[2] The assumption that the messengers of God are exalted beings apparently led to the transformation of the expressions "messenger of God" and "messenger of the Lord" to mean a heavenly being, who might serve as a member of the divine court or fulfill the symbolic role of leader of a human nation.[3]

Demythologization

In his works, Maimonides does not give angels the mythological role of national leaders. This is in contrast to his contemporary, Rabad (R. Abraham ibn Da'ud), author of *Ha-emunah ha-ramah*, who develops an angelology integrating the Aristotelian system of intellects, reincarnated

---

1. This word is the same in Arabic: *mal'akh*.

2. *Enziqlopediah miqra'it* (1967), s.v. *"Mal'akh ha-Shem, Mal'akhim."*

3. For a collection of sources, see R. Margaliot, *Mal'akhey 'Elyon* (Jerusalem, 5724).

souls, and stars with mythical figures of national leaders.[4] In order to demonstrate this process of demythologization in Maimonides' work, we will examine his first interpretation of the dream of Jacob's ladder,[5] which he bases on a midrash in *Pesiqta de-Rav Qahana* (23):

> The Torah says, "And he dreamt, and behold! A ladder, etc." (Gen 28:12)....These are the ministers of the nations of the world....This teaches that the Holy One, blessed be he, showed our forefather Jacob the minister of Babylon ascending and descending, the minister of Media ascending and descending, the minister of Greece ascending and descending, and the minister of Edom ascending and descending....Thus your children will be enslaved by these four kingdoms in this world.

In his *Mishneh Torah (Hilkhot yesodei ha-Torah* 7:3), Maimonides contextualizes this allegory.

> The things imparted to the prophet in a prophetic vision are conveyed to him in the form of an allegory. Its interpretation is immediately impressed on his mind during the vision, so that he knows what it means. For example, the ladder that our forefather Jacob saw, with the angels ascending and descending upon it, was an allegory for the foreign kingdoms and their subjugation. This is like the beasts the Ezekiel envisioned (Ezek 1, 10), and the bubbling pot and the staff of the almond tree that Jeremiah saw (Jer. 1), the scroll of Ezekiel (Ezek 2), and the *ephah* of Zechariah (Zech 5).

Maimonides' description of the first image, Jacob's ladder, includes the appearance of angels: "For example, the ladder that our forefather Jacob saw, with the angels ascending and descending upon it, was an allegory for the foreign kingdoms and their subjugation."

According to the allegory in the midrash, the angels ascending and descending the ladder are "the ministers of the nations of the world...the minister of Babylon ascending and descending, the minister of Media ascending and descending, the minister of Greece ascending and descending, and the minister of Edom ascending and descending." The midrash concludes with the interpretation: "Thus your children will be enslaved by these four kingdoms in this world." Maimonides refrains from integrating the mythological figures of the ministers of the nations into his work, borrowing from this midrash only the concept of subjugation of kingdoms mentioned at the end of the section. Yet the question remains, if the angels are not the ministers of the foreign nations and their messen-

---

4. See Abraham ibn Da'ud, *Sefer ha-emunah ha-ramah*, ed. S. Weil (Frankfurt am Main, 1852), article 2, principle 4.

5. For an intensive, in-depth analysis of Maimonides' various interpretations of Jacob's ladder, see Sarah Klein-Braslavy, "Maimonides' Commentary on the Dream of Jacob's Ladder," [in Hebrew] *Bar Ilan* 22–23 (5748): 329–49.

gers, what, according to Maimonides, is the connection between the angels on the ladder in the allegory and the four nations in the interpretation?

I think we can propose an intriguing solution for the question of the relationship between the allegory (the angels on the ladder) and its interpretation (the kingdoms and their subjugation). When we examine the other allegories that Maimonides mentions in this context—the beasts in Ezekiel, the bubbling pot and the staff of the almond tree in Jeremiah, the scroll of Ezekiel, and the *ephah* of Zechariah—we find that in at least one, the relationship between the allegory and its interpretation seems to be linguistic instead of semantic. Maimonides himself explains this in *Guide of the Perplexed*:

> Know that just as the prophets see things whose purpose it is to constitute a parable—as for instance...Ezekiel's scroll...and the seething pot that was seen by Jeremiah, and other similar parables whose purpose it is to imitate certain notions—they also see things whose purpose it is to point to what is called to the attention by the term designating the thing seen because of that term's derivation or because of an equivocality of terms...For instance the intention in the dictum of Jeremiah concerning *maqqel shaqed* [a rod of an almond tree]...did not concern the notion of rod or that of almond. Similarly Amos saw *qluv qayiz* [a basket of summer fruit], so that he should infer from it the end of the period. It accordingly says: *Ba' haq-qez*. [The end is come.][6]
>
> Stranger than this is the intimation aroused through the use of a certain term whose letters are identical to those of another term; solely the order of the letters is changed; and between the two terms there is in no way an etymological connection or a community of meaning...Through this method very strange things appear, which are likewise secrets, as in its dictum with regard to the Chariot: "brass" and "burnished" and "foot" and "calf" and "lightening."

We might, therefore, propose that the connection between "the angels ascending and descending" and the "allegory for the foreign kingdoms and their subjugation" is morphemic: *mal'akhim* (angels) represent *malkhuyot* (kingdoms) because of the resemblance between the letters of

6. Ibn Ezra comments on Amos 8:2, which reads, "He said, 'What do you see, Amos?' I replied, 'A basket of summer fruits [*qluv qayiz*].' God then said to me, 'The end has come.'" Ibn Ezra interprets this as follows: "'He said'—this was all through visions of prophecy, just as God said to Jeremiah (1:11–12), 'What do you see?', and he replied, 'The staff of an almond tree,' and God answered, 'I hasten to fulfill my word.' In other words, I will not move nor depart until I have fulfilled my word. Since the 'fruit' will not arrive until the end, in this way 'the end has come.'" See *Shnei perushei R. Abraham Ibn Ezra le-Trei 'Asar*, ed. U. Simon (Ramat Gan, 1991), 251.

both words. Support for this resemblance lies in the affinity for Arabic present in the background of Maimonides' work the *Mishneh Torah*, even though its language is Hebrew. In the Qur'ān, the word parallel to *m.l.'a.kh* is *m-l-kh* (the *alef* is absent). Furthermore, Maimonides sometimes used the Arabic orthography for this word (see his introduction to *Perek ḥelek*). Thus, we see that here Maimonides preserves the historical meaning of the allegory of Jacob's ladder as subjugation of the foreign kingdoms, while abandoning the mythological feature of the angels representing ministers of the nations. Below, we will examine how in his other works Maimonides proposes other meanings for the angels ascending and descending the ladder.

The *Mishneh Torah* contains yet another reference to the term *mal'akh* that reflects demythologization, but is usually interpreted as a polemic against magic. In this context, Maimonides responds to the verse in Psalms, "The angel of God encamps around his reverent ones and rescues them" (Ps 34:8). At first study, this verse seems to raise the question: How can one angel encamp around God's reverent ones and rescue them?

Maimonides first directs his opposition to the magical belief in the protective power of angels by protesting the activity of "those who write the names of angels inside the *mezuzah*" (*Hilkhot mezuzah* 5:4). Later, he proposes an alternative relationship between the term *mal'akh* and three types of religious articles: *tefillin* (phylacteries), *tzitzit* (ritual fringes), and *mezuzah* (*Hilkhot mezuzah* 6:13).

> One should carefully observe the precept of *mezuzah*....Whenever a person enters or leaves a home that has a *mezuzah*, he will meet with the Oneness of the Holy One, blessed be he, and remember his love we owe to him. He will be roused from his sleep and indulgence in temporal vanities. He will know that nothing endures forever and for all eternally except knowledge of the Creator of the universe, and he will straight away return to his senses and walk in upright paths. The early sages declared, "Anyone who has *tefillin* on his head and on his arm, *tzitzit* on his garment, and a *mezuzah* on his doorpost is strengthened against sinning, for he has many reminders. They are the veritable angels that rescue him from sin, as it is written, 'The angel of God encamps around his reverent ones and rescues them.'"

Maimonides bases his explanation on the Babylonian Talmud (Tractate *Menahot* 43b):

> Our rabbis taught: Beloved are Israel, for the Holy One, blessed be he, surrounded them with *mitzvot*: *tefillin* on their heads, *tefillin* on their arms, *tzitzit* on their garments, and *mezuzot* on their doorposts. Concerning these, David said, "Seven times a day I have praised you for your righteous ordinances" (Ps 119:164). As David entered the bath and saw himself standing naked, he exclaimed, "Woe is me that I stand naked without any precepts around me!" But when he reminded himself of the circumcision

in his flesh, his mind was set at ease. When he came out he sang a hymn of praise concerning it, as it is written, "For the conductor, with string music; on the eighth. A psalm by David" (Ps 6:1), that is concerning circumcision that was given for the eighth [day].

R. Eliezer ben Jacob said, "Whoever has *tefillin* on his head, *tefillin* on his arm, *tzitzit* on his garment, and the *mezuzah* on his doorpost, these are all strengtheners against sin, as it is written, "A three-ply cord is not easily severed" (Ecc 4:12) and also, "The angel of God encamps around his reverent ones and rescues them."

In this context, the guardian *mitzvot* appear in relation to several numbers: seven ("seven times a day"), eight ("For the conductor...on the eighth"), and three ("three-ply cord"). R. Eliezer ben Jacob refers to the three *mitzvot* as "strengtheners," as they apparently create power. These *mitzvot* surround the person performing them and guard him. Yet these concepts of plurality and guarding that the Talmud associates with the *mitzvot* do not form an explicit identification of the encamping angel with these *mitzvot*.[7] It is Maimonides himself who transforms the single encamping angel into multiple angels identified with the ritual objects that surround and guard a person. We will find it useful to compare the wording of the original source in the Talmud and Maimonides' citation in the *Mishneh Torah*.

---

7. In another context, the Mishnah (*Avot* 4:13) cites R. Eliezer ben Jacob as declaring, "Whoever performs a mitzvah acquires an advocate." In other words, in performing a mitzvah, a person acquires an advocate on high, and there is a direct relationship between the number of *mitzvot* and these advocates. In *Midrash Rabbah* (to Exod 32:6), an angel replaces the advocate. "'Behold! I send an angel before you' (Exod 23:20)—this is what is written, 'The angel of God encamps around his reverent ones and he releases them' (Ps 34:8). When a person does a mitzvah, God gives him an angel to guard him, as it says, 'The angel of God encamps.'" We discern three interpretations here. (1) R. Eliezer ben Jacob's exegesis in the Talmud, in which he cites the verse on the encamping angel and mentions the three ritual objects, but does not specifically identify angels with the *mitzvot*. (2) R. Eliezer ben Jacob's exegesis in the Mishnah, which outlines a direct relationship between the *mitzvot* and the advocates for human beings. (3) The explanation in the Midrash, which describes the heavenly reward of a guardian angel in return for each mitzvah and cites the same verse regarding the encamping angel. This text also does not identify the angel directly with the mitzvah itself, but describes how God grants the angel to a person in reward for performing a mitzvah.

Talmud	Mishneh Torah
R. Eliezer ben Jacob said,	The early sages declared,
Whoever has	Anyone who has
tefillin on his head,	*tefillin* on his head
tefillin on his arm,	and on his arm,
tzitzit on his garment,	*tzitzit* on his garment,
and a *mezuzah* on his doorpost,	and a *mezuzah* on his doorpost,
these are all strengtheners against sin,	is strengthened against sinning
as it is written, "A three-ply cord is not easily severed"	
	for he has many reminders
	and they are the veritable angels that rescue him from sin
and also, "The angel of God encamps around his reverent ones and rescues them."	as it is written, "The angel of God encamps around his reverent ones and rescues them."

In his explanation, Maimonides does not mention the number "three," which appears in the numerological exposition in the Talmud. Instead, he makes the vague statement "many reminders." In addition, he explicitly identifies the "angels" (who rescue from sin) with the "reminders" of *tefillin*, *tzitzit*, and *mezuzah*.[8] Thus these *mitzvot* do not imply the magical meaning of rescue. Instead of viewing the "names of angels" written inside the *mezuzah* in the magical role of guardians of the threshold, Maimonides proposes a metaphoric role for the *mezuzah* as an angel rescuing human beings from sin. The person who passes beside a *mezuzah* encounters the name of God and "remembers his love." As a result of recognizing the real truth, the person abandons his inappropriate behavior.

In these two interpretations in the *Mishneh Torah*, on Jacob's ladder and on the encamping angel, Maimonides aims mainly to expropriate the mythological and magical significance of these biblical verses. In the commentary on Jacob's ladder, that mythological meaning is the ministers of the nations, whereas in the one on the encamping angel, the magical sig-

---

8. See also *Hilkhot Tefillin: Hilkhot Mezuzah: Hilkhot Sefer Torah* 4:25.

nificance is the names of the angels in the *mezuzot*. Usually, though, Maimonides does not express the demythologization of the angels only in this conceptual manner. Rather, he applies the logical principle known as "Occam's razor," according to which the simplest explanation based on the fewest possible assumptions is the most preferable. Following this principle, Maimonides identifies the angels with beings already present in the natural world.

The works of al-Farabi and Ibn Sina led to identification of the angels with the Separate Intellect, or one of the ten Separate Intellects emanated by God. In Maimonides' writings, we find the term "angels" used in this sense in his commentary on the Mishnah (for example, in the introduction to *Perek ḥelek*) and in the *Mishneh Torah* (such as in *Hilkhot yesodei ha-Torah*, chapter 2). We also find this type of explicit linguistic identification of the term "angels" in the first part of the *Guide of the Perplexed* (1.149): "the angels are also not corporeal; rather, they are intellects separated from the material." Often, Maimonides identifies the angel with the active intellect, the tenth in the system of separate intellects, the one that maintains a connection with events taking place on earth. At times, Maimonides even grants the title "angel" to a prophet or a sage,[9] either because of that person's special relationship with the active intellect or because of his virtue.

A change becomes apparent in the second part of the *Guide*,[10] when Maimonides explains the term "angel" as indicating a messenger as well. At the same time, the term "messenger" acquires a unique significance in Maimonides' work. According to him, the world operates as a causative chain originating with God and his primordial will, such that each person who performs an action is indirectly performing the will of God (*Guide* 2.48). Thus a "messenger" is actually an intermediary. Because all creatures and natural powers are considered intermediaries whose primary cause is God, the term "angel," in fact, relates to every active entity in the world.[11] But we should note that according to Maimonides, the angel when carrying out his mission does not necessarily express an intentional

---

9. See *Perush ha-Mishnah, Avot* 5:13.

10. Elsewhere, I have proposed that early material written by Maimonides is integrated into the first part of the *Guide*, and that this material is perhaps *Sefer ha-nevu'ah* [The Book of Prophecy], which he began to compose in an early period of his life. See "Is There an Early Stratum in the *Guide of the Perplexed*?" *Maimonidean Studies* 3 (1995): 105–29.

11. A similar approach is found in the work of Abraham Ibn Ezra, for example, his commentaries on Zech 1:8, Ps 33:4, Ps 73:28. See Y. Cohen, *Haguto ha-philosophit shel R. Abraham ibn Ezra* (Jerusalem, 1996), 94–96.

and desired plan, but rather the primordial will of God, according to which nature follows its given rules.

From this point on, Maimonides uses both meanings, intellect and messenger, in parallel. He does this explicitly in chapter 6 of the second part of the *Guide*, which is entirely dedicated to a discussion of angels. This section begins by reminding the reader that

> Now a chapter making it clear for us that the angels are not bodies occurs previously in this Treatise[12] that the angels are incorporeal. This is also what Aristotle says. But there is a difference in the term; for he speaks of separate intellects and we speak of angels.
>
> As for his saying that these separate intellects are also intermediarier between God, may He be exalted, and the existents; and that it is through their intermediation that the spheres are in motion....[13]

The typical angels, in other words, the exalted beings, are incorporeal. The philosopher Aristotle shares this metaphysical assertion. The difference on this issue between the religious tradition and Aristotle is merely terminological: Aristotle uses the traditional term "angels" only to indicate their nature as intellectual beings that are incorporeal. After this, Maimonides clarifies the reason for use of the term "angel" to indicate "the separate intellects": these beings are "intermediarier between God, may He be exalted, and the existents." Maimonides goes on to generalize:

> Every act of God is described as performed by angels. But "angel" means "messenger," thus every one that performs a mission is an angel....Even the movements of beasts...the Torah describes these as caused by an angel....the elements are also called angels.

In this context, Maimonides points out that the term "angel" is used in the Bible not only in relation to the exalted beings ("the separate intellects") but also in regard to the lowest entities ("movements of beasts" and "the elements"). He then lists these systematically.

There is no doubt that the word "angel" is used regarding:

1. a messenger from among human beings;
2. the prophets;
3. the separate intellects perceived by prophets in prophetic visions;
4. animal powers...for every one of the physical powers is an angel, as are the powers spread throughout the world....The meaning of "angel" is any kind of activity.

---

12. See *Guide* 1.49, "The angels also are not corporeal; rather, they are intellects separate from the material."

13. *Guide* 2.6, trans. Pines, 262.

Because the term "angel" is an unequivocal term meaning "messen-ger," Maimonides presents the entities bearing this name in this specific order. First he notes the application of this term to the clearest form of messenger: "a messenger from among human beings" (1). Next, he lists the human messenger sent by God, the prophet (2). Then he recalls the separate intellect (3), the entity that connects God to the prophet. Accord-ing to this list, the use of the term "angel" as referring to the separate intel-lect is relegated to third place, whereas before he considered it the clearest definition. At the end of the list Maimonides presents the use of the term "angel" in relation to the powers of animals (4). He then explains this broad usage of the term "angel" by investing this term with a dynamic, very general meaning: "the meaning of 'angel' is any kind of activity." This dynamic meaning apparently does not permit Maimonides to recall the elements again, and instead, he mentions them at the beginning of the next chapter: "We have already explained that the term "angel" is a hom-onym, and that it includes the intellectual beings, the spheres, and the ele-ments—for all these are engaged in performing a command." In this state-ment, he presents the term "angel" as a multivalent term (homonym) because he specifies the different levels of reality ("the intellectual beings, the spheres, and the elements"), but he also gives the shared semantic core ("for all these are engaged in performing a command").

At times, Maimonides relates to the term *mal'akhim* simultaneously as a metaphysical concept meaning the separate intellects and as a biblical term referring to the role of intermediary in such a way that they do not overlap. Thus, in one place, he interprets the term *mal'akhim* in one verse as an indication of a natural entity that is not the separate intellects, while he delineates another term in that verse as indicating the separate intel-lects. In this text (*Guide* 3.13), Maimonides interprets two verses in the book of Job (4:18–19) based on two other verses from the same book (15:15–16).

Job 4:18–19	*Job 15:15–16*	*Guide 3:13*
18: If he cannot have faith even in his ser-vants	15: Behold, he cannot have faith even in his holy beings,	separate intellects
and finds fault with his messengers (*mal'akhav*),	and the heavens are not pure in his eyes,	heavenly spheres

19: then surely [he does the same with] those who dwell in clay houses, whose foundation is in the dust,	16: surely it is so for the loathsome and tainted one,	human beings
who are crushed before maggots.	man, who drinks iniquity like water.	

In this section of the *Guide*, Maimonides understands the status of humanity based on that of the other entities.

> If [man's] being is compared to that of the spheres and all the more to that of the separate beings, it is very, very contemptible. Accordingly it says: "Behold, He puteth no trust in His servants, and His angels He chargeth with deficiency [*tahalah*]. How much less in them that dwell in houses of clay, whose foundation is in the dust!" (Job 4: 18-19). Know that "His servants" that are referred to in this verse do not belong at all to the human species; this is proven by its saying: "How much less in them that dwell in houses of clay whose foundation is in the dust!" But "His servants" mentioned in this verse are the angels. Similarly, also, "His angels" referred to in this verse are indubitably the spheres.[14]

Maimonides deciphers the two sections of the first verse using the parallel phrases in the second verse:

1. His servants (Job 4:18) = his holy beings (Job 15:15) = angels (*mal'akhim*) = separate intellects
2. His messengers (*mal'akhav*) (Job 4:18) = heavens (Job 15:15) = heavenly spheres

In this section, Maimonides uses the term *mal'akh* in two different roles: as a biblical word with a general meaning (of intermediary), in this context indicating the heavenly spheres; and as a term indicating the separate intellects.

Maimonides further challenges us regarding the word *mal'akh* when he offers multiple interpretations for this term using the same verse as a source text. For example, at the beginning of the *Mishneh Torah*, in *Hilkhot yesodei ha-Torah* 2:4, within a description of metaphysics as an esoteric system, Maimonides presents angels in the following manner.

> Thirdly, there are those creations that have a form but no shape. These are the angels, which have no bodies, but whose forms vary from angel to angel.

---

14. *Guide* 3.13, trans. Pines, 455.

If so, what did the prophets mean when they said that they saw angels of fire with wings?[15] This is due to the riddles of prophetic vision, for angels in reality have no bodies and are not affected by physical limitations, as it is written, "For the Lord your God is a consuming fire" (Deut 4:24). This fire is merely analogous, as it is written, "He makes the winds his messengers" (*mal'akhav*) (Ps 104:4).

Because Maimonides describes the angels as incorporeal entities, he is forced to confront the question of how the prophets can describe them as entities with a certain appearance, made of fire and having wings. Maimonides argues that this characterization is allegorical: it expresses their differentiation from physical bodies. The wings symbolize lightness as well as fire, the fourth element and the lightest of all (above earth, water, and air). The wind, or the air moving underneath this fire, indicates that the angels are dissimilar from physical entities, which are made of earth and water. The meaning of the verse is, therefore, that God presents his angels, in other words, the separate intellects, in the form of wind and fire. The characteristic described here is the absence of the physical dimension.

Yet Maimonides offers an opposing interpretation of this same verse in *Guide* 2:6: "Even the elements are called messengers: 'He makes the winds his messengers (*mal'akhav*), the flaming fire his attendants' (Ps 104:4)." The direct objects in the verse are "winds" and "flaming fire." Thus, according to Maimonides, the verse means that God makes the winds and the flaming fire his messengers-attendants. The term *mal'akhim* here does not indicate the defined entity of the separate intellects, but rather the fulfillment of an active role. As said above, the interpretation in the *Mishneh Torah* follows the Midrash in *Genesis Rabbah*, whereas in the *Guide*, Maimonides interprets the same verse in a similar manner as Rashi (on Ps 104:4) and Ibn Ezra (on Ps 148:8).

As we saw, in the *Mishneh Torah* Maimonides gives a concise interpretation of Jacob's ladder as having the metaphorical meaning of "the king-

---

15. According to the *Mishneh Torah*, the fact that the angels have wings characterizes them as incorporeal entities. In *Guide*, the wings of the angels do not indicate their ontological status but rather the epistemological difficulty of humanity in attaining them. In the section of *Guide* on the meaning of the word "wing" (1.43), Maimonides offers the interpretation that "whenever the word 'wing' appears in reference to angels, it means 'concealment'." This interpretation relates to the term "wings" as a collective noun, and refers to the use of this term whenever it means something other than the organ of flight. Further in *Guide* (1.49), Maimonides finds that when Scripture describes angels as having "wings," this refers to their ability to fly: "because it is the most perfect and sublime movement of the brute creatures." In addition, the speedy characteristic of flight implies both revelation and disappearance.

doms and their subjugation." But in the *Guide*, aside from mentioning it at the beginning of the book without any interpretation, he gives two variant interpretations of this metaphor. The first instance is in 1:15:

> For the "angels (*mal'akhey*) of God" (Gen 28:13) are the prophets...How well put is the phrase "ascending and descending" (Gen 28: 12), in which ascent comes before descent. For after the ascent and the attaining of certain rungs of the ladder that may be known comes the descent with whatever decree the prophet has been informed of—with a view to governing and teaching the people of the earth.[16]

In this additional description of the beings ascending and descending the ladder, Maimonides prefers to use the term *mal'akh* to mean "prophet." The ascent and descent of the prophets on the ladder at whose peak stands the Divine characterizes their dual activity: intellectual elevation followed by descent to the people after they achieve the level that enables them to lead and instruct. Here Maimonides emphasizes the order of the actions as a key to understanding the metaphor: ascent precedes descent.

In *Guide* 2.10 he interprets Jacob's ladder as an allegory with yet another meaning. In this section, he mentions several categories, each of which contains four entities.

- four spheres [the heavenly spheres];
- four elements moved by them;
- and four forces that proceed from them into that which exists in general, as we have stated above;
- Furthermore, there are four causes of the motion of every sphere.

Maimonides continues,

> This number four is wondrous and should be an object of reflection. They said in Midrash Rabbi Tanhuma, "How many steps were in Jacob's ladder? Four, which refers to the dictum: "And behold a ladder was set upon the earth." (Gen 28:12) And in all the *midrashim* it is mentioned and repeated that there are four hosts of angels...But all the manuscripts and all the *midrashim* agree that the angels of God whom [Jacob] saw ascending and descending were only four and not any other number—two ascending and two descending—and that the four gathered together upon one step of the ladder, all four being in one row, namely, the two who ascend and the two who descend.[17]

In the first metaphor, all the angel-prophets ascended, and then they descended. But in this one, the angels' roles are divided: two ascend while two descend. Based on this division, apparently the four angels should be

---

16. Trans. Pines, 41

17. Trans. Pines, 272.

identified with the four elements: the two ascending are fire and air, while the two descending are water and earth. Their meeting on one rung means they all belong to the same category. Yet the continuation of this passage leads us to complexity and ambiguity.

> They even learned from this that the width of the ladder seen in the vision of prophecy equaled the dimension of the world plus one-third. For the width of one angel in the vision of prophecy is equal to one-third of the world, as it says, "His body was like *tarshish* (two-sixths)" (Dan 10:6). The width of the four angels, therefore, equaled that of the world plus one-third....In the words of our Sages in *Genesis Rabbah* (68), "the angel is one-third of the world"....The created entities consist of three parts, (1) the separate intellects, which are the angels (*mal'akhim*); (2) the bodies of the spheres; and (3) first matter, or the bodies below the sphere, which are subject to constant change.[18]

One possibility is to assume that Maimonides interprets the sages' statement that "the angel is one-third of the world" based on his conviction in a previous chapter (2:6): "The angel consists of burning fire and is as big as one-third of the universe." If the angel is a body made of the element of fire, then he is only one-fourth of the four earthly elements, which together make up one-third of the "created entities." This means that the angel is one-twelfth of the created entities, unless the angel-fire represents "the changing bodies below the lunar sphere" and this is "the third part that is inferior to the other parts of the created entities" (according to the interpretation Narbonne).[19]

In the next part of this passage Maimonides adds another element to the identification of the angel:

---

18. Apparently, Maimonides relies on the following midrashic sources:

    Genesis Rabbah 68: "R. Berakhiah said, He showed him the whole world plus one-third of the world. Ascending—there were at least two, and two descending. How do we understand that the angel is one-third of the world? As it is written, 'His body was like *tarshish*, his face like the appearance of lightning, his eyes like flaming torches, and his arms and legs like the color of burnished brass' (Dan. 10:6)."

    BT *Hullin* 91b: "He dreamt, and behold! A ladder was set upon the earth. A *tanna* taught: What was the width of the ladder? Eight thousand parasangs. For it is written: 'And behold the angels of God ascending and descending on it.' Two were ascending and two were descending, and when they met each other [on the ladder] there were four. Of the angel, it is written: 'His body was like *tarshish*,' and we have a tradition that *tarshish* is two thousand parasangs long."

19. Klein-Braslavy, 335n14.

Accordingly, the breadth of the four [angels] is equal to that of the world plus one third. In his parables, Zechariah—when describing that "there came out four chariots from between the two mountains, and the mountains were mountains of brass" (Zech 6:1)—says in interpretation of this: "these are the four airs of the heavens that go forth after presenting themselves before the Lord of all the earth." (Zech 6:5). They are accordingly the cause of everything that comes to pass in time. In regard to his mentioning brass and likewise the dictum "burnished brass" (Ezek 1:7), perceive in them a certain equivocality. You shall hear an indication regarding this.[20]

Daniel 10:6 reads, "His body was like *tarshish,* his face like the appearance of lightning, his eyes like flaming torches, and his arms and legs the color of burnished brass." The phrase "His body was like *tarshish,*" which Maimonides interprets as meaning the angel makes up two-sixths, or one-third, of the world, adjoins the phrase "burnished brass." In the passage cited here, Maimonides thus makes the connection to another instance of the term "brass" ("and the mountains were mountains of brass" in Zechariah), appearing in conjunction with the number "four": "four chariots" and "four winds of heaven."[21] Maimonides clarifies that the four winds are "the causes that produce all changes," and in this context they might be interpreted as the four heavenly spheres or the four forces proceeding from them. Based on the letters in the words, Maimonides seems to interpret the "brass" (*nehoshet*) as representing the corrupted (*nishhat*) world, that is, the sublunar world of constantly recreated and defective reality.[22]

Another possibility is to relate to the identification at the conclusion of this section, according to which "the separate intellects…are the angels (*mal'akhim*)," as clarifying Maimonides' argument that the angel is one-third of the world. Indeed, in their biblical context, the phrases "His body was like *tarshish*" and "burnished brass" form part of a description that Maimonides interprets in additional ways. The text in Daniel reads,

> I was still speaking in prayer, when the man Gabriel, whom I had seen in the earlier vision, was lifted in flight approaching me, at about the time of the afternoon offering. He made me understand and spoke with me. He said: Daniel, I have gone forth now to teach you understanding.…I raised my eyes and saw, behold one man clothed in linen, his loins girded with fine gold. His body was like *tarshish,* his face like the appearance of lightning, his eyes like flaming torches, and his arms and legs like the color of burnished brass; the sound of his words like the sound of a multitude.…So I remained alone. I saw this great vision. No strength remained

20. *Guide* 2.10, trans. Pines, 272–73.

21. See also *Guide* 2.29, 2.43, 3.2, 3.22.

22. See Profiat Isaac ben Moshe ha-Levi Duran [the Efodi] on *Guide* 2.10.

in me; my robustness changed to pallor, and I could retain no strength. I
heard the sound of his words, and when I heard the sound of his words I
was in a deep sleep upon my face, with my face toward the ground. (Dan
9:21–22, 10:5–6, 10:8–9)

In Maimonides' introduction to *Perek ḥelek* in his commentary on the
Mishnah, he describes the angel Gabriel as an intermediary that revealed
itself to Daniel.

> Because of this meaning, they said of him that he spoke with God without
> the intervention of the angels....No prophet would speak to God himself
> except through an intermediary, while Moses did so without an interme-
> diary....The prophet, when prophecy comes to him, even though it is in
> a vision and through an angel....As Daniel explained when Gabriel spoke
> with him in a vision, "No strength remained in me; my robustness
> changed to pallor, and I could retain no strength"; and "I was in a deep
> sleep upon my face, with my face toward the ground"; and "during the
> vision my joints shuddered." (Dan 10:16)

According to this, the phrases "His body was like *tarshish*" and "burnished brass" in the biblical text describe the angel Gabriel as he is
revealed to Daniel. Just as the Muslims identify the angel Gabriel with the
active intellect that speaks with the prophets,[23] Maimonides refers similarly to Gabriel's conversation with Daniel. The angel Gabriel, identified
with the active intellect, is, therefore, the one whose "body was like *tarshish*...like the color of burnished brass." This explanation in the introduction to *Perek ḥelek* does not fit the description at the beginning of section 10
in the *Guide*, according to which the *tarshish* and brass refer to the four
angels, two ascending and two descending.

Maimonides confronts another test of his understanding of the term
mal'akh in the story of the angel who conquers the Land of Israel. The biblical text reads,

> Behold! I send an angel before you to protect you on the way, and to bring
> you to the place that I have made ready. Beware of him—listen to his voice,
> do not rebel against him, for he will not forgive your willful sin—for my
> name is within him. For if you hearken to his voice and carry out all that
> I will speak, then I will be the enemy of your enemies and persecute your
> persecutors. For my angel will go before you and bring you to the Amorite,
> the Hittite, the Perizzite, the Canaanite, the Hivvite, and the Jebusite, and
> I will annihilate them. (Exod 23:20–23)

---

23. See also the Qur'an, sura 2, in the message of the cow regarding the revelation
of the angel Gabriel. See also the Rabad's statement in *Ha-Emunah ha-Ramah*,
principle 6, section 1: "The Ishmaelites never said that God spoke with the
prophets or revealed Himself to them, rather, He was present—they called
Him 'Gabriel' and 'the faithful spirit'" (ed. Weil, Frankfurt am Main, 1852).

In *Guide* 2.34, Maimonides points out the conflict within this text: "Now there is no doubt that this injunction is addressed only to the multitude. An angel, however, does not manifest himself to the multitude and does not give them orders and prohibitions; consequently they could not be ordered not to disobey him."[24]

According to Maimonides the verses in Exodus contain three contradictory assertions:

1.   The angel is one of the separate intellects, the active intellect;
2.   The active intellect reveals itself only to prophets;
3.   The command "Beware of him—listen to his voice, do not rebel against him" is addressed to the general public.

He thus offers the following resolution:

> Accordingly, the meaning of this dictum is that he, may he be exalted, gave them knowledge that there would be a prophet among them to whom an angel would come speak and give orders and prohibitions. Thus God forbade us to disobey that angel whose words the prophet would transmit to us.[25]

In other words, the angel here is the active intellect that speaks to the general public through the prophet. Maimonides reinforces this assertion using verses taken from another context in which the public is commanded to listen to a prophet. He establishes the following connection, among others:

> It makes that clear in Deuteronomy, saying, "Unto him ye shall hearken." And it also says, "And it shall come to pass, that whosoever shall not hearken unto My words that he shall speak in My name, and so on" (Deut 18:19)—this being the explanation of the dictum, "For my name is within him."

Previously, in *Guide* 1.64, Maimonides has interpreted the phrase "For my name is within him" as meaning "he is an instrument of my will and volition." In this context, he understands "the name of YHVH" as "the word of YHVH" or "the speech of YHWH." According to his statement in *Guide* 2.7, this instrument is one of the supreme forces, either the spheres or the intellects.

> We have explained the equivocality of the term "angel" and that it includes the intellects, the spheres, and the elements...For the spheres and the intellects apprehend their acts, choose freely, and govern....Scripture also says, "Take heed of him, and hearken unto his voice. Be not rebellious against him; for he will not pardon your transgression; for my name is in

---

24.   Trans. Pines, 366.

25.   Ibid.

him" (Exod 23:21). All this indicates to you that they [the spheres and the intellects] apprehend their acts and have will and free choice.[26]

Returning to *Guide* 2.34, we see that Maimonides repeats the role of the designated angel.

> However, an angel whom I shall send to your prophets will conquer the country for you, will smooth out the land before you, and will let you know what you should do. He will let you know what you should approach and what you ought to avoid.[27]

Apparently, Maimonides' intention in describing the role of the angel ("he will conquer the country for you, will quiet the land for you") parallels the continuation of the biblical passage.

> For My angel will go before you and bring you to the Amorite, the Hittite, the Perizzite, the Canaanite, the Hivvite, and the Jebusite, and I will anni-hilate them....I will send the hornet-swarm before you and it will drive away the Hivvite, the Canaanite, and the Hittite before you. I will not drive them away from you in a single year, lest the land become desolate and the wildlife of the field multiply against you. Little by little will I drive them away from you, until you become fruitful and make the land your heritage. (Exod 23:20–30)

According to what Maimonides has said thus far, the angel represents the revelation of the active intellect to the prophets. At the end of this sec-tion, Maimonides delineates the status of the angel in relation to all the prophets (in this case, apparently he is referring to Joshua): "to every prophet except Moses our Master, prophetic revelation comes through an angel. Know this." From what we have learned above, we may conclude that the prophecies of all the prophets, except that of Moses, came through the active intellect. The assertion that the prophecy of Moses did not come through an angel appears previously, in the commentary on the Mishnah, in the Introduction to *Perek helek*. There (in the seventh principle), Mai-monides presents Moses as having achieved the level of a true angel.

> He [Moses], may peace be with him, achieved the level of exaltedness among humanity, even reaching the level of the angel....He left no phys-ical trace...and remained as intellect alone. Because of this, they say that he spoke with God without the intervention of the angels....For God does not speak with any prophet, no matter which one, except through an inter-mediary. But with Moses, [he spoke] without an intermediary....The prophet, when prophecy comes to him, even though it is in a vision and through an angel...as Daniel explained when Gabriel spoke with him in a vision.

---

26. Trans. Pines, 266.

27. Ibid., 367.

Here Moses achieves the level of the separate intellects. He has no need of the intermediary role of the angel, since he has a direct relationship with God. The angel who mediates between God and the other prophets is identified as Gabriel, in other words, Gabriel is the active intellect.

Still, we find that Maimonides offers another interpretation for the angel as the mediator of prophecy. He gives this explanation later in *Guide* 2:45, within a discussion on the possibility of hearing speech directly from God. He notes that in "the vision of prophecy," the prophet does not hear that God himself is speaking to him.

> With regard to the question whether it is possible that a prophet would also see in a vision of prophecy that God, as it were, addressed him -- this, in my opinion, is improbable, for the power of the act of the imagination does not reach this point....Our principle states that all prophets hear speech only through the intermediary of an angel, the sole exception being Moses our Master....Know then that this is in fact so, and that in these cases the intermediary is the imaginative faculty....Moses our Master, on the other hand, heard him "from above the ark cover, from between the two cherubim" (Exod 25:22), without action on the part of imaginative faculty.[28]

From the statement that "all prophets hear speech only through the intermediary of an angel...and that in these cases the intermediary is the imaginative faculty," we may conclude that the angel-intermediary is the "imaginative faculty." As we recall, the term "angel" also represents the animal forces, and the imaginative faculty is one of these. The description "from above the ark cover, from between the two *cherubim*" therefore intends to indicate the nonintermediary nature of the imaginative faculty in Moses's prophecy.[29] Thus, in one of the previous sections (2:6), Maimonides differentiates the *cherubim* from the imaginative faculty: "the imaginative faculty is also called 'angel' and the intellect is called 'cherub.'"

Others have noted that in the writings of Maimonides that precede the *Guide*, he does not mention the imaginative faculty as a characteristic of prophecy.[30] Still, in the *Mishneh Torah* we find a description of the rev-

---

28. Ibid., 402–403.

29. Later (*Guide* 3.45), Maimonides clarifies that the command to sculpt the *cherubim* was intended to fortify the belief in the inspiration of prophecy through the angel, which represents the separate intellect, and the command to form two of them was meant to prevent the identification of this separate intellect as God.

30. On this phenomenon, see J. Macy, "The Theological-Political Teaching of *Shemona Peraqim*: Reappraisal of the Text and of Its Arabic Sources," *Eighth World Congress of Jewish Studies* (Jerusalem, 1982), Division C, 36. See also the methodical discussions of Haim Kreisel in *Prophecy: The History of an Idea in Medieval*

elation of the active intellect to the prophets through the intermediary of images.

> What did the prophets mean when they said that they saw angels of fire with wings? This is due to the riddles of prophetic vision…. (*Hilkhot Yesodei ha-Torah* 2:4)

> The tenth level consists of the *ishim* [men], who are the angels who speak with the prophets and appear to them in prophetic visions. (ibid., 2:7)

> The other prophets received their prophecies via an angel. Therefore, what they saw was by way of parable and riddle. Moses, on the other hand, did not receive his prophecies via an angel….He saw each prophecy absolutely clearly without any parables or riddles. (ibid., 7:6)

At any rate, in the *Guide* Maimonides specifically mentions the imaginative faculty as one of the characteristics of prophecy. In that work, as we saw, Maimonides identifies the term "angel" as indicating both the active intellect and the imaginative faculty.[31]

In conclusion, Maimonides presents varied definitions or identifications for the *mal'akh* or angel of God in the Bible, as he does for the biblical accounts of miracles and certain other biblical stories.[32] He does this both

---

Jewish Philosophy (Dordrecht/Boston: Kluwer Academic Publishers, 2001), esp. 236–37 regarding the angel.

31. In another context in the *Guide*, Maimonides finds a way to interpret the angel both as the active intellect and as one of the animal forces. According to Maimonides, the "angel of pregnancy" can be either one of the animal forces ("with the power of seed, the molder shapes and outlines these limbs") or the active intellect ("the forms are all created entities, and this is the angel who is 'the minister of the world'"). Maimonides does this in order to remove any possibility of mythological interpretation: "God sends the angel who enters the abdomen of the woman and forms the fetus there….An angel is a body of burning fire whose breadth is one third of the world." (*Guide* 2.36) Maimonides attempts to avoid using the term "angel" in such a way that will create the absurd situation of a dangerous "body of burning fire" with the enormous dimensions of "one third of the world" entering the woman's womb. He, therefore, offers two alternative interpretations of "angel," one taken from the metaphysical world of philosophy (Separate Intellect), which he identifies with an exalted entity, and the other relating to its meaning of "messenger," or "functionary," as one of the animal forces. Either way, this interpretation, by creating complexity and ambiguity of meaning, is intended to perform the role of demythologization.

32. Hannah Kasher, "Biblical Miracles and the Universality of the Natural Law," *The Journal of Jewish Thought and Philosophy* 8 (1988): 25–52. Idem., "Maimonides' Commentaries on the Story of the Cleft of the Rock," [in Hebrew] *Daat* 35 (5755): 29–66.

throughout his works and within integral ones. This trend enables him to offer various alternatives to the reader, and to prevent comprehension of these instances as describing mythological phenomena that are foreign to his world view.

THE HERMENEUTICS OF ORDER IN MEDIEVAL JEWISH PHILOSOPHICAL EXEGESIS

Robert Eisen
George Washington University

IN RECENT YEARS, there has been growing interest among Jewish scholars in the exegetical aspects of medieval Jewish philosophy. There is now an awareness that the major medieval Jewish philosophers such as Maimonides, Samuel ibn Tibbon, Joseph ibn Kaspi, and Gersonides cannot be properly understood without taking into account how they mined the biblical text for philosophical insights.[1] Yet, an issue that has yet to receive adequate treatment is the hermeneutics of these thinkers. Little has been written on the fascinating interpretive methods that medieval Jewish philosophers used to make sense of Scripture.[2]

---

1. A number of book-length studies on the exegesis of the medieval Jewish philosophers have been published. See, e.g., Sarah Klein-Braslavy, *Maimonides' Interpretation of the Adam Stories in Genesis: A Study in Maimonides' Anthropology* [in Hebrew] (Jerusalem, 1986); idem, *Maimonides' Interpretation of the Story of Creation* [in Hebrew] (Jerusalem, 1988); Maurice R. Hayoun, *L'exégèse philosophique dans le judaïsme médiéval* (Tübingen, 1992); Robert Eisen, *Gersonides on Providence, Covenant, and the Chosen People: A Study in Medieval Jewish Philosophy and Biblical Commentary* (Albany, N.Y., 1995); idem, *The Book of Job in Medieval Jewish Philosophy* (New York, 2004); Mordechai Z. Cohen, *Three Approaches to Biblical Metaphor: From Abraham Ibn Ezra and Maimonides to David Kimhi* (Leiden, 2003). Several dozen articles have also appeared in recent years dealing with exegetical matters in medieval Jewish philosophy. A number of critical editions of exegetical works by medieval Jewish philosophers have been published. These include Hannah Kasher's edition of Joseph ibn Kaspi's *Shulḥan kesef* (Jerusalem, 1996) and Howard Kreisel's edition of Nissim ben Moshe's *Ma'aseh nissim* (Jerusalem, 2000).

2. This issue has been addressed by Cohen, Hayoun, and my two studies listed in the previous note. See also Sarah Klein–Braslavy's chapter on medieval Jewish philosophical exegesis in *Hebrew Bible/Old Testament: The History of Its Interpretation*, ed. Magne Sæbø, vol. 1, pt. 2 (Göttingen, 2000), 302–20.

An obstacle that has prevented scholars from taking this issue more seriously is the widespread and erroneous assumptions that the exegesis of medieval Jewish philosophy consists primarily of allegory and that the allegorical method was applied arbitrarily to the biblical text so as to elicit preconceived philosophical ideas from it. While allegory was certainly an important tool for the medieval Jewish philosophers, it was by no means the only one, and it was not applied as arbitrarily as scholars have assumed. One has to keep in mind that medieval Jewish philosophers, particularly after Maimonides, were well-rounded intellectuals well versed in many areas of knowledge, including the rich traditions of biblical exegesis represented by such leading lights as Rashi, Ibn Ezra, and Nahmanides. Many of them also had mastery of the nuances of biblical grammar. Thus a full understanding of the exegetical enterprise of medieval Jewish philosophers requires a good deal more than investigating their views on allegory. One must also examine a host of other issues, such as how the philosophers responded to the major nonphilosophical exegetes who preceded them, how they viewed such issues as *peshat* and *derash*, and how their expertise in grammar played into their readings of the biblical text.[3]

One hermeneutic concern that highlights the confluence of the philosophical and exegetical schools in medieval Judaism is the issue of order within the biblical text. The major medieval Jewish exegetes who were not part of the philosophical tradition had a great deal to say about this question.[4] Their reflections on this issue were frequently focused on the principle of *ein muqdam u-me'uḥar ba-torah*. This principle literally means "there is no 'earlier' or 'later' in the Torah," and it specifies that the Torah is not always ordered in a chronological manner. It first appears in a passage in

---

3. The lack of scholarly appreciation for the complexity of medieval Jewish philosophical exegesis is exemplified by Moshe H. Segal's treatment of this form of biblical interpretation. In his *Biblical Exegesis* [in Hebrew] (Jerusalem, 1952), Segal characterizes the philosophers as interpreters who merely created "philosophical midrash" on the biblical text (p. 52), a comment that greatly underestimates their sophistication as exegetes, and he dismisses all post-Maimonidean exegetes in medieval Jewish philosophy as contributing nothing original to the study of the biblical text (p. 60). More sympathetic to the exegesis of the medieval Jewish philosophers are the various authors in *Jewish Biblical Exegesis: An Introduction* [in Hebrew], ed. Moshe Greenberg (Jerusalem, 1983). However, in this work, there is no section devoted to Maimonides, despite the fact that he is the most important philosophical exegete in medieval Judaism.

4. This concern has roots in rabbinic literature. See Isaac Heinemann, *Darkhey ha–aggadah* (Jerusalem, 1970), 135–36, 140–43.

the Talmud to explain the fact that Num 1:1–19 is dated to "the first of the second month of the second year" after the Exodus (1:1) while a passage appearing later in Num 9:1–8, is dated to "the first month" (9:1) of the same year.[5] The use of this principle was greatly expanded by prominent medieval Jewish exegetes, such as Rashi, Rashbam, Ibn Ezra, and Nahmanides, who applied it in numerous instances in their biblical commentaries.[6] What is less known is that medieval Jewish philosophers were also concerned with the question of order in the biblical text, and on occasion they too invoke the principle of *ein muqdam u-me'uhar ba-torah*, imparting to it their own original philosophical understanding.

In his paper, I would like to examine how four medieval Jewish philosophers dealt with the question of order in the biblical text: Maimonides, Samuel ibn Tibbon, Joseph ibn Kaspi, and Gersonides. Most of my attention will be devoted to Kaspi and Gersonides since these two philosophers were particularly interested in this issue.

The question of order in the biblical text did not seem to preoccupy Maimonides to any great extent. I have been able to locate only a handful of passages in the *Guide of the Perplexed* dwelling on this issue. Yet, as is often the case, Maimonides' meager comments are amplified in later philosophers and become programmatic for their thinking. Maimonides' remarks on the question of order must therefore be carefully examined.

The first example appears in Maimonides' introduction to the *Guide*. There Maimonides points out that the Torah begins with the account of creation (*ma'aseh bereshit*), which he identifies with physics, because physics must precede the study of the account of Ezekiel's chariot (*ma'aseh merkavah*), which he equates with metaphysics. Implied here is the notion that sometimes the biblical text is ordered as it is for pedagogical reasons. Physics must come before metaphysics in the proper sequence of study, and therefore the biblical text must present its philosophical lessons in that order.[7]

A much more extensive engagement with the question of order in the biblical text is found in Maimonides' discussion of the first chapter of Ezekiel. In *Guide* 3.5, Maimonides discusses what he considers to be the

---

5. BT *Pesahim* 6b.

6. To my knowledge, no major study has been done on this hermeneutic device, but it has been analyzed in several articles. See Isaac Gottlieb, "*Ein Mukdam U-me'uhar ba-Torah* in Nahmanides' *Commentary on the Torah*" [in Hebrew], *Tarbiz* 63 (1984): 41–62; Yaakov Elman's discussion of Nahmanides in Sæbø, *Hebrew Bible*, 423–27; Devorah Rosenvasser, "*Ein Mukdam U-me'uhar ba-Torah*" [in Hebrew], *Shema'tin* 152–53 (2003): 41–61.

7. Maimonides, *Guide of the Perplexed*, trans. Shlomo Pines (Chicago, 1963), 9.

three major components of Ezekiel's vision: the living creatures (*ḥayot*), the wheels (*ofanim*), and the figure of the man sitting on the throne. Maimonides' commentary is highly cryptic here and would require a discussion beyond the scope of this paper to be thoroughly explained. For the sake of simplicity, let us go with the interpretation of a number of commentators who argue that according to Maimonides the living creatures represent the spheres, the wheels represent the four elements in the sublunar realm, and the figure of the man represents the Separate Intellects.[8] What is most important for our purposes is that Maimonides gives a rationale for the ordering of these components in the biblical text:

> You ought to have your attention directed to the order of these three apprehensions. Thus he has put first the apprehension of the *living creatures*, for they come first because of their nobility and of their causality—according to what he says: "For the air of the living creatures was in the wheels"—and because of other things too. After the *wheels* comes the third apprehension, which is higher than that of the *living creatures*, as is clear. The reason for this lies in the fact that the first two apprehensions necessarily precede the third apprehension in the order of knowledge, the latter being inferred with the help of the other two.[9]

Maimonides tells us that the living creatures are mentioned in the biblical text before the wheels for two reasons: the living creatures are of greater nobility than the wheels, and the living creatures are prior in the chain of causation. Translated into philosophical terms, Maimonides' claim is that the order of the biblical text teaches us that the spheres precede the four elements in the sublunar realm both with respect to nobility and cause.

In the continuation of the passage, Maimonides goes on to relate that the living creatures and wheels are mentioned in the biblical text before the figure of the man because one must have an understanding of the first two entities before comprehending the third. That is, an understanding of the spheres and the sublunar realm necessarily comes before a comprehension of the Separate Intellects. In short, according to Maimonides, the ordering of elements in the Ezekiel text is accounted for by several principles: the more noble subject matter precedes that which is less noble, causes are mentioned in their proper sequence, and philosophical concepts are communicated to the reader in their logical order for pedagogical purposes. This last principle echoes Maimonides' explanation as to why the Torah begins with the account of creation.

---

8. See, for instance, the remarks of the medieval commentator Efodi in standard Hebrew editions of the *Guide*, and those of the modern commentator, Solomon Munk *Le Guide des égarés*, ed. and trans. Solomon Munk (Paris, 1855–66), 3:33n2.

9. *Guide* 3.5, 426.

Another example of Maimonides' concern for order is his well-known interpretation of Jer 9:22–23 in the final chapter of the *Guide*. In this chapter Maimonides discusses four perfections for which human beings should strive, and, in ascending order of importance, they are: perfection in acquiring material possessions, perfection of the body, perfection of the moral virtues, and perfection of the rational virtues that is equated with knowledge of God. Maimonides finds support for this sequence of virtues in the verse in Jeremiah:

> Jeremiah says concerning these four perfections: "Thus saith the Lord: Let not the wise man glory in his wisdom, neither let the mighty man glory in his might, let not the rich man glory in his riches; but let him that glorieth glory, glory in this, that he understandeth and knoweth me" (Jer 9:22–23). Consider how he mentioned them according to the order given them in the opinion of the multitude. For the greatest perfection, in their opinion, is that of *the rich man in his riches*, below him *the mighty man in his might*, and below him *the wise man in his wisdom*. [By the expression, "the wise man in his wisdom,"] he means he who possesses the moral virtues; for such an individual is held in high esteem by the multitude to whom the discourse in question is addressed.[10]

Maimonides argues that the first three virtues mentioned by Jeremiah are ordered in ascending degree of importance in accordance to the perspective of the masses. Thus, the perfection of morals is followed by the perfection of the body, which in turn is followed by the perfection of material wealth since the masses value these items in the order specified.

Yet, the statements in the *Guide* that become most influential on the opinions of later philosophers regarding the issue of order in the biblical text do not actually concern Scripture. I am referring to Maimonides' views on the order of subject matter in his own treatise. Maimonides states in his introduction to the *Guide* that the chapters in his treatise will be disordered so as to hide his true views from the masses. As Maimonides puts it, the chapters are "not set down in order or arranged in coherent fashion ... but rather are scattered and entangled with other subjects that are to be clarified."[11] The reason why Maimonides' views on order—or lack thereof—in his own treatise become important is that he consciously models his style of esoteric discourse on what he believes is the style of discourse in the Bible. Therefore, when Maimonides claims that the order of the subject matter in the *Guide* can be understood only on an esoteric level, he is implying that the same principle applies in the exegesis of the biblical text. And while Maimonides never explicitly makes

---

10. *Guide* 3.54, 636.

11. *Guide*, introduction, 6.

the connection between order and esotericism in his exegesis, later philosophers would.

Samuel ibn Tibbon is the first philosopher to develop that association. His *Ma'amar yiqqavu ha-mayim* and *Commentary on Ecclesiastes* are both devoted to implementing Maimonides' program of philosophical exegesis that had been laid out only in outline in the *Guide*, and it is therefore no surprise that in these works he elaborates on Maimonides' insights on the question of order.[12] Thus, while the quest for understanding order in the biblical text cropped up only occasionally in Maimonides' exegesis, it becomes a common theme in Ibn Tibbon's. An excellent example is his extensive discussion of *ma'aseh merkavah* in *Ma'amar yiqqavu ha-mayim*, which encompasses not only the first chapter of Ezekiel, but also the sixth chapter of Isaiah and Jacob's dream in Gen 28:10–19, both of which he relates to the metaphysical conceptions encompassed in *ma'aseh merkavah*. Ibn Tibbon approaches these three chapters with the premise that all of them teach how the human intellect achieves perfection by ascending in stages through the lessons of physics and metaphysics, and he attempts to show that each one lays out a pedagogical program for inculcating the truths of these subjects in a properly ordered sequence.[13] Ibn Tibbon therefore makes use of Maimonides' notion that the biblical text is at times ordered in accordance with pedagogical considerations.

Ibn Tibbon also makes use of Maimonides' notion that one mixes up the order of subject matters in philosophical writing to conceal esoteric truths. While Maimonides had applied this technique only to his own treatise, Ibn Tibbon turns it into an exegetical principle, a move that, as noted earlier, makes sense given the parallel that Maimonides draws between his own esoteric writing style and that of the Bible. Thus, Ibn Tibbon at times concludes that the biblical text is deliberately disordered in order to hide an esoteric message. For instance, Ibn Tibbon notes that there is esoteric meaning in the fact that in the creation story, the creation of light on the first day precedes the creation of luminaries on the fourth.[14] Exegetes have long been troubled by this difficulty, but for Ibn Tibbon the issue takes on esoteric meaning. Ibn Tibbon's solution to this peculiarity need not detain us here.[15] The important point is that for Ibn Tibbon an

---

12. *Ma'amar yiqqavu ha-mayim* was published by M. L. Bisliches (Pressburg, 1837). The *Commentary on Ecclesiastes* was recently edited and partially translated by James T. Robinson, "Samuel ibn Tibbon's *Commentary on Ecclesiastes*" (Ph.D. diss., Harvard University, 2002).

13. *Ma'amar*, 25–57.

14. *Ma'amar*, 156.

15. Ibn Tibbon refers us to a number of biblical verses in Psalms and Ecclesiastes

apparent lack of order in the biblical text can be a clue for esoteric doc-trines.

Ibn Tibbon sometimes finds esoteric meaning when there is an appar-ent disorder of words or phrases in a single biblical verse. An example is his explication of Ps 148:14 in *Ma'amar yiqqavu ha-mayim*. The biblical verse reads as follows: "He [God] has exalted the horn of his people, [brought] glory for his devout ones, for the Children of Israel, the people close to him. Hallelujah."[16] Ibn Tibbon explains the verse in the following manner:

> [The verse] mixed up the order [of components] in it for the sake of concealment. The order that was intended in it is as follows: "He [God] exalted the horn of glory for his people, for the Children of Israel, the people close to him, and for all his devout ones" ... for it is with them [i.e., the pious ones] that the greatest degree of providence is found in the world...[17]

Ibn Tibbon's point here is not easy to decipher, but he appears to be saying that the author of the Psalm should have placed the entities experiencing God's favor, which for Ibn Tibbon means divine providence, in ascending order of importance. Thus, the verse should have first mentioned "his people," then the "Children of Israel," and finally the "devout ones," the last reference apparently taken by Ibn Tibbon to refer to those who have intellectual perfection and therefore the highest degree of providence. According to Ibn Tibbon, the biblical text placed these entities in incorrect order to conceal the fact that the highest degree of providence is reserved for those with intellectual perfection. While Ibn Tibbon never explains why this truth needs to be concealed, he obviously believes that the mass-es have to be shielded from the fact that only the philosophical elite can experience providence in its highest form.[18]

Among the philosophers examined here, it is Joseph ibn Kaspi who provides the most extensive treatment of order in the biblical text. What distinguishes Kaspi is not just the number of instances in which he deals with this issue, but the fact that he is the only one of our thinkers who

---

that he claims will solve the mystery of this peculiarity, but an analysis of Ibn Tibbon's explication of those verses both in *Ma'amar yiqqavu ha-mayim* and in his *Commentary on Ecclesiastes* would require a separate article in its own right.

16. The translation is my own and attempts to render the verse in the manner in which Ibn Tibbon understands it. In the New Jewish Publication Society trans-lation, the verse reads as follows: "He exalted the horn of his people for the glory of all his faithful ones, Israel, the people close to him. Hallelujah."

17. *Ma'amar*, 168.

18. A similar example in which Ibn Tibbon argues that there is disorder in a bib-lical verse for the sake of concealment can be found in *Ma'amar*, 166.

reflects extensively on its theoretical underpinnings. An important programmatic statement appears in *Tirat kesef*—one of Kaspi's two commentaries on the Torah—in remarks he makes on a seemingly insignificant biblical verse. In Gen 5:32, we read that "[w]hen Noah had lived 500 years, Noah begot Shem, Ham, and Japeth." The chronological relationship between the first half of the verse noting Noah's age, and the second half of the verse referring to the birth of his sons, inspires Kaspi to discuss the issue of order in the biblical text as a whole. In the key portion of this discussion, Kaspi says as follows:

> It is necessary to examine whether the order of verses [in the biblical text] goes according to the order of chronology, because this is not always the case. For it is not obligatory that one who writes things in order, should write them in their order of chronology, unless he explains it explicitly and says "and so it was afterward ..." and [expressions] similar to this. Therefore, our Sages said "the Torah departs from chronological order" (*ein muqdam u-me'uhar ba-torah*). That is, we cannot render judgment from the order [of verses in the Torah] regarding chronological order. Perhaps this statement also applies to the order of causation; there is no question that this way of interpreting our Scriptures is most correct—even though it is not logical. [This is true] all the more so with our Torah, and for many reasons. The most important of them is to hide secrets. Indeed, how very dangerous this principle is. There is nothing like it among all the secrets of the Torah. By God! There are few people who are sensitive to this [issue], and if they are sensitive to it [there are few] capable of avoiding confusing one type [of principle of order] with another.[19]

Kaspi expands on these ideas a little later in the same passage:

> I have already informed you that in some instances that which is stated later [in Scripture] is the cause of that which is [stated] earlier. Everything goes according to the language of the verses. I have also informed you that the meaning of their [i.e., the Sages'] saying *ein muqdam u-me'uhar ba-torah* does not refer to the sequence of the order [of the text], because it is clear that this exists in the Torah and every book, for things cannot be said in one statement or written at one time. What they were referring to was all the other types of sequence. That is, the order [of the biblical text] does not necessitate the other types of order. Therefore, there is no need for us to say in any place "this occurred earlier," as Ibn Ezra says frequently, as if this matter [of the Torah lacking chronological order] is found only in a few instances that he identifies. In addition, he says this in many places. I don't agree with him [with respect to this point], as will be explained in our book.[20]

In these passages, Kaspi imparts new meaning to the principle of *ein muqdam u-me'uhar ba-torah*. First, he argues that this principle refers not

---

19. *Tirat kesef*, in *Mishneh kesef*, ed. Isaac Last (Pressburg, 1905), 1:61.

20. Ibid., 61–62.

just to chronology but also to the order of causes in the biblical text, an insight that Kaspi elsewhere claims is his own.[21] That is, *muqdam* and *me'uḥar*, "earlier" and "later," can be understood in terms of that which is prior or posterior in a causal chain. Thus, if "A" is the cause "B," in the biblical text "A" may not necessarily precede "B." Another innovation is Kaspi's view that the departure of Scripture from causal order serves the purposes of esotericism. The Torah is written in disordered fashion so that only the trained philosopher will discern the proper order of causes in the biblical text. In a creative move, Kaspi has therefore given a common exegetical principle a philosophical spin.[22]

There are other instances in Kaspi's works in which he invokes the principle of *ein muqdam u-me'uḥar ba-torah* as an esoteric technique for concealing philosophical secrets. Perhaps the most interesting is a discussion appearing in *Shulḥan kesef*, a work in which Kaspi deals with a number of topics in philosophy and exegesis. In his introduction, Kaspi argues that the Bible is untranslatable because there are elements in it that cannot be rendered in a language other than Hebrew. Kaspi directs his remarks specifically against the Christians who attempt to prove the truth of their faith by reference to the Latin Vulgate. According to Kaspi, their arguments are not to be taken seriously because of their reliance on a translation.[23]

Kaspi's primary proof for the untranslatable nature of the Bible is that there are fourteen mysterious instances in the biblical text in which a new pericope begins in the middle of a verse. What is odd here is not just that there is a complete break in the middle of a verse, but that the new pericope begins without any chronological or causal connection to the previous one. Thus, for instance, in Gen 35:22, the first half of the verse reads as follows: "While Israel stayed in that land, Reuben went and lay with Bilhah, his father's concubine, and Israel found out." The second half of the

---

21. See Kaspi's second commentary on Proverbs in *Asarah keley kesef*, ed. Isaac Last (Pressburg, 1905), 2:127.

22. Kaspi's criticism of Ibn Ezra is worth highlighting here. His complaint is that Ibn Ezra points out far too frequently when an element in the biblical text is out of chronological order. For Kaspi the departure from chronological order in the Bible is common enough that one need not make an issue of it every time it occurs. Kaspi's displeasure with Ibn Ezra's handling of the issue of order can be found in other passages in his writings. In some instances, Kaspi reiterates the same criticism noted here. In other places, he criticizes Ibn Ezra for claiming that an element in the biblical text is out of order when it is not. See, for instance, *Maẓref La-kesef*, in *Mishneh kesef*, ed. Isaac Last (Cracow, 1906), 2:17, and *Tirat kesef*, 106.

23. *Shulḥan kesef*, ed. Hannah Kasher (Jerusalem, 1996), 57–65.

verse introduces an entirely new pericope with no apparent connection to
the first half, with the statement, "Now the sons of Jacob were twelve in
number."[24]

Kaspi devotes a lengthy discussion to this phenomenon.[25] Why, he
asks, would the Torah place a break between two pericopes in the middle
of a verse? Kaspi answers as follows:

> ... [the biblical books] in some places made a break in the text, even though
> there is no period (*sof pasuq*), in order that the matter [under discussion in
> the biblical text] will conclude there. From this, we will know that in
> numerous places [in the Bible], there is a pause in the matter [under discus-
> sion], even though there is no period. From this [awareness], great secrets
> can be explained.[26]

Kaspi informs us that these instances are intended to teach us that the
order of the biblical text does not always follow a chronological or causal
sequence. If one pericope can end and another one begin right in the middle of a verse with no chronological or causal connection between the two,
this is a clue that in other instances the Torah will depart from chronological or causal sequence, even when the biblical text indicates no break
between pericopes. According to Kaspi, the reason for this phenomenon is
again related to the Torah's esoteric style. The Torah sensitizes those
adept in philosophy to the fact that it is not always arranged chronologically or causally and that this is the case because it conceals esoteric wisdom.[27]

Yet, Kaspi's interpretation of *ein muqdam u-me'uḥar ba-torah* runs into
some difficulty in his commentaries on the books of the latter prophets. In
a number of passages in these works, Kaspi insists emphatically that the
components of the prophetic speeches are perfectly ordered and that the
interpretation of any single passage must therefore take its textual context
into account. The explicit target of this position is the Christians who, Kaspi claims, read sections in the prophets out of context in order to interpret
them as prefigurations for the coming of their messiah. A passage in Kaspi's commentary on the tenth chapter of Isaiah brings across his main
point:

> Be mindful lest you think, as the Christians claim, that it is correct for a
> prophet to write something that has no relationship whatsoever with that
> which precedes it [in the text] or comes after it. Rather, I will say emphat-

---

24. Ibid., 70–72.
25. Ibid., 65–101.
26. Ibid., 69.
27. Ibid., 69–70.

ically that each and every book of the prophets is carefully ordered. This is correct even though the [books] were not dictated or written down at one time, as is the case with every one of Aristotle's books. And whoever wants to dispute with me about this, let him come to me. Yet, necessity caused the Christians to say this [i.e., that the prophetic books are not ordered] because they say that the passage "Indeed, my servant shall prosper" (Isa 52:13) is about their messiah. So it is with "the young woman [is with child]" (Isa 7:14). etc.[28]

The problem with Kaspi's position here is that it flies in the face of his strong support for the principle of *ein muqdam u-me'uhar ba-torah*, which, we have seen, is found in numerous places in his biblical commentaries. If the books of the prophets are perfectly ordered, what then of the notion that Scripture deliberately disorders its subject matter so as to conceal its esoteric truths from the masses? In a passage in his commentary on Jeremiah, Kaspi appears to be aware of this tension, and he tries to resolve it. Kaspi engages the problem in his commentary on the first verse of Jeremiah 35, which introduces a prophecy that takes place "in the fourth year of King Jehoiakim":

> It is known that Jehoiakim lived before the time of Zedekiah, who was mentioned earlier [in the book of Jeremiah]. Jeremiah was capable of ordering his book such that the prophecies in the days of Jehoiakim were [placed] prior to his prophecy in the days of Zedekiah. However, he did it [this way] here and elsewhere to make us aware that the Torah departs from chronological order (*ein muqdam u-me'uhar ba-torah*) and to teach us that the prophecies were like sermons given in different places and different times. This is not unlike many of the preachers who, at the end of their lives, collect all the sermons that they gave in their time, and there is no necessity that they write [their sermons] in the order of years, for what is the benefit of this? ... Yet, one should not deduce from what we have said that it is correct that Isaiah and Jeremiah and others have written their prophecies about the messiah of the Christians or our messiah who will build the third temple because we need not examine what [passage] is before it or after it. The matter is not like this; for we must nonetheless examine the adjacent [texts] that come before so that we can get insight into the precise intention of the author.[29]

Kaspi notes that Jeremiah's prophecies in the days of Jehoiakim come after those in the days of Zedekiah but that the order of their appearance in the biblical text is reversed, and he gives two reasons for this. First, the biblical text teaches us once again the principle of *ein muqdam u-me'uhar ba-torah*. Second, the prophets wrote down their prophecies in the same manner that preachers write down their sermons. Preachers commonly collect

---

28. *Adney kesef*, ed. Isaac Last (London, 1911), 1:105. See also 140–41, 143, 165.

29. *Adney kesef*, 2:18.

their sermons at the end of their lives without regard to chronological order. Yet, Kaspi is aware that his position here comes dangerously close to the Christian approach according to which biblical passages can be taken out of their literary context to support prefigurations of the Christian messiah. Kaspi therefore argues that the principle of *ein muqdam u-me'uḥar ba-torah* does not give one liberty to ignore order and context entirely. Even if a passage is out of order, an examination of the adjacent texts is required to make sense of the author's intention.

Kaspi's discussion does not give us much guidance here as to how one precisely negotiates the balance between order and lack of order in the biblical text. Yet, one can appreciate Kaspi's dilemma. His interpretation of *ein muqdam u-me'uḥar ba-torah* runs the danger of creating anarchy in the reading of Scripture. If passages in the biblical text can be taken out of context and reshuffled so as to reveal esoteric wisdom, who is then to say that the Christians are wrong in doing something similar with their prefigurative readings? Kaspi therefore argues for a balance between the two alternatives. The text can be reordered but context cannot be entirely shunted aside. A passage must still be understood broadly within the book of which it is a part.

One major difficulty in Kaspi's intriguing discussions of order in the biblical text is that in none of the instances in which he invokes the principle of *ein muqdam u-me'uḥar ba-torah* does he provide an example of esoteric secrets that can be discovered by this device.[30] Now in all fairness, esoteric secrets are meant to be hidden and therefore we should not expect Kaspi to be forthcoming with them. However, esoteric writers like Maimonides and those in his school will often provide at least some hint of the esoteric doctrines that are being concealed. In this instance, Kaspi is not so generous to his readers. Perhaps a close and careful examination of Kaspi's biblical commentaries will reveal more information about this issue. That challenge, however, must be left for another occasion.

It should be noted that Kaspi does not always link the principle of *ein muqdam u-me'uḥar ba-torah* to his esoteric agenda. Sometimes, a lack of chronology in the biblical text can be explained by other reasons. Thus, for example, in *Tirat kesef* Kaspi claims that the ceremony described in Numbers 7 upon completion of the building of the Tabernacle seems out of place and should have come at the end of Exodus. Kaspi explains this anomaly by arguing that the ceremony could not have been placed at the end of Exodus because the heads of the various tribes involved in the cer-

---

30. In addition to the sources discussed here, see also other places in which Kaspi uses *ein muqdam u-me'uḥar ba-torah* as an esoteric principle: *Tirat kesef*, 155–56; *Maẓref la-kesef*, 9.

emony would not have been known to the reader at that point in the biblical narrative. The ceremony is thus placed in Numbers only after the appointment of the heads of the tribes is described in the first chapters of that book.[31]

On some occasions, Kaspi insists that the lack of order in the biblical text serves no purpose whatsoever. For instance, in *Mazref la-kesef*, he argues that the laws enumerated in Exodus 21–23 are not ordered in any particular way.[32] A similar judgment is made in the same work in Kaspi's discussion of the laws listed in Leviticus 19–20.[33] In a passage in one of his two commentaries on the book of Proverbs, Kaspi also declares that there is no necessary connection between the dozens of aphorisms found in that book. Proverbs, he claims, belongs to the genre of ethical treatises that will often list statements of ethical advice with no principle governing their order.[34]

An interesting contrast to the thinkers we have examined thus far is Gersonides. In his exegetical works, Gersonides frequently takes up the question of order in the biblical text, especially in his commentary on the Torah, and in most cases he deals with it with the help of philosophical insights. However, unlike Maimonides, Ibn Tibbon, and Kaspi, Gersonides has no esoteric agenda.[35] Thus, absent in Gersonides is any suggestion that the biblical text is at times disordered so as to conceal hidden truths. Instead, he consistently tries to demonstrate that every element in the text is in its proper place.

---

31. *Tirat kesef*, 159–60. A similar point is made in *Tirat kesef*, 113, and in *Mazref la-kesef*, 214.

32. *Mazref la-kesef*, 210.

33. Ibid., 232. That Kaspi twice takes this approach toward legal portions of the biblical text may indicate that as a philosopher he was far more interested in biblical narrative than in biblical law. This surmise is supported by Kaspi's remarks in other writings that reveal an ambivalence toward the strictures of Jewish law. See Isadore Twersky, "Joseph ibn Kaspi: Portrait of a Medieval Jewish Intellectual," in *Studies in Medieval Jewish History and Literature*, ed. Isadore Twersky (Cambridge, Mass., 1979), 243–46.

34. Second commentary on Proverbs, 95.

35. See Charles Touati, *La pensée philosophique et théologique de Gersonide* (Paris, 1973), 93–94, 95–96. Touati is most emphatic in denying any suggestion that Gersonides engages in esoteric discourse. A comprehensive discussion of Gersonides' views on esotericism can be found in my *Gersonides on Providence*, 99–113. There I argue that Gersonides was not unaware of the dangers of revealing philosophical secrets to the masses but chose to protect those truths in ways other than concealment.

In a number of instances, Gersonides acknowledges that the biblical text is out of sequence chronologically—though, to my knowledge, he never cites the principle of *ein muqdam u-me'uḥar ba-torah*. In such cases, he attempts to demonstrate that the reordering of events is deliberate and that it serves a pedagogical function in inculcating philosophical or moral lessons. For instance, Gersonides surmises that the incident in Leviticus of the Israelite gathering wood on the Sabbath should have come earlier in the biblical text.[36] He argues that it appears where it does because this incident comes right after a passage dealing with punishments involving idol worship (Num 15:30–31),[37] and the two sections have similar lessons to teach. Violating the Sabbath is akin to idol-worship, because the Sabbath teaches us that the world was created by God and that God therefore exists. Therefore, failure to observe the Sabbath denies God's existence as idolatry does.[38]

Gersonides' interest in order is greatest in his comments on sections of the Torah that contain lists of commandments. He expends enormous effort imposing conceptual order on these sections, an approach that stands in stark contrast to Kaspi who, as we have seen, declares that such sections are not ordered at all. Here too Gersonides often makes use of philosophical and moral principles to organize the material, though other issues come into play as well. Thus, for instance, in his commentary on Exodus, Gersonides provides a lengthy discussion explaining the order of the Ten Commandments. According to Gersonides, the commandments are given in descending order of importance, with those inculcating proper intellectual belief coming before those concerned with moral action. Moreover, within each of these groups, Gersonides argues that the Torah deliberately places positive commandments before prohibitions.[39] Far more elaborate conceptual schemes are posited for explaining lengthier sections of commandments, such as Exodus 21–23.[40] In some places, Gersonides attempts to show that even individual items listed in a biblical passage are arranged in a specific order.[41]

---

36. Num 15:32–36.

37. This is not obvious from the biblical text. Gersonides is following a rabbinic interpretation of this passage. See BT *Keritot* 7b.

38. Gersonides, *Perush 'al ha-Torah* (Venice, 1547), 187c. Gersonides takes a similar approach in other passages. See ibid., 72c, 181a–b.

39. Ibid., 78a–f.

40. Ibid., 100c, 121c, 150c, 164b.

41. In such instances, he often claims that the items appear in descending order of nobility—an approach similar to that used for the Ten Commandments. See, e.g., ibid., 220, 240a. Yet, note p. 240b where the reverse is the case.

What is lacking in Gersonides is any kind of theoretical discussion regarding order in the biblical text of the kind that we saw in Kaspi. However, one passage in his commentary on the Torah gives us some insights into this thoughts on this issue. While explicating a passage in Exodus concerning the ritual of tefillin, Gersonides explains why the sections of the Torah on parchments inside the tefillin must appear in the same order as they do in the biblical text:

> It is fitting for it to be this way [i.e., that the sections be ordered in the tefillin according to their order in the Torah] for it is incumbent upon us to believe that in the Torah we find the utmost perfection so that it contains nothing that is without benefit. From this it follows that the order of sections [in the Torah] is intended from God, as has been explained in the third [chapter] of *Menahot*.[42]

Gersonides argues here that if every aspect of the Torah is perfect because of its divine origin, its order should be perfect as well.

Yet, an understanding of Gersonides' approach toward order in the biblical text is best achieved by looking at his remarks in the introduction to his major philosophical work, *The Wars of the Lord*. There, Gersonides devotes a discussion to the question of order in his own philosophical treatise. He maintains that his treatise has been ordered very carefully, and he describes seven principles that have guided the sequence of its discussions.[43] A summary of the first three principles gives some idea of their contents:

1. Presentation of a subject will be preceded by another when the former cannot be understood without the latter.
2. Discussion of a given subject will proceed from the more general to the more specific.
3. Easier material is presented before more difficult material.[44]

What is implied here is that good philosophical writing is *ordered* philosophical writing. What also jumps out at us is that Gersonides' views here are in sharp contrast to those of Maimonides who, in his introduction to the *Guide*, makes a virtue out of the *lack* of order in his treatise. Moreover, in his introduction to the *Guide*, Maimonides presents seven principles as well. The purpose of Maimonides' principles is to explain why treatises, including his own, contain contradictions, and, as is well known, it is here that he introduces the notion that some of the contradictions in

---

42. Ibid., 67c, *shoresh* 4; BT *Menahot* 34b–35a.
43. *The Wars of the Lord*, trans. Seymour Feldman (Philadelphia, 1984–99), 1:98–104.
44. Ibid., 99–101.

the *Guide* are meant to conceal esoteric truths from the masses.[45] Gersonides' seven principles seem to be in direct opposition to those of Maimonides. Rather than dictate how his treatise will obfuscate philosophical
truths, Gersonides' principles demonstrate how his work is a model of
clarity in being perfectly ordered.

Most important for our purposes is that we have critical insight as to
why order in the biblical text is of such great concern to Gersonides. The
Torah is a text of divine origin meant to impart philosophical truths, and it
must therefore exhibit the best features of philosophical writing, which
includes perfect order.[46] It is for this reason that whenever Gersonides
encounters passages that lack order, he seeks some philosophical or moral
reason to explain why this is the case. By imposing order on the Torah,
Gersonides is demonstrating its worth as a clear and coherent work of
philosophy. All philosophical treatises of value must present their teachings in a sensible and orderly manner so that all can share in their truth.
Thus, the Torah, God's guide to human perfection, must be no exception.

The issue of order is more than just a pedagogical or stylistic concern
for Gersonides. It is also an ontological principle in that the physical and
metaphysical worlds are perfectly ordered. Now in truth all medieval philosophers argue for order in the universe—Jews, Christians, and Muslims.
The very nature of the philosophical enterprise in the Middle Ages was
predicated on the belief that the universe was rational in its design. Yet,
my sense is that Gersonides dwelled on this issue more than others. This
is exemplified in the fact that God is frequently referred to in his writing
as *Ha-siddur*, "The Order." That is, he is the Law that orders everything in
the universe. Order is therefore at the center of Gersonides' metaphysics.
In sum, the issue of order is a common thread that unites Gersonides'
views on philosophical writing, revelation, and ontology.[47]

One other possibility worth considering here is that Gersonides' concern for order in the biblical text has roots in Nahmanides. Nahmanides
was obsessed with the issue of order in his commentary on the Torah, and
this obsession is one of the primary factors guiding his exegesis. It is well
known that, in opposition to Rashi and Ibn Ezra, Nahmanides severely
constricts the principle of *ein muqdam u-me'uhar ba-torah* to only those cases in which the Bible is explicit about presenting its material out of chro-

---

45. *Guide*, introduction, 17–20.

46. The term that Gersonides often uses when discussing the value of the Torah as
a source for philosophical guidance is *haysharah*, or "guide." See, e.g., Gersonides' introduction to his *Perush 'al ha-Torah*, 2a–c.

47. This issue is discussed by Touati, 105–6.

nological order.[48] Like Gersonides, he attempts to show that the biblical text is ordered on all levels—pericopes, verses, and even words. The scholarship on Gersonides has not, to my knowledge, investigated a relationship between him and Nahmanides. However, in an unpublished paper, Leonard S. Levin has persuasively argued for such a relationship with respect to Gersonides' views on the reasons for the commandments.[49] Thus, Nahmanides' influence on Gersonides with respect to order in the biblical text may not be out of the question.

What emerges from the foregoing analysis is that the positions that medieval Jewish philosophers adopted regarding order in the biblical text were closely connected to their views on philosophical writing in general. Maimonides laid the groundwork for this connection by implying that his own esoteric writing style would mirror that which he imputed to the biblical text. That connection was later brought to bear on the issue of order in the biblical text by Ibn Tibbon and Kaspi, with Kaspi providing the richest treatment of this question. Kaspi develops the nexus between esoteric writing and the issue of order in the biblical text with his widespread and novel application of the principle *ein muqdam u-me'uhar ba-torah*. For Kaspi this principle teaches us that the biblical text is deliberately disordered in order to hide esoteric truths in the same manner that any philosophical treatise would. In Gersonides, there is also a connection between the question of order in the biblical text and the issue of philosophical writing. Gersonides, however, stands apart from the other three thinkers in rejecting esoteric discourse and in believing that the hallmark of good philosophical writing is its presentation of ideas in perfect sequence. Therefore, for Gersonides the biblical text is always ordered and he expends great effort in his biblical commentaries, especially in the legal portions of the Torah, to show that this is the case.

Our analysis also demonstrates a confluence between medieval Jewish philosophy and medieval Jewish exegesis. The principle of *ein muqdam u-me'uhar ba-torah* was used widely by the major medieval Jewish exegetes, but it was also adopted by medieval Jewish philosophers, particularly Kaspi, who gave it philosophical meaning in his reading of the biblical text. An analysis of the hermeneutic methods of medieval Jewish philosophers must, therefore, take into account influences from exegetes outside the philosophical sphere.

---

48. In such cases, he consistently attempts to find justification for the reordering of the biblical chronology. On Nahmanides' views on sequence in the biblical text see Gottlieb and Elman.

49. "Gersonides on the Reasons for the Commandments" (paper, Boston, Mass., AJS Conference, December 17, 2000).

AMBIGUITIES OF SCRIPTURAL EXEGESIS
JOSEPH IBN KASPI ON GOD'S FOREKNOWLEDGE

Charles H. Manekin
University of Maryland

OF THE VARIOUS ATTEMPTS in medieval Jewish philosophy to solve the divine foreknowledge/human choice antinomy, Joseph ibn Kaspi's reconciliation is the most unexpected and uncharacteristic. Kaspi (1279–1340) has been described by historians of Jewish philosophy as extreme in his rationalism;[1] a student of Aristotle, Maimonides, and Averroes;[2] and not entirely original.[3] As such he would be expected to adopt one of the solutions to the antinomy advanced by Maimonides or the Arab Aristotelians, still very much influential in fourteenth-century Jewish philosophy, or at most to offer a slight variation of his own.

---

1. Guttmann introduces him as "More extreme in his rationalism [than Levi b. Hayyim of Villefranche]"; see Julius Guttmann, *Philosophies of Judaism: The History of Jewish Philosophy from Biblical Times to Franz Rosenzweig* (New York, 1964), 196.

2. E. Knupfer, "Kaspi, Joseph ben Abba Mari ibn," in *Encyclopedia Judaica* (Jerusalem, 1971) 10:809–11.

3. C. Sirat, *A History of Jewish Philosophy in the Middle Ages* (Cambridge, 1985), 329. For recent bibliographical material, see the literature cited in Robert Eisen in "Joseph ibn Kaspi on the Scroll of Esther," *Revue des études juives* 160 (2001): 379–408, esp 380n1; cf. Joseph ibn Kaspi, *A Table of Silver* [in Hebrew], ed. Hannah Kasher (Jerusalem, 1996), 11–36; Basil Herring, *Joseph Ibn Kaspi's "Gevia Kesef": A Study in Medieval Jewish Philosophical Bible Commentary* (New York, 1982), 3–32; Isadore Twersky, "Joseph ibn Kaspi: Portrait of a Medieval Jewish Intellectual," in *Studies in Medieval Jewish History and Literature*, ed. Isadore Twersky (Cambridge, Mass., 1979), 231–57; Barry Mesch, *Studies in Joseph Ibn Caspi: Fourteenth-century Philosopher and Exegete* (Leiden, 1975), 43–58. The name "Kaspi" (the man of Silver) refers to the author's home town of Argentière. But he became so enamored of the name that at a point in his literary career he decided to use the word *kesef* (silver) in all his book titles.

Instead, Kaspi's position in his late collection of scripturally inspired homilies, *The Silver Is Concluded* (*Tam ha-kesef*) appears to be entirely unprecedented: God knows future possible choices, acts, and events through what he calls "*shi'ur sikhli*," which we provisionally translate as "intellectual assessment."[4] Just as experts are able to assess an outcome with varying success, depending upon the extent of their knowledge of the relevant factors, so God, who knows *all* the relevant factors, will be able to know what a person will do. Yet this knowledge does not causally determine the outcome, and the person still has "complete choice" (*beḥirah gemurah*). God knows the circumstances that are brought to bear on an individual's choices and actions, and through an intellectual assessment he is able to determine what the individual will choose or do in the future.

What is unusual about this solution is that it appears to assume, unabashedly and unapologetically, that God knows particular individuals, acts, and events *qua* particulars. As is well known, this was rejected by all the Arab Aristotelians. Even Maimonides, who appears to have held that God knows particulars, took great pains to justify the deviation from the philosophers and to argue that we cannot know *how* God knows things, that God's mode of knowing is essentially different from our own.[5] Yet not only does Kaspi present his solution without qualification, he states explicitly that God's knowledge of the future resembles the knowledge of "wise men." The solution also has been understood to exclude from the scope of divine foreknowledge the free choices and actions of human individuals.

Shlomo Pines was the first to draw attention to what he considered to be Kaspi's deviation from the dominant philosophical tradition in fourteenth-century Jewish Provence and, as was his practice, searched for parallels among contemporary scholastic philosophers.[6] Although he didn't find any close matches, he saw signs of scholastic influence in the way Kaspi frames the question, in his belief in the contingency and the free-

---

4. "Assessment" is used here in a broad sense, so as not to exclude either conjecture or knowledge. The reason for this will be apparent below.

5. See *The Guide of the Perplexed*, 3.19–21, trans. Shlomo Pines (Chicago 1863), 477–90. On different ways of interpreting Maimonides' position, see Charles H. Manekin, "Maimonides on Divine Knowledge—Moses of Narbonne's Averroist Reading," *American Catholic Philosophical Quarterly* 76, no. 1 (2002): 51–74.

6. "Joseph ibn Kaspi's and Spinoza's Opinion on the Probability of a Restoration of the Jewish State [in Hebrew]," *Iyyun* 14 (1963), rept. in S. Pines, *Studies in the History of Jewish Philosophy: The Transmission of Texts and Ideas* (Jerusalem, 1977), 277–305, esp. 279–84.

dom of human choice, and in the distinction he makes between God's foreknowledge and his knowledge of the past and present.[7]

I wish to examine Pines' interpretation of Kaspi's statement on God's knowledge of future possibles,[8] and to propose and examine several other interpretations. I will argue that none of the interpretations is entirely satisfactory in the broader context of Kaspi's biblical exegesis, although some are better than others. Kaspi's penchant for revealing the secrets of other exegetes was criticized in his own lifetime, but his desire to conceal his own secrets, coupled with his apparent disinterest in sustained philosophical analysis,[9] makes a unified account of his thought difficult, perhaps impossible. In the case of his views on God's knowledge of future possibles, the best one can do is explore and rank a range of interpretations, rather than argue for an exclusive one. This pluralistic interpretative approach may be appropriate not only for Kaspi, but also for all medieval Jewish philosophers who struggle to chart a course between the demands of Scripture and "wisdom."

I.

The Silver Is Concluded is a series of eight investigations on various scriptural and philosophical topics, written toward the end of Kaspi's literary career.[10] In the third investigation Kaspi discusses two well-known scriptural passages that seem to suggest that God predetermines sinful actions. The first, Exod 7:3, is where God informs Moses that he will harden Pharoah's heart so that the latter will not free the Hebrew slaves. The second, Gen 15:13, is where God informs Abraham that a foreign nation will afflict and oppress his progeny. Both passages imply the inevitability of the future events, either because of divine ordainment or, at the very least and perhaps with a different sort of implication, divine foreknowledge.

Kaspi uses Maimonides' explanation of these passages in the latter's *Code of Law* (*Mishneh Torah*) as a springboard for his own discussion of

---

7. Ibid., 283.

8. I prefer this phrase to "future contingents" because during this period Jewish philosophers do not distinguish terminologically between "possible" and "contingent"; that is a scholastic innovation that was unknown in the Arabic/ Hebrew philosophical tradition. Later Jewish philosophers use the distinction, a sign of scholastic influence.

9. This point is also made by Robert Eisen in "Joseph Ibn Kaspi on the Scroll of Esther," 391–92n49.

10. Ed. Isaac Last (London, 1913). This edition is based on the sole extant manuscript of the work, Elkan N. Adler Collection, 1519, which has been consulted for this article.

divine knowledge and justice. Although he dismisses Maimonides' solutions in the law code as geared to the multitude, he finds in the *Guide of the Perplexed* a general principle that absolves God of responsibility for the evil actions of humans:

> God is the remote efficient cause of everything that happens, whether by nature, accident, or by human choice.[11]

Because God is the *remote* cause of accidents and events, implies Kaspi, humans are accountable for their own choices. However, since the Bible often speaks of God as possessing proximate causal agency, Kaspi proposes the following hermeneutical principle, also based on *Guide* 2.48, that will render Scripture and philosophy in agreement:

> When the biblical authors ascribe historical actions and events to the proximate causal agency of God, this is to be taken merely as a scriptural *façon de parler* and hence not literally true.

In our case, because God is the remote agent for Pharoah having the power of choice, the Bible says that God hardens Pharoah's heart. God is the agent, but not the *proximate* agent. As Kaspi writes in his exoteric commentary on Torah, *A Refining Pot for Silver* (*Mazref la-kesef*):[12]

> The Lord is without a doubt the agent of everything, for he (may he be blessed) says to [Pharoah], "Choose or accept for yourself whatever you desire." So when Pharoah himself arouses this hardness in his heart, the Lord is its agent, I mean by virtue of his giving [Pharoah] the [power] of choice to do as he wishes."[13]

God is the agent of Pharoah's particular choice only in the sense that he is the agent of everything, including Pharoah's power of choice. Because he is not the proximate cause of that particular choice, he is not considered to be responsible for it. The naturalistic picture presented here is in keeping with Kaspi's general naturalist interpretation of God's role in history.[14]

It is not clear why Kaspi believes Maimonides' explanation of God's causal activity in the *Mishneh Torah* to be intended for the multitude. Maimonides interprets the notion of "God's hardening Pharoah's heart" as

---

11. *Guide* 2.48; trans. Pines, 409–12.

12. *A Refining Pot of Silver*, ed. I. Last (Cracow, 1896), 152–53.

13. Ibid., 153. In the continuation of this passage Kaspi concludes that "there is no limit to the sorts of ways in which it is true to say of God that he is the agent of all things. Yet it is just as true to say of him that he is not the agent of evil or even of good." I.e., God is the agent of all things as remote cause, and the agent of nothing as proximate cause. Cf. ibid., 280 (on Deut 5:26).

14. See Pines, "Joseph ibn Kaspi's and Spinoza's Opinion," 285–98.

God's removing the power of repentance from Pharoah so that "he die in the wickedness that at first he did voluntarily."[15] If Kaspi interprets this to mean that God miraculously intervenes in nature to remove the power of repentance from Pharoah, then such an interpretation certainly goes against the grain of his philosophical naturalism. But since Kaspi is willing to interpret the biblical verse naturalistically, it seems odd that he does not give the same naturalistic reading to Maimonides' interpretation of "God's hardening Pharoah's heart." He could have said that Pharoah sinned so many times that his disposition to act wickedly naturally became an ingrained habit of which he could not rid himself[16] Whatever the reason for his characterization of Maimonides' explanation in the *Mishneh Torah* as designed for the multitude, Kaspi prefers the general and hermeneutical principles of *Guide* 2.48.

Kaspi next takes up Gen 15:13, which implies God's ordainment, or at least knowledge, of the Israelites' future affliction by a foreign nation. Why, he asks, were the Egyptians punished, inasmuch as God had already decided that a "foreign nation" would enslave the Israelites? He answers that God knew how the Egyptians would choose and on what basis; yet this did not cause or necessitate their choice. They were justly punished because they acted voluntarily. It is at this point that he makes the statement about God's knowledge of future possibles that caught Pines' eye:

> God knows future possibles. For it is known that in respect to a future possible, the contradictory opposites are not divided according to truth and falsehood in a complete manner today, inasmuch as the thing [to which the contradictory opposites refer] is future. For today they are unknown[17] to us and by nature, as has already been demonstrated in Logic. Consequently, the philosophers took pains to explain how God could have knowledge of the future possible before it takes place, and how is it [that he knows] which of the two possible alternatives will occur, to the extent that he often reveals this secret to his servants, the prophets, without there being any compulsion coming from him. This is what R. Akiva, the most perfect sage of those entering the paradise of the theoretical sciences, said: "All is observed and power is granted."[18] What more can be said?

---

15. *Laws concerning Repentance* 6:3. Cf. *Exodus Rabbah* 13.3.

16. See David Shatz, "Freedom, Repentance, and Hardening of the Hearts," in *The Jewish Philosophy Reader*, ed. Daniel H. Frank, Oliver Leaman, and Charles H. Manekin (London and New York, 2000), 51–59, esp. 55–57.

17. Reading *muskal* (with *samekh*) for *muskal* (with *sin*). Aside from making more sense, this reading is based also on Kaspi's *The Bundle of Silver* (*Ẓeror ha-kesef*), Vatican Ms. 283 (IMHM 340).

18. *Avot* 3:17.

For example, God, may he be blessed, revealed to Jeremiah that Jerusalem would be destroyed by Nebuchadnezzar if Zedekiah did not surrender to Nebuchadnezzar, and that it would not be destroyed if he surrendered to him. And he revealed to him that Zedekiah would choose of his own accord to rebel against Nebuchadnezzar. It is as if he said to him: "Know that Zedekiah the accursed will choose evil for himself."

This is analogous and similar to our scholars who are experts in assessing (shi'ur) and estimating (omed). For they will assess that a person accursed in his actions and affairs will make a bad choice tomorrow, or the day after, whether in marriage or some other worldly affair such as a business matter, or a journey. Now, if we are only rarely mistaken in our speculations, then certainly God, the master of intellectual assessment, as well as of established knowledge, can focus securely on the considerations that enter into our choices. There is no doubt that the prophets likewise are the supreme experts in assessing and estimating, as the Teacher [=Maimonides] explained in his book.[19]

So what is so remarkable about the fact that Moses assessed that after his death the people would rise up and go astray with other gods? The most minor of prophets would be able to assess this, as Moses claimed: "While I am yet alive with you this day, you have been rebellious against the Lord, etc. [and how much more after my death]" (Deut 31:27). How much more so does God know all future possibles and know today what we will choose tomorrow or the following day with the total choice that is fixed in our hearts.

All this is clear to me.[20]

Two preliminary points before we examine the interpretations of the passage. First, Kaspi affirms here that future possible actions and events are metaphysically and not just epistemically possible; that is, they are not only possible with respect to our knowledge of them, but they are possible in their very nature. To support this claim he appeals to "what has been demonstrated in Logic," i.e., Aristotle's doctrine in De interpretatione 9 that a pair of contradictory statements referring to future possible actions and events "do not divide truth and falsity in a complete manner,"[21] i.e., nei-

19. *Guide* 2.38; trans. Pines, 376–78.

20. *Tam ha-kesef*, "Third Investigation," 20–21.

21. For Kaspi's own discussion of this material, see his logical compendium, *The Bundle of Silver* (*Ẓeror ha-kesef*), Vatican Ms. 283 (IMHM 340), fols. 232r–v. This seems to me based at this point not on Averroes *Middle Commentary* of the *De Interpretatione* (perhaps because of its length; see Paris, Bibliothèque Nationale Ms. Héb 923, 63v–67v,) but rather on Alfarabi's *Short Treatise* on the *De Interpretatione* (cf. Paris, Bibliotheque Nationale Ms. Heb 898 [IMHM 26854], fol. 62r–64r.), both of which were translated into Hebrew and available in the thirteenth and fourteenth centuries. These works are available in English translations from the Arabic: see *Alfarabi's Commentary on the "De Interpretatione,"* trans. with introd. and notes, F. W. Zimmerman (Oxford, 1981), 244–46, and

ther of the statements is completely true or completely false *now*, because the states of affairs to which they refer are not yet determined. Presumably this implies for Kaspi that they cannot be known with "established knowledge" (*ha-mada'ha-meyushav*), since such knowledge implies truth, and where there is not yet truth, there is not yet knowledge. Hence Kaspi must come up with a different kind of knowledge, one that preserves the metaphysical contingency of such future things, and of human choice.

Second, Kaspi appeals to "the philosophers" who have explained how God knows future possibles before they take place, and how God can inform the prophets that they will occur, without that knowledge or information compelling the future events to take place. He does not mention who these philosophers are or of what their explanations consist. Instead, he attributes "intellectual assessment" to God, and he compares it to the sort of speculation employed by prophets and sages.

Taken in isolation, Kaspi's statement on God's knowledge of future possibles admits of at least three different interpretations. I shall label Pines' interpretation "libertarian/incompatibilist" and the other two "determinist/compatibilist" and "libertarian/compatibilist" respectively. Let us now see the virtues and defects of each interpretation.

The Libertarian/Incompatibilist Interpretation (Scholastic Philosophers?)

The libertarian/incompatibilist interpretation, advanced by Pines and supported by Colette Sirat,[22] understands Kaspi as holding that humans have free choice and that God foreknows future possibles. If one assumes that infallible foreknowledge is incompatible with human choice and metaphysical possibility, then some concessions have to be made, and, according to Pines, the concession is found in the concept of *shi'ur sikhli*. Pines traces the term *"shi'ur"* to the Arabic term *"shu'ūr"* as used by Maimonides in *Guide* 2.38, namely, the activity of divination, which manages to produce accurate predictions. God's knowledge is understood by Pines as predictive and probabilistic, albeit with a high degree of probability, one "which approximates certainty."[23] Going further, Sirat reads Kaspi as claiming that "God knows all the contingent things with a probable knowledge, to a perfect degree."[24]

Averroes' Middle Commentaries on Aristotle's "Categories" and "De interpretatione," trans. Charles E. Butterworth (Princeton, 1983), esp. 147.

22. Sirat, *History of Jewish Philosophy*, 313–14.
23. Pines, "Joseph ibn Kaspi's and Spinoza's Opinion," 282.
24. Sirat, *History of Jewish Philosophy*, 314.

There are several difficulties with this interpretation. First, as Hannah Kasher has pointed out, Kaspi never says that God's knowledge of future possibles is probable. On the contrary, he contrasts God's "intellectual assessment" of the future with that of the wise men who seldom err, suggesting that the difference between them lies *precisely* in the former's infallibility: "How much more so does God know all future possibles and know today what we will choose tomorrow or the following day with the complete choice that is fixed in our hearts!"[25]

Second, while it is true that Kaspi mentions the *shi'ur* of wise men and prophets, and that this term in *Guide* 2.38 refers to a cognitive process associated with the sense and imagination, Kaspi specifically speaks here of *shi'ur sikhli*, an *intellectual* assessment. Nothing suggests that this latter type of speculation is an inferior or fallible kind of knowledge. This is not to say that *shi'ur sikhli* should be identified necessarily with demonstrative knowledge, the model of scientific certainty for the Aristotelians. If the objects of the divine assessment are the particular circumstances surrounding a possible choice or action, then it is difficult, perhaps impossible, to reconcile that with demonstrative knowledge, which concerns itself with the universal rule or essence rather than the concrete particular. But whether *shi'ur sikhli* is the same as demonstrative knowledge or not, it still seems to be, from this passage, certain.

Third, Kaspi does not imply that divine omniscience is in fact incompatible with human choice. Of course, it *appears* to be so, or else the problem would never arise in the first place. But Kaspi could be claiming that the problem is only apparent because God's infallible knowledge can be interpreted in such a way as to make it compatible.

Fourth, Kaspi does not claim that human choice is "free," either terminologically or substantively, certainly if free choice is given a strong libertarian sense of "uncaused" or "metaphysically autonomous." The phrase *behirah gemurah* may, indeed, mean "free choice" in the strong libertarian sense, but this cannot be assumed without argument.[26]

One of the attractions of the libertarian/incompatibilist interpretation is that it allows Pines to see evidence of scholastic influence in Kaspi's thought. Although he concedes that Kaspi's specific solution was not found among the scholastics, he points to similarities in terminology and doctrine with Christian philosophers who interpreted God's knowledge of future possibles as probabilistic. Since we have just seen that the pas-

---

25. This point was already made by Hannah Kasher in "Joseph ibn Kaspi as Philosophical Exegete [in Hebrew]" (Ph.D. diss., Bar Ilan University, 1979), 62–71.

26. In ibid., 68, Kasher cites a passage from *A Refining Pot for Silver* that appears to indicate a strong libertarian understanding of free choice:

sage does not imply that God's knowledge is probabilistic, there is no need now to examine these alleged similarities. But the issue of scholastic influence is interesting in its own right. Pines points to features of Kaspi's solution that he claims are unprecedented within the Arab tradition, such as the use of the Hebrew equivalent of the Latin phrase *"contigentia futura,"*[27] the concern with the apparent incompatibility of divine foreknowledge and human free choice and future contingency, and the implied distinction between divine foreknowledge and past knowledge.[28]

But these claims can be disputed. Even if Kaspi uses a Hebrew phrase that is equivalent to the Latin *"contigentia futura"*—which is not at all certain—that does not show that he was familiar with Latin discussions about God's knowledge of future contingents. One would have to show *inter alia* that the phrase does not appear in the Arabic texts or in their Hebrew translations. And, indeed, the equivalent phrase, *"ha-devarim ha-efsharim ha-'atidiyim"* (the future possible things), is found in Alfarabi's *Short Treatise* on the *De interpretatione*,[29] the likely source for the discussion of the truth value of future statements in Kaspi's logical compendium, *The Bundle of Silver*, where Kaspi uses the phrases *"ha-efshari ha-'atid"* (the future possible), *"devar 'atid efshari"* (the future possible thing), and *"'atid efshar"* (the possible future) (all sic!) interchangeably. True, Alfarabi does not connect the logical dimension of the issue to the question of God's knowledge of future possibles in the *Short Treatise*, but he does in the *Long Commentary* on the *De interpretatione*,[30] and it is not a difficult connection to make, as can be seen from many discussions of God's knowledge of future possibles in the Arabic, Hebrew, and Latin traditions.

> Our material possessions and even our own bodies do not belong to us but are from God (may he be exalted). He may do with them as he wishes, but we cannot. Hence let us strip away from all external possession and body so that we remain for ourselves merely a soul without a body. Now only this, I mean, the soul, possesses choice, and it (*ve-hi*) is free and sovereign (*hofshit ve-gevirah*) to do as it wishes, for it is for itself.

This certainly sounds like a strong libertarian position, but note that what is characterized as "free and sovereign" is not choice, but the soul, and that we are not told exactly the nature of the freedom, specifically, whether it excludes any external causality.

27. Pines repeats this point in his "Scholasticism after Thomas Aquinas and the Teachings of Hasdai Crescas and His Predecessors," in S. Pines, *Studies in the History of Jewish Thought* (Jerusalem, 1997), 489–590, esp. 497.

28. Pines, "Joseph ibn Kaspi's and Spinoza's Opinion," 283–84.

29. Bibliothèque Nationale Ms. Heb 898, fol. 62r. Cf. Zimmerman, *Alfarabi's Commentary on the De Interpretatione,"* 244.

30. Ibid., 92–95. Apparently this work was not translated into Hebrew.

Moreover, although the divine knowledge/human choice antinomy was not always discussed in the Arab Aristotelian philosophical tradition in terms of divine foreknowledge, it certainly was discussed in Jewish philosophy prior to contacts with scholastic philosophy. We shall see below that Kaspi's solution can be read within the Hebrew philosophical tradition of the thirteenth and fourteenth centuries. We shall see also that there is no need to interpret intellectual *shi'ur* as a species of foreknowledge, nor must one read Kaspi as distinguishing between God's knowledge of the future and knowledge of the past, two of Pines' alleged criteria for scholastic influence.

Still, even though there is no evidence that Kaspi was familiar with scholastic discussions on this issue, none of the aforementioned arguments go so far as to *exclude* his coming up with a libertarian/incompatibilist position on the question of God's foreknowledge and human choice and accountability, especially if we confine ourselves to this passage.

The Determinist/Compatibilist Interpretation (Avicenna/Alghazali)

As odd as it may sound, Kaspi's solution to the antinomy can also be given an interpretation that is both determinist and compatibilist, i.e., that humans choose and are accountable for their actions although their actions are causally determined.[31] Such an interpretation solves some of the philosophical issues mentioned above and can claim some textual support, although it is not without difficulties.

Let us begin with the textual support. It should be recalled that Kaspi compares God's knowledge with the knowledge of "our scholars...who assess that a person accursed in his actions and affairs will tomorrow, or the following day, make a bad choice, whether in marriage or some other worldly affair such as a business matter, or a journey." Now if this description is referring to scholars such as astrologers,[32] Kaspi may be comparing God's "intellectual assessment" to the sort of speculation made by the astrologers, who, through their knowledge of the properties and influences of the stars, are able to predict with varying degrees of success a person's future. The difference is that God, unlike the astrologers, knows *all* the astral influences that will determine the outcome in a given situation, because of the assumption of astral determinism.

If Kaspi is comparing God's knowledge to that of the astrologers, then he is following in the footsteps of Alghazali in the *Opinions of the Philoso-*

---

31. This is sometimes referred to as "soft determinism," following William James.

32. Pines, "Joseph ibn Kaspi's and Spinoza's Opinion," 282, understands Kaspi as referring to "simply sharp men experienced in practical life."

phers (Maqāsid al-falāsifa), Hebrew translations of which were available in fourteenth-century Jewish Provence:[33]

> The First (may he be praised) knows originated events by their causes, since motives and causes ascend to the Necessary of Existence. But everything originated, and which is possible, is necessary by virtue of its cause and impossible when its cause is absent. For if its cause would not exist, then it would not exist. And that cause is also necessary, [etc., going backward] until one arrives at the essence of the Necessary of Existence. And since he knows the hierarchy of the causes, he necessarily knows the effects.
>
> The astrologer investigates some of the causes of existence of an event but is unable to encompass all of them; so, indubitably, his judgment concerning the realization of this event rests on an hypothesis.... If the astrologer is informed of the greater part of the causes, then his hypothesis is strengthened; if his information covers all of them, he has achieved certain knowledge....This then is the manner of knowing possibles.[34]

According to Alghazali, who is summarizing Avicenna's position, God's knowledge is like that of an astrologer who knows all the future possible events because he knows the hierarchy of the causes that causally determines them, except that God, unlike the astrologer, has complete knowledge of the causes. If Kaspi has this doctrine in mind, then he is committed to accepting the deterministic implications of Avicenna's doctrine, namely, that there is a hierarchy of causes that determines future possibles. There is nothing in Kaspi's solution cited above that excludes this interpretation. Even the metaphysical possibility of future possibles and their unknowability by nature are compatible with their being determined—*not* for a libertarian/incompatibilist, to be sure, but for someone like Avicenna, who maintains that particular events are possible in themselves and necessitated by their causes.

One advantage of the determinist interpretation over the libertarian interpretation is that there is no need to devalue *shi'ur sikhli* as a form of knowledge, for now intellectual assessment is conceived as the knowledge of the universal causes that determine the particular effects, which has nothing to do with the imagination. Another advantage is that God need not have as the objects of his knowledge the particular circumstances

---

33. According to Steven Harvey, the *Opinions* was not as popular in fourteenth-century Provence as has been claimed. See his "Why Did Fourteenth-century Jews Turn to Alghazali's Account of Natural Science," *Jewish Quarterly Review* 91 (2001): 359–76. But it was still read. For ibn Kaspi's acquaintance with Alghazali, see ibid., 365; I am not aware that the exegete mentions the *Opinions* anywhere.

34. Paris, Bibliotheque Nationale Ms. Héb, 956 (IMHM 32606), fol. 159r.

leading to a future possible choice or action, at least not in all their parti-
culiarity, as the medievals would say. Avicenna famously held that God
knows particulars from their universal aspect, and although there is much
disagreement about how this idea should be understood,[35] it is generally
taken to imply that God knows the universal features, properties, rules,
etc., that govern and determine the generation and destruction of material
particulars. On this "Avicennan" interpretation of Kaspi's solution, God
does not apprehend all the *particular circumstances or factors* that will lead
to a given choice, but rather all the *general principles* of which these particular circumstances or factors are instantiations, and that determine that a
choice or action will occur at a particular time.

On the basis of the statement from *The Silver Is Concluded* alone, it is
impossible to determine which is the better interpretation, the libertarian/
incompatibilist or the determinist/compatibilist. Conducive to the libertarian reading are the claims that events occur by nature, accident, and
human choice, that divine "intellectual assessment" is compatible with
"absolute choice," and that divine causality is remote. Even so, we cannot
rule out an Avicennan approach, nor can we infer that the philosopher
was a strong libertarian/incompatibilist, for the reasons given above.

Perhaps Kaspi merely wishes to claim that God's perfect knowledge
does not *causally* determine future possibles, without addressing the issue
of whether it implies the necessity of their occurrence in any other way.
After all, both Saadia Gaon and Judah Halevy claimed that God's knowledge, while certain, does not causally "compel" the existence of future
possibles.[36] So does Maimonides, but the latter is sensitive to the problem
(as old as Boethius) that although divine knowledge does not causally
determine future possibles, there is a sense in which they have to occur.
Yet with respect to this point or distinction Kaspi has nothing to say.

The Libertarian/Compatibilist Interpretation (Averroes)

In Pines' "libertarian/incompatibilist" interpretation, the mental
activity of *shi'ur* consists of forming an hypothesis that takes into consideration particular causal factors in order to predict the occurrence of a
future possible. Pines traces Kaspi's understanding of the term to the way
it is used in *Guide* 2.38 in conjunction with prophecy and divination. But

---

35. See Michael E. Marmura, "Some Aspects of Avicenna's Theory of God's
    Knowledge of Particulars," *Journal of the American Oriental Society* 82 (1962):
    299–311.

36. Saadia Gaon, *The Book of Beliefs and Opinions* 4.4, trans. Samuel Rosenblatt
    (New Haven, 1948), 191; Judah Halevy, *The Book of Kuzari* 5.20, trans. Hartwig
    Hirschfeld (New York, 1946), 249.

we also saw that Kaspi qualifies *shi'ur* by the term *"sikhli"* (intellectual), and he attributes this mode of knowing *only* to God. So he may be referring not to a predictive speculation based on particular causal factors at a particular time, but rather to an *eternal determination of the causal order that brings things into existence*. In that case, the Arabic equivalent would not be *"shu'ūr,"* but rather *"qadar,"* as that term is used in the well-known phrase in Muslim theology, *"al-qada' wa-l qadar,"* i.e., the divine decree and existential determination of that decree.[37] We find that the thirteenth-century philosopher and translator Shem Tov b. Joseph ibn Falaquera renders *"al-qada' wa-l qadar"* by the phrase *"ha-gezerah ve-ha-shi'ur"* in a passage that he translated for his commentary on the *Guide*.[38] And Kaspi reproduces Falaquera's translation in his own commentary on the *Guide*, *Silver Pillars* (*Amudei kesef*). This is clear evidence that, at the very least, Kaspi was familiar with the meaning of *shi'ur* as the eternal divine determination of existing things.

The long passage cited by Falaquera is an excerpt from Averroes' *The Exposition of the Methods of Proof concerning the Principles of Religion* (*Al-kashf 'an manāhij al-adilla fi 'aqāidi al-millah*), his chief theological work, which was translated into Hebrew in the Middle Ages.[39] In his introduction Averroes maintains that religion consists of two parts, external and interpreted, the former for the multitude, the latter for the learned; this work is addressed to the multitude and treats the external dogmas that are incumbent upon them. But it would be wrong to dismiss the *Exposition* as not reflecting Averroes' true philosophical opinion; certainly, there is no internal evidence for that conclusion. In any event, there is no indication that Kaspi treated the extract Falaquera translated from Averroes' chapter on *al-qada' wa-l qadar* as exoteric (although we should note that there is also no indication that Kaspi was familiar with anything more of the *Exposition* than the extract). Because of the importance of Averroes' influence in fourteenth-century Jewish philosophy and his influence on Kaspi, we shall consider some of his views on these questions and how they are to be distinguished from those of Avicenna.

---

37. *Taqdīr* has the sense of "conjecture," "estimate," "gauge"; the Hebrew *shi'ur* can capture both the sages' *taqdīr* and God's *qadar*.

38. See Shem Tov b. Joseph Ibn Falaquera, *Moreh ha-moreh*, ed. Yair Shifman (Jerusalem, 2001), 311–13.

39. See M. Steinschneider, *Die hebräischen Übersetzungen des Mittelalters und die Juden als Dolmetscher* (Berlin, 1893; rept. Graz, 1956), 277–79. I have used here the Arabic edition by Mahmud Qasīm (Cairo, 1964), and the English translation by Ibrahim Najjar, *Faith and Reason in Islam: Averroes' Exposition of Religious Arguments* (Oxford, 2001).

Averroes begins the chapter by noting that the question of divine decree and determination is one of the most difficult ones posed by religion. One can find support in both tradition and reason for the position that only God acts and determines everything, as well as for the opposite position that humans can act independently of God. Averroes himself stakes out an intermediate position, according to which God creates within us faculties by which we may choose between alternatives. But these choices cannot be brought to fruition unless there is a concurrence between our internal desires and choices and external causes. He then continues:

> However, since the external causes proceed according to a pattern and an arranged order, because of what their creator has determined (*shi'er*) for [them][40] and since our will and actions exist only through the concurrence of the external causes [it follows that our actions occur according to a defined pattern—they take place at specific times and in a determined measure. This must be the case because our actions are effects of these external causes].[41] Now every effect that occurs through defined and determined causes (*mi-sibbot mugdarot mesho'arot*) is, of necessity, itself defined and limited....The determined arrangement of the external and internal causes, i.e., that which does not corrupt, is the degree (*gezerah*) and determination (*shi'ur*) that God has written for his servants....[42]

All things are brought into existence through causes, and the order and arrangement of the causes are what we call the divine degree and determination.[43]

Averroes next takes up the question of God's knowledge:

> God's knowledge (may he be exalted) of these causes, and what follows from them, is the cause of their existence. That is why only God (may he be exalted) encompasses the knowledge of these causes. Hence, only he knows truly the hidden things. And knowledge of causes is the same as knowledge of hidden things, because what is hidden is the knowledge of whether a future thing is existent or nonexistent.
>
> Now, inasmuch as the order and arrangement of things is what brings about[44] the existence of something at a certain instant, [it follows

40. This is based on the Arabic; Kaspi has *'alav*.

41. The material within the brackets is found only in the Arabic.

42. Ed. Salomo Werbluner (Frankfurt a. M., 1848), 126–27.

43. Later on in the chapter, Averroes mentions that God has instilled natures within celestial and sublunary bodies as part of the *causal framework* that is the divine decree. See *Al-kashf*, ed. Qasīm, 229, trans. Najjar, 111.

44. Hebrew: *yehayyev*; Arabic: *tājib*. Najjar translates *tājib* as "calls for." A more literal translation is misleading ("necessitates," "obligates," or "requires") because it suggests strict causal determinism. These terms should be save for the phrase *yehayyev be-hekhreah*.

that the knowledge of the causes of a certain thing is equivalent to the knowledge of the existence of that thing or its nonexistence at a certain instant,][45] and the knowledge of the causes without qualification, is the knowledge of what thing exists or does not exist at any instant all the time. May he who encompasses the origination and knowledge with respect to all causes of existing things be praised![46]

Averroes does not use the term *qadar* or *taqdīr* or any other form of the root "*q-d-r*" in the discussion of divine knowledge, and this is admittedly a disadvantage when trying to draw a connection to *shi'ur sikhli*. He does say, however, that God's knowledge is the cause of the existence of things, which is what he says also about the divine determination. So it does not seem too much of a stretch to interpret *shi'ur* in the context of a divine knowledge that determines the existence of existing things.

There is much that Averroes leaves unsaid about his views on divine knowledge in the *Exposition*, as, for example, that God intellectually cognizes himself and nothing outside himself, that neither the object nor the manner of his knowledge is particular or universal, that God does not know himself *qua* cause, that the term "knower" is applied of God and other knowers with "pure equivocation," etc. These doctrines are explained at length in his more strictly philosophical works,[47] and he no doubt considers at least some of them out of place in a popular religious work, especially since he opposes teaching philosophical interpretations to the multitude.

Indeed, were we to possess only the *Exposition* and not the philosophical writings, we would not be able to see much of a difference between Averroes' and Avicenna's views on divine knowledge and causal determinism. Both argue that God knows existing things by virtue of knowing their causes, and that these causes bring about the existence of existing things. Averroes explicitly writes that "the external causes that God has made subservient to us not only complement or impede the actions we want to do, they are also the causes of our choice of one of the two opposites." This does not leave any room for uncaused phenomena, mental or external, that some libertarian/incompatibilists require for their interpretation of free will. If the belief in free will requires that humans can choose by virtue of an autonomous power that is not subject to natural causality (as libertarians often argue) then Averroes does not believe in free will.

---

45. The material within the brackets is not found in the extant manuscripts of Falaquera's extract.

46. *Silver Pillars*, ed. Werbluner, 127. (*Al-kashf*, ed. Qasīm, 228; trans. Najjar, 110.)

47. For a review and analysis of the pertinent passages, see Thérèse-Anne Druart, "Averroes on God's Knowledge of Being Qua Being," in *Studies in Thomistic Theology*, ed. Paul Lockey (Houston, 1995), 175–205.

But interpreted in the light of other statements by Avicenna and Averroes, the passage from the *Exposition* presents a doctrine quite different
from the *Opinions of the Philosophers*, both in the nature of divine knowledge and how it determines the existence of actually existing things. Avicenna, as we have seen, holds that God knows particulars with a "universal knowledge," or "in their universal aspect," i.e., as types rather than
tokens. For example, God knows that the sun and the moon exist (because
they are emanated from him), and he knows all the properties of their
movements, and that after a certain amount of time, for example, there
will be a solar eclipse.[48] This implies, according to Ghazzali in the *Incoherence of the Philosophers*, that God does not know that a solar eclipse is
occurring *now*, because otherwise his knowledge changes before, during,
and after the eclipse.[49] Averroes, in the *Incoherence of the Incoherence*,
rejects Avicenna's view that God knows particulars in their universal
aspect because the universal aspect of particulars, i.e., the patterns governing them that we recognize, are mental abstractions from sensory
experience. God does not know in the way that we know; he is neither a
superknower nor a superpredictor based on knowing the universal rules
of science, because the universal rules of science involve abstraction and
conceptualization.[50]

Perhaps this reticence to embrace Avicenna's view explains why
Averroes distinguishes in the aforementioned passage between knowledge of the causes *of a certain thing* and knowledge of causes *without qualification*; only the latter produces knowledge of what exists or does not
exist at any instant all the time. If we read this in light of Averroes' views
on divine knowledge, we may wish to say that God's knowledge conforms to the latter, which in a sense includes the former, but without the
implication that what God knows are the *universal* causes that necessitate
particulars. In other words, God knows himself and the pattern and order
of reality that is his essence; that pattern and order is *not* conceived by him
as a detailed encyclopedia of science, as human knowers would view it,
but something else entirely. In so far as that pattern and arrangement is
the cause of the existence of things, then God can be said to know existing
things. But his knowledge is not like that of an omniscient astrologer or
scientist.

---

48. Paris, Bibliotheque Nationale Ms. Héb, 956, fol. 159r–v.

49. *The Incoherence of the Philosophers*, Discussion 13, trans. Michael E. Marmura
(Provo, Ut., 2000), 136–37.

50. *The Incoherence of the Incoherence*, Discussion 6, trans. Simon van den Bergh
(Oxford, 1954), 203–4.

As for the question of determinism, Averroes' position, while not libertarian/indeterminist in the sense described above, differs from the strict determinism of Alghazali (in the *Opinions of the Philosophers*) and Avicenna. Unlike them, he does not refer to future possibles as "possible by virtue of themselves, yet *necessitated* by their causes," nor does he accept the emanationist picture that presents events as proceeding necessarily from God through a series of hypostases. Like many other Aristotelians, Averroes appears to hold that universal causation does not imply necessitation because there are different sorts of causes, including accidental ones. And further on in the *Exposition* he sharply distinguishes his "intermediate" position on human voluntary movements from the intermediate position of the Asharite theologians, who claim that humans "acquire" such movements, which are created by God, in so far as they desire or acquiesce to them. According to Averroes, if a voluntary movement is created by God, then the only difference between voluntary and reflex actions is verbal; in both cases we have no power to refrain from them and "accordingly we are compelled to act."[51] In other words, Averroes would consider an act to be "compelled" even when there is no felt compulsion, when an agent feels that she is acting voluntarily. Such a position goes against the grain of those determinist/compatibilists who maintain that humans are accountable for their actions as long as they do not feel themselves compelled.[52]

For these reasons Averroes' position may be called "libertarian/compatibilist": "libertarian" because he adopts the Aristotelian position that actions must be voluntary in order to be appropriately blamed and praised, and that voluntary actions are not necessitated; "compatibilist" because he considers such blame and praise to be compatible with a universal causation that does not allow for causal "gaps" in nature. Averroes explicitly rejects fatalism, and may also consider praise and blame to be inappropriate given a causal determinism of the Avicennan variety.[53]

One further point that is pertinent to our discussion of Kaspi: in Averroes' *Book of Eternal Knowledge* (called by Müller and subsequent scholars,

---

51. *Al-kashf*, ed. Qasīm, 232; trans. Najjar, 115.

52. For a different reading of Averroes' position, see J. Guttmann, "The Problem of Free Will in Hasdai Crescas and the Islamic Aristotelians," in *Religion and Knowledge: Essays and Lectures* [in Hebrew], trans. Saul Esh, ed. S. H. Bergman and N. Rotenstreich (Jerusalem, 1955), 149–68.

53. Hence the reader should note that the term "compatibilist" in the phrases determinist/compatibilist (Avicenna) and libertarian/compatibilist (Averroes) is ambiguous; according to the former, human accountability is compatible with causal determinism; according to the latter, with universal causation.

the *Appendix* [*Damima*] to the *Decisive Treatise*), the author writes, "How is it conceivable that the Peripatetic philosophers could have held that the eternal Knowledge does not comprehend particulars, when they held that is the cause of warning in dreams, of revelation, and of other kinds of inspiration?"[54] I have argued elsewhere that the so-called Arabic recension of the *Parva naturalia* may have served as the source for this comment and, hence, that Averroes had grounds for believing that this was truly Aristotle's position.[55] Whether this speculation is correct or not, Averroes presents himself and the Aristotelians as arguing that we can infer that God knows particulars from the well-attested phenomenon of revelation and veridical dreams.

We do not know whether Kaspi was familiar with the *Book of Eternal Knowledge* or the *Decisive Treatise*, both of which were translated into Hebrew.[56] But if one wished to interpret Kaspi's statement on the knowledge of possibles in an Averroist light, it would go something like this:

God's knowledge comprehends future possibles, because God's knowledge is the cause of everything that was, is, and will be. God is rightly called the cause of the future event in so far as he is the remote cause of humans having desires, choices, and external causes to motivate those choices. God's knowledge does not causally necessitate that a future event will occur in a strong deterministic sense; rather, in so far as future events causally depend upon human choice, they are (a) possible, (b) not known to us, or by nature, and (c) known to God. This explanation was provided by the philosophers (i.e., the Arab Aristotelians[57]), who also showed how God's knowledge was imparted to his servants, the prophets, without there being any compulsion coming from him.

The attractiveness of this interpretation lies in its emphasis on the sort of naturalism and libertarian/compatibilism that one associates with the Aristotelian position and that one finds in Averroes and Maimonides,

---

54. See George Hourani, *Averroes on the Harmony of Religion and Philosophy* (London, 1961), 75. A similar remark appears in the *Decisive Treatise*, p. 55); cf. n. 98, 99. Both works were translated into Hebrew in the High Middle Ages, although there is no evidence that either was known to Kaspi.

55. See Manekin, "Maimonides on Divine Knowledge" (cited in n. 5 above).

56. For the former, see Georges Vajda, "Deux versions hébraiques de la dissertation d'Averroès sur la science divine," *Revue des Études Juives* N. S. 13 (1954): 63–66; for the latter see Norman Golb, "The Hebrew Translation of Averroes' 'Fasl al-maqāl,'" *Proceedings of the American Academy for Jewish Research* 25 (1956): 91–113, and 26 (1957): 41–64.

57. And maybe Aristotle and his school, if Kaspi read Averroes' *Book of Eternal Knowledge*.

Kaspi's philosophical mentors. No doubt it seems odd to claim that a future possible is not known "by nature" yet known to God. But here the sense of "not known by nature" is "not *fore*known by nature," because future possibles are undetermined now. And this inability of future possibles to be foreknown is compatible with their being known to God. For in an Averroist interpretation, not only is God's knowledge not *fore*knowledge, it shares only the name "knowledge" in common with human knowledge.[58]

This interpretation also accords well with a passage in *A Silver Candelabrum* (*Menorat kesef*), Kaspi's commentary on Isaiah, in which Kaspi interprets "his glory fills the earth" (Isa 6:3) to explain how God knows things outside of him:

> Aristotle and all his students found difficult the question of how God knows what is beneath him, a fortiori [things] in the sublunar world called "*ha-aretz*"; likewise [the question of] how God watches over our world, and how powers in this world emanated from his power and his glory. The book of Job in its entirety was composed for the sake of this question, and Ptolemy devoted chapter seven of his book to it. Alfarabi also spoke a great deal about it. So what is the great surprise that Isaiah taught us this extraordinary secret....
>
> The understanding of "his glory" is like "from his glory," and the understanding of "fills all the earth" is the creatures and existence that is in the earth, as their saying, "And the earth was filled with them."
>
> The understanding [of the entire verse] is [as follows]: All creatures of the sublunar world exist from his power and from his glory, i.e., he is their cause. He supervises them and knows them. Now it was mentioned before that God (may he be exalted) is a threefold cause of everything, i.e, efficient, formal, and final, as the *Guide* already explained....[59]
>
> Isaiah apprehended this extraordinary secret with a clear knowledge, without the premises and conclusions that the philosophers composed in their books. And I am astonished how this was hidden from the Teacher, considering what he (of blessed memory) wrote in the last chapter of the *Guide*, on the verse, "Who exercises loving-kindness...and righteousness in the earth" (Jer 9:24).[60]

---

58. I do not deny that there is a sense in which God's eternal knowledge can be called foreknowledge, just as my knowledge at t_1 that seven plus five will equal twelve at t_2 can be called foreknowledge. But this is not the sense of foreknowledge that underlies our discussion. (I also realize that the last example is an imperfect analogy, but this is to be expected when talking about a divine attribute that is claimed to be utterly different from its human counterpart!)

59. *Guide* 1.69, trans. Pines, 69–70.

60. Ibid. 3.54, 637. See *The Silver Candelabrum* in '*Asarah Kelei Kesef*, ed. I. Last (Pressburg, 1905), 1:115.

Kaspi refers here to the Maimonides' identification of the divine attributes of "loving-kindness" and "righteousness," (and presumably "judgment," although that is not explicitly mentioned by Kaspi) with the divine actions. According to Kaspi, Maimonides could have understood how God knows the world had he simply recalled that God is the threefold cause of the world and that it is through God's attributes of actions that God supervises the world.

The passage from *A Silver Candelabrum* seems to take God's knowledge in an Averroist direction, especially the connection between divine causality and knowledge, although some characteristic elements of Averroes' theory are missing, such as the claim that God knows the world by virtue of (a) self-intellection and (b) the world being included, in a more noble form of existence, in the divine essence. The passage certainly stands in stark contrast to Kaspi's claim in *The Silver Is Concluded* that God's knowledge of future possibles is like the knowledge of experts. If one wishes to reconcile the passages, one will have to reconcile the "how" of divine knowledge of particulars in both cases.

To sum up the discussion to this point: Kaspi, in *The Silver Is Concluded*, proposes a solution to the divine foreknowledge/human choice antinomy in which God is said to know future possibles in such a way as to preserve human choice. That way is called "intellectual assessment," which is likened to the speculation of the prophets and the scholars. We have suggested so far three possible interpretations of the solution: one libertarian/incompatibilist (unnamed scholastic philosophers), another determinist/compatibilist (Avicenna), still another libertarian/compatibilist (Averroes). According to the first, Kaspi preserves human free choice and metaphysical contingency by ascribing to God a probabilistic type of knowledge. The interpretation rests on understanding "absolute choice" as a type of choice that is incompatible with any form of causality, determinism, or necessitation, and on understanding "intellectual assessment" as inferior to demonstration, or at least as less certain.

According to the second interpretation, Kaspi preserves divine knowledge at the expense of libertarian free choice, but allows for a kind of choice that is compatible with determinism. While it seems unlikely that Kaspi opts for a strong Avicennan version of causal determinism, nothing in his remarks rules this out or rules out his acceptance of a weaker version of "theological determinism," in which God's infallible knowledge implies that future events must occur in the way God knows them, but not that it causally determines then.

According to the third interpretation, Kaspi accepts the Aristotelian view that identifies divine ordainment with natural, volitional, and accidental causality. On the one hand, there are no causal "gaps" in nature; on the other hand, not everything that occurs happens of necessity because some things are chosen, or they occur by accident. It is God's knowledge of the order and arrangement of existing things within himself that determines the way things are; this order and arrangement differs fundamentally from the order and arrangement in existing things. Still, God is said to know everything that exists and occurs, including future possibles, although not *qua* particulars or universals, but as they exist within the divine essence. Some of Kaspi's phrases and comments are reminiscent of Averroes' writings, especially his theological writings.

II.

So far we have viewed Kaspi's statement on God's knowledge in *The Silver Is Concluded* in light of his philosophical antecedents. But what if the nub of that position reached him from outside the philosophical tradition? When we compare elements of Kaspi's discussion to the glosses of Abraham b. David's on the *Mishneh Torah* that deal with the same subject, we find rather striking similarities. Perhaps Kaspi's treatment here is inspired by the more traditional treatment of Abraham b. David. Let us examine what can be said on behalf of this more traditionalist interpretation.

The Traditionalist Interpretation
(Abraham b. David)

It will be recalled that the context of Kaspi's statement on divine knowledge is his exegesis of Gen 15:13, which is also discussed by Maimonides in his *Mishneh Torah*. Maimonides maintains in that work that we are unable to understand how God knows future actions without determining those actions. In a well-known gloss, the rabbi and kabbalist Abraham b. David criticizes Maimonides for raising the question and leaving it unanswered. In lieu of a convincing answer, Abraham b. David finds it useful to provide a "partial answer":

> God's knowledge of [what humans will do in the future] is like the knowledge of the astrologers, who know what this person's manner will be because of [astral] force. For it is known that every human accident, great or small, was delivered by God to the power of the stars. But God gave man intellect because it fortifies him to depart from the [power of] the star, and this is the power given to man to be good and bad. Now the creator knows the force of the star and its minutes and whether intellect has the force to remove *this* man from his dominion or not, and this knowledge does not constitute divine decree.
> But all this is of no value.[61]

---

61. Abraham b. David, *The Animadversions of Rabad to the "Mishneh Torah* [in Hebrew]," ed. Bezalel Naor (Jerusalem, 1980), 44–45. Cf. I. Twersky, *Rabad of*

According to Abraham b. David, God's manner of knowing future possibles is comparable to that of the astrologers, who predict what will happen to an individual based on stellar influence. The difference is that God knows the not only the power of the stars but the power of a given individual's intellect to act otherwise than what the stars decree. Although humans can avoid astral determinism through acting according to intellect, whether they do so or not will be known to God, because he knows the relative forces of intellect and the stars bearing upon human choice.

The notion that individuals can avoid astral determinism through rational choice is a common trope in the astrological literature as far back as Ptolemy; it is prominent in Ibn Ezra and later in Gersonides.[62] It should be noted that Abraham b. David presents God as an infallible predictor of this *particular* individual's choices and actions because he has complete and intimate knowledge of the present circumstances surrounding this man.

Although the terminology differs, Abraham b. David's solution possesses the two elements that are peculiar to Kaspi's statement in *The Silver Is Concluded*: the notion that God assesses human action based on his complete knowledge of the circumstances surrounding this individual, and the notion that this knowledge does not render human choice "decreed." He also holds that God's manner of knowing future possibles is akin to that of the astrologers, which, we suggested, were likely to be the "scholars who are experts in speculating and estimating" mentioned by Kaspi.

But the similarities between Abraham b. David and Kaspi are not limited to the question of divine knowledge. In his very next gloss on the *Mishneh Torah*, Abraham b. David writes:

> The matter of the [justice in punishing the] Egyptians is not a problem for two reasons: First, it is well known that the creator does not exact punishment from a wicked man save through one more wicked than he, and after he exacts it from the former, he will exact it from the latter. Thus he says, "O Assyria, rod of my anger…when you cease to despoil then you will be despoiled" (Isa 10:6, 33:1). The explanation of this is that [you will be despoiled] because of your haughty heart and your glorying yourself over me. Now the Egyptians were wicked and deserving of the plagues. Had they listened to Moses from the beginning and sent Israel away then they would not have drowned or been afflicted. But Pharoah's malicious and demeaning behavior toward the creator (may he be blessed) before he sent

---

Posquières: A Twelfth-century Talmudist, rev. ed. (Philadelphia, 1980), 281–82 and sources cited in nn. 48 and 49.

62. See Charles H. Manekin, "Freedom within Reason?: Gersonides on Human Choice," in *Freedom and Moral Responsibility: General and Jewish Perspectives*, ed. Charles H. Manekin (Bethesda, 1997), 165–204.

[Israel] away caused [the punishment of the Egyptians. The second reason [why no injustice was done the Egyptians] is that the creator said, "They will afflict them and oppress them" (Gen 15:13), and "they enslaved them ruthlessly" (Exod 1:13) and killed them. They were held accountable, as it is written, "for I was only angry a little, but they overdid the punishment" (Zech 1:15)."[63]

According to Abraham b. David, the Egyptians were justly punished, because they were haughty before God, and because they acted with excessive cruelty toward Israel. These are the very two reasons cited by Kaspi in the continuation of *The Silver Is Concluded*:

> Our teacher Moses explained and related in his Torah, written from the mouth of the Almighty, that "the Egyptians enslaved the Israelites ruthlessly" (Exod 1:13). He also wrote: "They made life bitter for them with harsh labor" (Exod 1:14). These things, and certainly the killing of the male [children], were not in accordance with God's eternal will. The intent of this was that God wanted Moses to publicize in his[64] Torah that the Egyptians sinned and rebelled against God, since they continued to inflict great evil upon the Israelites over and above what he (may he be exalted) wished...
>
> This is also the point in the book of Zechariah, who states as a principle: "And I am very angry with those nations that are at ease; for I was only angry a little, but they overdid the punishment" (Zech 1:15)
>
> Regarding Sennacherib, Isaiah likewise followed Moses's opinion by providing two reasons [for his punishment]: The first resembles the one we mentioned concerning the Egyptians; the second he added when he stated: "O Assyria, rod of my anger," etc. "[I sent him against an ungodly nation...] But he has evil plans" (Isa 10:5–7)...
>
> Our nation's prophets acted astutely, foremost among them Moses, [whose prophecy] proceeded from the mouth of God. They provided for this matter [of divine punishment of the instruments of his wrath] a *legal and juridical reason*: [a] the excessive malice that inflicts greater evil than willed by God, and [b] the denial of God, by virtue of which they say that "My own power and the might of my own hand have obtained this wealth for me" (Deut 8:17) and that "the Lord did not make all this" (Deut 32:27). This is all true, as it is written in the books.[65]

Both Abraham b. David and Kaspi provide similar explanations of the manner of divine knowledge of future things. They also provide virtually identical justifications for the punishment of the foreordained (or foreknown) instruments of God's retribution against Israel. Abraham b. David appeals to the "well-known" rule that

---

63. B. David, *Animadversions*, 45–46.

64. It is not clear from the text whether the possessive pronoun refers to God or to Moses.

65. Ed. Last, 21.

the creator does not exact punishment from a wicked man save through one more wicked than he, and after he exacts it from the former, he will exact it from the latter, and after he exacts it from the former, he will exact it from the latter. Thus he says, "O Assyria, rod of my anger…when you cease to despoil then you will be despoiled" (Isa 10:6, 33:1).

And so too Kaspi:

As a rule, evil is always defeated by greater evil, as it is written, "I create the instruments of havoc" (Isa 54:16). This is a truth concerning all men with respect to other men, and all nations with respect to other nations, as I wrote in the book entitled *The Silver Beds* (*Mittot Kesef*).[66] …Regarding Sennacherib, Isaiah likewise followed Moses' opinion by providing two reasons [for his punishment]: The first resembles the one we mentioned concerning the Egyptians; the second he added when he stated: "O Assyria, rod of my anger," etc.[67]

It should be recalled that the context of the exegesis on Gen 15:13, as found in Maimonides' *Mishneh Torah*, is certainly the same for both men. Some of the proof texts adduced by Abraham b. David are found in Kaspi as well.

From all the above it is not unreasonable to conclude that Kaspi was familiar with Abraham b. David's glosses on the *Mishneh Torah*, or some other writing based on them, and that this played a role in the formulation of the statement on divine knowledge in *The Silver Is Concluded*.

But this raises an obvious difficulty. If Abraham b. David was, indeed, the main source for Kaspi's statement on God's knowledge of future possibles,[68] then why would a philosopher of Kaspi's Aristotelian temperament rely on a traditionalist like Abraham b. David for his theodicy and theory of divine knowledge? An eleventh-hour conversion to a more traditional approach is hardly likely, given Kaspi's thoroughgoing naturalism in The *Silver Is Concluded*, as we have already seen, and as is evident in the preceding passages. Are we to read the solution as merely exoteric, and, if so, are there any hints to what the esoteric solution would be?

In answer to the first question, there is strong evidence to suggest that Kaspi's theodicy in The *Silver Is Concluded* is intended for the multitude.

---

66. Not extant.

67. *Silver Is Concluded*, ed. Last, 23.

68. Ibid., 21n2, cites Nahmanides as a source for Kaspi, and it may be that Kaspi was influenced by Abraham b. David's views through their elaboration in Nahmanides' comments on Gen 15:14 and Exod 18:11. Nahmanides has both of Abraham b. David's reasons for the wicked kings deserving their punishment (i.e., their excessive wickedness and hubris), but he lacks the treatment of divine foreknowledge as well as the principle that the wicked receive their just punishment through the agency of the more wicked.

First, he calls the defense of God's justice in punishing the Egyptians "legal and juridical." If his own philosophical solution is correct, namely that God, as remote cause, is not directly responsible for human actions, then this obviates the need for any such legal and juridical explanation; it constitutes an entirely sufficient theodicy in itself. And, in fact, Kaspi makes this very point in his esoteric commentary on the Torah, *A Silver Goblet (Gevia' kesef)*. After referring to Maimonides' rule in *Guide* 2.48 that God is only a remote cause, he writes:

> Even though Scripture decreed and ordered in the case of Pharaoh and the Egyptians that they should do this [i.e., enslave the Israelites], the truth of the matter is that they did this out of their own complete choice. The Lord did not cause them in any essential way. It is the same with Nebuchadnezzar, as recounted in the narratives of Isaiah. "It is only that he who gave the Torah provided a common reason for the benefit of the masses when he said that Pharoah and his people acted with more evil intent than what the Lord desired and had decreed."[69]

This passage, of course, pertains to the question of divine ordainment rather than that of divine knowledge. But I suspect that just as God's ordainment acts as a remote cause, so too God's knowledge. If so, then the passage in *The Silver Is Concluded*, far from being a daring and original solution to the problem of divine foreknowledge and human choice and accountability, is actually a conventional and traditional explanation of God's knowledge addressed to the multitude!

This traditionalist interpretation is not without precedent. The Jewish Averroist Isaac Albalag, after severely criticizing Alghazali's comparison of God's knowledge to that of astrologers, allowed that it would be proper to teach such a conception to the multitude.[70] If Kaspi was familiar with Albalag's translation and emendation of the *Opinions of the Philosophers* then he may have been inspired by this comment to offer an exoteric interpretation of God's foreknowledge, based on Abraham b. David's views (which itself bears a family resemblance to Alghazali's view in the *Opinions*). But even if he was not, it is not unlikely that two Jewish Aristotelians would come up with the similar idea.

As for Kaspi's *esoteric* view of God's knowledge of future possibles, any appeal to the esoteric/exoteric distinction opens up a Pandora's box of readings, as students of medieval Jewish philosophy well know. But since our goal is to provide *possible* interpretations of Kaspi's statement on divine knowledge in *The Silver Is Concluded*, let us offer a "moderately esoteric" interpretation of the statement on God's knowledge of possibles:

---

69. *A Silver Goblet*, chap. 15, in Herring, *Kaspi's "Gevia' Kesef,"* 238n31.

70. Isaac Albalag, *Improvement of the "Opinions"* [in Hebrew], sec. 49, ed. Georges Vajda (Jerusalem, 1973), 75–76.

esoteric, because the correct interpretation is hidden from the nonphilosophical reader; moderately so, because what is presented to the reader
requires only a philosophical interpretation of its various elements in
order for it to reflect the true, i.e., philosophical, opinion.

In fact, Kaspi appears to offer a moderately esoteric interpretation of
the Bible's explanation of why the Egyptians were justly punished. On the
exoteric level he agrees with Abraham b. David's principle that "the creator does not exact punishment from a wicked man save through one
more wicked than he, and after he exacts it from the former, he will exact
it from the latter." But at the hands of a philosophical naturalist such as
Kaspi this becomes a general principle of history that applies to "all men
in respect to other men and all nations in respect to other nations," namely, that evildoers are always defeated by those more evil than they:

> As a rule, whenever there are two people or many wicked nations, it is
> divine wisdom, as well as complete justice, that one of them will destroy
> the other in a manner that is deserved, such as the sword, while subse-
> quently another wicked (agent) comes and destroys the earlier victor. So
> it is always.[71]

On this thoroughly naturalistic view, which fits in nicely with Kaspi's
view of God as remote cause, there is no need to appeal to the two "legal
and juridical" reasons of haughtiness and excessive cruelty in order to justify God's punishing Pharoah, Sennacherib, and other biblical "destroy-
ers." Their punishment is simply part of the way of the world.

In the next section I will offer a moderately esoteric interpretation of
Kaspi's statement on God's knowledge of possibles in light of his interpretation of the notion of divine "test" (*nissayon*). Once interpreted in this
manner, Kaspi's statement on God's knowledge of future possibles fits
squarely within the Jewish exegetical and Arabic/Hebrew philosophical
tradition. That, of course, is not a sufficient reason to adopt the interpretation, which is only advanced here as tentative—at best, a plausible route
for Kaspi to have taken, given his general philosophical and exegetical
inclinations.

The Moderately Esoteric Interpretation

The story of the Binding of Isaac has aptly been called a test case for
how philosophically minded commentators understood God's knowledge of future possibles.[72] In the story God tests Abraham's devotion by
demanding him to sacrifice his son Isaac. After Abraham convinces God

---

71. Cf. *A Silver Goblet*, chap. 15, in Herring, *Kaspi's "Gevia' Kesef,"* 34–37 (Hebrew
    text), 240 (English trans.).

72. See Seymour Feldman, "The Binding of Isaac: A Test Case of Divine Fore-

of his readiness to do just that, God replies (speaking through a messenger), "Now I know that you are God-fearing—you have not spared your son, your only son, from me." (Gen 22.12)The implication of God's reply is that he was ignorant, or at least uncertain, of Abraham's devotion, and that through the test he gains knowledge or becomes certain.

Kaspi devotes two discussions to the philosophical aspect of the Binding of Isaac: one in an early esoteric commentary on the Torah, *A Silver Tower* (*Tirat Kesef*), the other in *A Silver Goblet*. A third text of importance is Kalonymous b. Kalonymous' polemical letter sent to Kaspi in which the doctrines of *A Silver Tower* are critically examined. All three works antedate *The Silver Is Concluded*, and hence are directly relevant to the proper interpretation of his view of divine knowledge of future possibles.

The discussion on God's knowledge in *A Silver Tower* is found in chapter 30 of the "General Matters" that precede and underlie Kaspi's esoteric reading of Scripture. The subject of that chapter is the meaning of the Hebrew term "*nissah*" (tested or tried) as in "God tested Abraham." Kaspi notes that his predecessors Ibn Ezra and Maimonides were troubled by Scripture's use of the term, apparently because of its implication of divine uncertainty and ignorance. Yet he himself is not troubled by it at all! For he has learnt from Maimonides' treatment of divine attributes such as "merciful" and "at rest" that the Bible attributes to God transient psychological states that are said to motivate divine action. It does so because such states motivate human actions, and "the Torah speaks in the language of men," i.e., treats God as a person. When, for example, a city is destroyed, the Torah says that "God destroyed it out anger" because humans destroy things out of anger. But actually God's activity is eternal and is not motivated by transient psychological states.

To explain how all this is pertinent to the notion of "God's testing Abraham," Kaspi first comments that the word *nissayon* is defined by the philosophers as a combination of sense knowledge and intellectual knowledge, i.e., "the memory of the concept within the sense" (*zikhron ha-musag ba-ḥush*). So the expression "*nissah*" is like the expression "saw and knew" and the sense of "God tested" is the same as "God examined." Kaspi continues:

> Now it is correct that although God knew with an intellectual knowledge (*yedi'ah sikhlit*) before this event that Abraham was God-fearing, he wanted now to know this with the knowledge of experience (*yedi'at nissayon*).

knowledge," in *Divine Omniscience and Omnipotence in Medieval Philosophy*, ed. T. Rudavsky (Dordrecht, 1985), 105–133.

All of this should be understand in the manner of "the Torah speaks in the language of men." For it is possible *for us* to know intellectually through a categorical syllogism that [the color] green is pleasing to our sight. Later, however, when we wish to have experiential knowledge, as when we paint our walls green and apprehend through our sense that it pleases our sight, we shall say, "Now we know that green is pleasing to our sight." We intend by this that we now know with an experiential knowledge. Likewise, God said, "Now I know that you are God-fearing." Moreover, our expression, "Now I know"...does not imply that this was not known beforehand.

Kaspi makes two separate points here. One is that the biblical phrase "Now I know" does not imply that the knower was previously ignorant or uncertain. Another is that the Bible appears to say (because of the principle that the Torah speaks in the language of men) that as a result of testing Abraham, God's knowledge underwent a shift from intellectual (discursive, syllogistic) knowledge to direct experiential knowledge.

This, at any rate, is how Kaspi was understood by his countryman Kalonymous b. Kalonymous, who strongly criticized Kaspi for introducing the philosophical sense of *nissayon* into the scriptural context. According to Kalonymous, the philosophers distinguished two types of experiential premises, neither of which is appropriate here. The first type is a universal generalization from experiences that confirms a hypothesis, e.g., the example that Kaspi himself brings. As this premise has not been formed through the repetition of experiences, our reasoning does not yield a necessary conclusion. Calling a reasonable hypothesis "intellectual *knowledge*" and defining it as "the memory of the concept within the sense" is nonsense. Moreover, if God had intellectual knowledge prior to his experiential knowledge, then why would he have had to test Abraham?[73]

The second type of experiential premise indicates to the examiner what was previously hidden and unknown, as when a physician or scientist infers the properties of a rare plant based on her experiments. To impute this to God is more reprehensible because it implies that God was *wholly* ignorant before the test. In short, concludes Kalonymous, the philosophical definition of *nissayon* will not help Kaspi here, for both sorts of experiential premises, the one that confirms a prior hypothesis and the other that discovers something unknown, imply imperfection—the first a probabilistic sort of foreknowledge, the second no knowledge at all—and, unlike other metaphorical terms that indicate either perfections or attributes of actions, cannot be attributed to God.[74]

73. Kalonymos ben Kalonymos, *Response to Joseph Kaspi* [in Hebrew], ed. Joseph Perles (Munich, 1879), 15.

74. Ibid., 16–17.

Oddly enough, Kalonymous does not pay attention to a critical line in the continuation of Kaspi's interpretation. After the latter writes that he has explained the true definition of *nissayon*, he writes:

> But in any event, I am surprised that any perplexity still remains. For inasmuch as we noted that "Torah speaks in the language of men," and *inasmuch as people test things in different respects, and they also test God, may he be exalted, it is correct to say that God tests humans*, as it is written, for example, "They infuriate me...and I will infuriate them.... They angered me...and I will anger them" (Deut 32:21). We have already referred to other metaphors like "And he regretted," "And he was saddened," "And he rested."
>
> This example is sufficient for all the metaphors attributed to God, and its interpretation everywhere will be the same as the Teacher taught us with respect to "merciful" and the like, as we mentioned.

Whatever Kaspi means in these cryptic remarks, he certainly does not mean that God's manner of knowledge *changes* from intellectual foreknowledge to direct experiential knowledge when the "foreknown" event actually transpires—no more than he understands the phrase "God regretted what he had done" as meaning that at a certain time God's inner state changed. Rather, events are such that we *project* a change of God's inner state in order to explain a change in the world. Well, what has changed in the world? The answer, as we shall see presently, is Abraham's state of mind. He has come to experience directly, perhaps intuitively, what he knew before intellectually, i.e., through proper reasoning.

Now I don't think Kaspi's point in interpreting *nissayon* is merely to teach us about how we should understand Abraham's illumination, any more than his point about divine attributes such as "merciful" or "just" is merely to teach us something about how we should act. Both teach us something about the way the world is. If God's knowledge does not change, then what Kaspi calls here "intellectual knowledge" may be understood simply as *God's eternal knowledge of the pattern according to which the world operates*. Now the phrase "intellectual knowledge" certainly sounds like the "intellectual assessment" of *The Silver Is Concluded*, especially when both are contrasted to experiential knowledge. If so, then *shi'ur sikhli* should not be distinguished from demonstrative and certain knowledge, as Pines explained it, but rather from experiential and intuitive knowledge.

But what does God's "experiential knowledge" mean? Kaspi's point may be that divine knowledge *can be described* in certain instances as nondiscursive, experiential, intuitional, and this is what the Bible means when it has God saying things like "Now I know." Again, this does not imply a change in God's mental or epistemic state. Rather, the world is such that when individuals, such as Abraham, receive prophetic illumination, they enter into what can be called a direct "experiential" relationship with God.

This may be what Kaspi has in mind when he writes, "inasmuch as people test things in different respects, and they also test God, may he be exalted, *it is correct to say* that God tests humans." With "test" understood as "experiences," we have the idea that Abraham's experiencing God can be described as God's experiencing Abraham. This accords well with Kaspi's "conjunctionist" model of the encounter between the divine and human intellect.[75]

As for the divine foreknowledge/human choice antinomy, the present passage adds little to what we already learned in *The Silver Is Concluded*, i.e., that humans have absolute choice and that future possibles are not knowable by nature. The same three interpretations that were available for that work are available here as well: (a) God's knowledge causally necessitates human choices, but humans have the sort of absolute choice that Avicennan compatibilism vouchsafes them; (b) God's knowledge necessitates human choices but not causally so; and (c) God's knowledge causes human choices but does not necessitate them. In each of these cases, God is said to know human choices without vitiating them.

Perhaps Kaspi's view on solving the antinomy was similar to that of his countryman and contemporary Levi ben Gershom (Gersonides). Gersonides claimed that God is ignorant of certain human choices, namely, those that are made in contravention of the celestial/astrological patterns that determine human affairs. This is because God's knowledge of human "accidents" is via the astral patterns that determine them, and human choices that are made according to reason are not determined by astral patterns. Gersonides distinguishes between this sort of divine knowledge and what he calls God's "particular knowledge," which is the direct particular-providential experience of one who chooses according to reason.[76] His distinction is highly reminiscent of Kaspi's distinction between divine intellectual and experiential knowledge. But once again, there is no hard evidence that Kaspi adopts this route; he certainly does not say, with Gersonides, that from a certain aspect God does not know human actions.

---

75. On the relation between God and intellect, and between the divine and human intellect during conjunction, see Kasher, "Joseph ibn Kaspi," 52–53.

76. For this distinction, see "On the Limited-Omniscience Interpretation of Gersonides' Theory of Divine Knowledge," in *Perspectives on Jewish Thought and Mysticism*, ed. A. Ivry, E. Wolfson, and A. Arkush (Reading, 1998), 135–70. Pines interpreted both Gersonides and Kaspi as limiting divine foreknowledge in order to make room for human free choice. I argued against this reading of Gersonides here. There is, indeed, a similarity between Gersonides and Kaspi in that they both appear to draw a distinction between "types" of divine knowledge: one intuitive and experiential, the other intellectual and, for lack of a better word, discursive.

Kaspi's discussion of the Binding of Isaac in *A Silver Goblet* adds little to our understanding of the divine-knowledge aspect of the story from *A Silver Tower*.[77] That aspect appears to be one of the "deep matters" that are said to be discussed elsewhere.[78] In *A Silver Goblet* he lists ten benefits that accrue from the story, first of which is the belief that God actually tests people. We learn four chapters later that this belief, as literally expressed, is intended for the multitude. The expressions, "he tested" and "now I know" are cases of the Torah speaking in the language of men; they are not literally true because they reflect the understanding of the hearers. Kaspi continues, "Now it is a commonly accepted opinion of the multitude that the Lord tests and that he will know in the future what he does not know now." So it was proper for Moses to use terms that imply this commonly accepted opinion. But it was even more proper

> because the terms "tests" and "Now I know" can truthfully be attributed to God by virtue of his being the remote mover of the entire affair, even though Abraham is the proximate mover. This is one of the reasons that Torah uses the phrase, "And the Lord tested," which refers precisely to Abraham himself, or to his imaginative faculty and nature, which is the principle and cause of his moving, as is written in the definition of nature, and included in the natural force.[79]

Once again Kaspi employs the familiar hermeneutical principle based on the *Guide* 2.48, that when the biblical authors ascribe historical actions and events to the direct causal agency of God, this is to be taken merely as a scriptural *façon de parler* and hence not literally true. To say that "God tested Abraham" means that the nature of the world is such, and the nature and experience of Abraham was such, that he performed (or dreamed about performing) the Binding of Isaac. If we join this naturalism together with the esoteric explanation of "*nissah*" from *A Silver Tower*, which Kaspi himself does not do, at least not explicitly, we have the idea that Abraham, through natural causes, including his own efforts, was elevated to a state of experiencing the deity during the Binding of Isaac, and through this

---

77. For other aspects, see Hannah Kasher, "'How Does God Command Us to Commit Such an Abomination?': A Critique of the Sacrifice of Isaac according to Joseph ibn Kaspi [in Hebrew]," *Et ha-daat* 1 (1997): 37–47, and Roland Goetschel, "Le sacrifice d'Isaac dans la *Gebia Kesef* de Joseph Ibn Kaspi d'Argentières (1279–1340)," *Pardes* 22 (1996): 69–82.

78. Yet in *A Refining Pot for Silver* Kaspi refers to *A Silver Goblet* and *A Silver Tower* as the places where he wrote "everything that he is able to write" about the Binding of Isaac, "and specifically the explanation of *nissah*." See ed. Last, 62.

79. Herring *Kaspi's "Gevia' Kesef,"* 39 (Hebrew text), 255–56 (English; I have altered somewhat Herring's translation).

experience, truths and benefits were made known that Moses communicated to the people. This is what is meant by "And God tested Abraham."

Whether this interpretation of Kaspi is correct or not, the passage from *A Silver Goblet* is important for our purposes, because it labels the proposition that God acquires new knowledge "a common belief for the multitude." Unless we want to say that God's knowledge remains predictive and probabilistic even after the once-future event has occurred, then it will be difficult to reconcile Pines' libertarian/incompatibilist interpretation with the passage in *A Silver Goblet*.

Conclusion

Our examination of Joseph ibn Kaspi's statement on God's knowledge of future possibles in *The Silver Is Concluded*, comparing it to the views of his predecessors and contemporaries, and to pertinent material in the author's other writings, has yielded no less than five interpretations. Of these, the least likely one views God as a very good but still fallible prognosticator who foreknows what people will choose without affecting that choice. That interpretation is based on a devaluation of the epistemic value of God's *shi'ur sikhli*, a strongly libertarian conception of human choice, the view that divine knowledge is incompatible with human choice and, in general, a *fore*knowledge model of how God knows particulars. This interpretation is not ruled out by Kaspi's statement, but it is not well supported by it and, more importantly, is at odds with other statements by Kaspi on God's knowledge and human choice.

Slightly more plausible are the traditionalist and the determinist/compatibilist interpretations, if only because under them God's knowledge is infallible. But the traditionalist interpretation is at odds with Kaspi's view that God's knowledge does not change, and the determinist interpretation does not fit well with the view that humans have absolute choice, although, as we mentioned above, it is possible to reconcile these views.

This leaves us with the Averroist and the moderately esoteric interpretation, which are so close as to be almost identical, the only difference being how one reads the words of Kaspi. According to the former, the deeper meaning of *shi'ur sikhli* is the eternal determination of the causal order that brings things into existence, a determination that causes, but does not necessitate, the coming into existence of future possibles. According to the latter, we *merely describe* God's knowledge of future possibles as *shi'ur sikhli* in order to designate that God knows the world via the causal order, in a manner similar to how scholars know the future, i.e., through inference rather than direct experience.

In fact, the moderately esoteric interpretation solves the problem we encountered when we tried earlier to read Kaspi's statement in an Averroist light: How could Kaspi attribute *shi'ur* both to God and to human scholars if he is influenced by the Averroist view that knowledge is predicated of God and other knowers with pure equivocation? The answer is that the phrases "intellectual speculating," "intellectual knowing," and "experiencing" are all human *façons de parler*, to be understood along the lines of Maimonides' theory of how passions and other qualities are predicated of God. Although such epistemic terms appear to represent transient states, they actually represent one eternal state variously described from the standpoint of the human encounter with the divine intellect.

Finally, we noted that Kaspi's distinction in *A Silver Tower* between God's intellectual and experiential knowledge could be profitably compared to Gersonides' distinction between God's knowledge of particulars and God's "particular knowledge," i.e., the providential knowledge that occurs within the framework of human (partial) conjunction with the divine intellect. If we understand divine knowledge as following from divine causality, then insofar as humans act in accordance with the (astral) rules that govern sublunar reality, they are "known" by God via intellectual assessment; insofar as they act in accordance with reason, often against their astrally determined predispositions, they are known experientially. But as attractive as this reading of Kaspi may be, there is, once again, little evidence to support it.

SPINOZA, HISTORY, AND JEWISH MODERNITY

Michael A. Rosenthal
University of Washington

IN DECEMBER, 1665, Henry Oldenburg, who was the secretary to the Royal Society in London, wrote to Benedict Spinoza:

> But I turn to politics. Here there is a widespread rumour that the Israelites, who have been dispersed for more than two thousand years, are to return to their homeland. Few hereabouts believe it, but many wish it ... I am anxious to hear what the Jews in Amsterdam have heard about it, and how they are affected by so momentous an announcement, which, if true, is likely to bring about a world crisis. (Letter 33)[1]

Oldenburg, of course, is referring to Sabbatai Zevi, whose movement dissipated less than a year after this letter was written when its leader was arrested and converted to Islam.[2] We do not know if Spinoza ever replied to Oldenburg's inquiry. But it is not hard to read Spinoza's subsequent work, the *Tractatus Theologico-Politicus* (TTP), on which he began work in 1665, partly as an extended response to the messianic fervor. Spinoza was hostile to the charismatic politics of such prophets, which he thought was authoritarian, and to the underlying eschatological metaphysics. Spinoza developed his historical methods of biblical criticism—which claimed that

---

1. References to Spinoza are as follows: *Letters* refers to *The Letters*, trans. Samuel Shirley (Indianapolis, 1995); *E* refers to *The Collected Works of Spinoza*, vol. 1 (Princeton, 1985), ed. and trans. Edwin Curley, using the system (part, proposition, scholium, etc.) found in *The Cambridge Companion to Spinoza*; references to the *Tractatus Theologico-Politicus* (hereafter abbreviated as TTP) are to the draft of the forthcoming *The Collected Works of Spinoza*, vol. 2, ed. and trans. Edwin Curley, with chapter and section number, followed by reference to *Spinoza Opera*, ed. Carl Gebhardt (Heidelberg, 1972), with volume and page number; and finally the *Political Treatise*, trans. Samuel Shirley (Indianapolis, 2000).

2. See Gershom Scholem, *Sabbatai Zevi: The Mystical Messiah* (Princeton, 1972).

113

the Hebrew Bible did not have a single author and ought to be understood in its various historical and linguistic contexts—specifically to undermine the divine authority of those who advocated a repressive state church and the messianic pretensions of those like Sabbatai Zevi.

Any account of events presupposes some narrative structure and in this case we have several, which together, I think, illustrate the predicament of Jewish modernity and Spinoza's place within it. First, we have the urgent messianic story of Sabbatai Zevi and its relation to the predicament of many Jews within the seventeenth century. Second, we have the story told by Oldenburg. He is an outside observer but not a disinterested one. His curiosity about the reaction of Amsterdam's Jews most likely reflects, I believe, a millenarian Christian eschatology in which the Jews play an important role in the events of the Second Coming of Christ. He, like Zevi, believed himself to be part of a story that is governed by some providential scheme and felt emboldened to predict a world crisis. Third, there is the story of Spinoza's reaction to this letter and the reported crisis, which I have claimed is expressed in the argument of the TTP. Finally, there is the historiographical narrative that tells the story of the significance of this event and the philosophical reaction to it, to us, at this moment and perhaps beyond. In other words, what is the significance of Spinoza for Jewish modernity?

In this essay I intend to work backward through some of these different levels of narrative to the letter itself. First, I want briefly to survey the debate in contemporary historiography over the place of Spinoza within Jewish modernity. We need to stipulate, if only for the sake of debate, the meaning of some key terms, and I want to question, along with some others, the typical way Spinoza has been depicted in this literature. Second, in the core section, I want to examine Spinoza's views expressed in the political works and in the *Ethics* over the nature of God's providence and the structure of history itself. I shall show that his discussion of how to read the Bible is the basis. More specifically, I shall analyze the various senses and use of the word "historia" in Spinoza's work on the Bible in the TTP and draw some conclusions about his conception of history there and in the *Ethics*. Third, I shall relate Spinoza's views on history to the messianic currents of his time. Spinoza's response, as I shall show, was not to replace the messianic conception of history with the stock Enlightenment view, one that would only eradicate the religions of the world and replace them with a purely secular world. Rather it was to offer some critical tools that would transform the belief systems from within. Spinoza's idea of history belongs at root to that of Renaissance Humanism. It offers a narrative of events, suited to a particular place and time, whose purpose is either to justify some state of affairs or to cause some change. Finally, I shall claim that the underlying philosophy of history in Spinoza, in which he translates concepts of providence and messianism into naturalistic terms, may be useful to contemporary Jewish thought.

Spinoza and Jewish Modernity: The Problem

Spinoza has had a difficult relationship with contemporary Jewish thinkers. In the eighteenth century Moses Mendelssohn came to the aid of his dead friend Lessing's reputation when he defended him from charges of having been secretly a Spinozist, which, since Bayle, if not earlier, was a charge tantamount to pantheism and hence heresy. In the nineteenth century Hermann Cohen was outraged by what he considered Spinoza's zeal to outdo Christianity itself in his critique of Judaism. Not only, as Leo Strauss states Cohen's view, did Spinoza take "the side of spiritual and trans-political Christianity against carnal and political Judaism," but he "put religion altogether [i.e., not merely Judaism] outside the sphere of truth." Cohen believes Spinoza was deservedly excommunicated from the Jewish community not just because he denies the validity of the law and lacks insight into its prophetic and ethical core, but for taking sides against Judaism.[3] Twentieth-century thinkers have been equally critical for the most part. Emmanuel Levinas, for example, agrees with Cohen that Spinoza was guilty of betraying his religion. For him, Spinoza's dogmatic rationalism is a Jewish intellectual's Christianity.[4]

Nonetheless, it has been common to recognize Spinoza as at least a problematic figure for, if not in, the tradition. For many, Spinoza represents a defining challenge to the tradition. Eliezer Schweid states the point most clearly when he writes: "the beginning [of modern Jewish thought] was the beginning of [its] confrontation with the doctrine of Spinoza."[5] Spinoza is the icon of modernity, in this view, and the success of a Jewish philosophical or theological program may be measured, to some large degree, in terms of how well it can answer his various challenges to what is assumed to be the metaphysical bedrock of Judaism, for example, the idea of an absolutely transcendent God who guides his people Israel with a special providence in history.

What lies behind this critical reception is a set of historical narratives that tell us what ideas and events constitute modernity, what kind of challenge modernity so construed posed for the Jewish people, and what role

3. Preface to *Spinoza's Critique of Religion* (New York, 1965), 18–19.
4. See "The Spinoza Case," in *Difficult Freedom: Essays on Judaism*, trans. Seán Hand (Baltimore, 1990), 106–10.
5. Cited by Seymour Feldman in "Spinoza," in *Routledge History of World Philosophies*, vol. 2, *History of Jewish Philosophy*, ed. D. Frank and Oliver Leaman (London, 1997), 627.

Spinoza played in all this. This is a vast and controversial set of topics and before I proceed I need to narrow the possible range of meanings a bit here, even though I cannot even begin to adequately defend my choices. First, let me describe modernity in terms of the very broad and profound set of changes that began to affect Western Europe in the sixteenth century. Robert Pippin, in his book *Modernism as a Philosophical Problem*, identifies several key features, such as the emergence of the nation state, the claim for the supreme authority of reason in human affairs over and against the claims of tradition (especially those of the church), the importance of natural science, the development of a free-market economy, and the belief in the improvability of man along with the belief in historical progress.[6] In general terms, I think that we can safely identify philosophical modernity with the Enlightenment and categorize the problems of modernity in terms of the various reactions to the various Enlightenment projects. Second, allow me to limit my consideration of the effect of modernity on the Jewish people to one issue: the emancipation of communal life from the intolerant strictures of premodern society and the difficult reconfiguration of Jewish life under the new regime of the increasingly secular nation state.[7] Emancipation posed profound problems for those who sought to maintain a more traditional life within the state and for those who eagerly sought emancipation, as the Dreyfus case illustrates.

Now there is little question that Spinoza contributed importantly to the development of philosophical modernity and the Enlightenment and much recent study of Spinoza's relation to the Jewish tradition has focused on his contribution to the development of these ideas. Jonathan Israel has even named Spinoza the central figure of the so-called "radical Enlightenment" and at least two recent studies (Smith and Sutcliffe) have examined Spinoza's relation to Judaism through his development of these ideas.[8] Stephen Smith has argued that Spinoza attempted to produce a new kind of state to produce a new kind of individual, a truly Enlighten-

6. Robert B. Pippin, *Modernism as a Philosophical Problem: On the Dissatisfactions of European High Culture* (Oxford, 1999), 4.

7. David Novak, in his book on *Natural Law in Judaism* (Cambridge, 1998), chap. 1, has identified two other events that define Jewish modernity—the Holocaust and the rise and problematic fulfillment of political Zionism—but here I will take them not as defining features of modernity but as consequences of emancipation.

8. See Jonathan Israel, *Radical Enlightenment: Philosophy and the Making of Modernity 1650–1750* (Oxford, 2001); Steven B. Smith, *Spinoza, Liberalism, and the Question of Jewish Identity* (New Haven, 1997; and Adam Sutcliffe, *Judaism and Enlightenment* (Cambridge, 2003).

ment figure of rational autonomy. While he is far more sympathetic to Spinoza's position *vis-à-vis* the Jewish community than some of his for-bearers, such as Cohen or Strauss, he still thinks that in the end Spinoza advocates assimilation and the withering of Jewish identity. Others have argued along the lines that Spinoza is not radically opposed to the Jewish tradition.[9]

This is not the place to engage in a systematic appraisal and critique of these complex and important contributions to our field. What I intend to focus on here is their explicit or implicit interpretation of Spinoza's views on history. Among the questions we need to raise and then, I hope, answer are: How does Spinoza conceive of "history"? Does Spinoza have a theory of historical progress? Is there any indication that Spinoza believes reason will triumph over superstition in history? Does Spinoza have a theory of history *per se*? Because the idea of history is so central to the discourse of the Enlightenment and the problem of Jewish identity within it, it will be useful to learn how Spinoza conceives of it.

Spinoza's Uses of History[10]

In order to answer some of these questions, we need to look at Spino-za's texts carefully. Interestingly the word "historia" occurs only once in the *Ethics*.[11] Of course that does not means the *Ethics* has nothing to teach us about this subject, and we will return to this issue. However, the place to look first must be in the TTP, where Spinoza repeatedly quotes histori-ans and frequently uses the terms "historia" and "narratio" (and their variants). Spinoza uses the term "historia" in several different senses and in this section I shall canvass them with some reference to other works.

The first term I want to examine is "fabula," because I think it clearly indicates one possible meaning of "historia." It is used twice in TTP, chap-ter 10, and in both cases it refers to some narrative that is not entirely cred-ible, as when it refers to prophecies of Isaiah that have not been preserved (10.7; 3/142), or apocryphal additions to the book of Ezra, which Spinoza characterizes as having been added by "some trifler" [*ab aliquo nugatore*]. In the *Political Treatise*, we find the phrase used in an important context, to which we will return later, where Spinoza writes, "we have seen that rea-

---

9. See many of the essays in *Jewish Themes in Spinoza's Philosophy*, ed. Heidi M. Ravven and Lenn E. Goodman (Albany, 2002), or Steven Nadler's *Spinoza's Heresy: Immortality and the Jewish Mind* (Oxford, 2001).

10. This and the subsequent section are drawn from my article, "Spinoza and the Philosophy of History," in *Interpreting Spinoza: Critical Essays*, Charlie Huen-emann, ed. (Cambridge: Cambridge University Press, 2008), 111–27.

11. E4p67s (G2/261/26).

son can indeed do a great deal to restrain and moderate the affects; but at the same time we have seen that the road that reason teaches us to follow is very difficult, so that those who are persuaded that the masses, or people who are separated into parties by public affairs, can be induced to live only according to the prescription of reason are dreaming of the golden age of the Poets, *or of a myth [fabulam]*" (TP, 1.5; 3/275).[12] A fable is obviously fabricated, possibly false, and very likely misleading. The word "historia" is sometimes used in just the same way. Spinoza makes the point quite clear when, in the crucial chapter 7 of the TTP, he writes that "it happens quite frequently that we read similar stories [*historias*] in different books and make very different judgments about them" (7.61; 3/110). For instance, we find a story of men flying in *Orlando Furioso*, Ovid, and in the books of Judges and Kings, yet "we make a very different judgment about each of them: that the first wanted to write only trifles [*nugas*]; the second, political; and the third, finally, sacred matters" (7.62; 3/110). It all depends not so much on the story itself but on our opinion of the writer.

The second sense of history must go beyond that of trifles and entertainments and point to something real, especially in politics. These we can, with Spinoza, call "chronicles" that relate some narrative of events.[13] These chronologies or annals (the terms are used interchangeably at 10.24, 3/145) are written by chroniclers (10.9; 3/142) or scribes or historiographers appointed by governors, princes, or kings (10.24; 3/145). The main point of distinguishing these chronicles is to indicate another kind of history, which I propose to call "superchronicles," because they are arranged by an historian or editor out of the work of other chroniclers. Spinoza thinks that such books as Daniel, Ezra, Esther, and Nehemiah are all written by one historian who sometimes even refers to his sources, such as, in the case of Esther, the "Chronicles of the Kings of Persia" (10.23; 3/145). Interestingly enough, many of the superchronicles, although they often take on the form of a narrative of events, are chronologically confused and inaccurate. Spinoza says that, in the case of Jeremiah, the sources "have been plucked up and collected from various chroniclers," and are "piled up confusedly, with no account taken of the times of the events recorded" (10.10; 3/142). In fact, as his work in chapters 8 and 9 show, conflicting and confused accounts in just about all the books of Scripture, including

---

12. Translations vary. For 3/142, Curley has "legend"; Shirley, "myth"; and Lagrée and Moreau, "*fable*"; for 3/146, Curley has "legend" again; Shirley, "story"; and Lagrée and Moreau, "*fable*"; and for 3/275, Curley has "myth"; Shirley, "fairy tale"; and Lagrée and Moreau, "*une histoire imaginaire*."

13. See, e.g., 10.9; 3/142.

the Pentateuch, exhibit the same composed nature, and testify to the fact that there was not a single author.

Spinoza's point in making this observation takes us to the next level, or sense, of history, which is the one most often referred to in commentaries, namely, the Baconian sense of the term.[14] In chapter 7, Spinoza states that "to liberate our minds from theological prejudices, and not to recklessly embrace man's inventions as divine teachings, we must discuss in detail the true method of interpreting Scripture" (7.6; 3/98). This he famously identifies with the method of interpreting nature, which requires that we "prepare a straightforward history of Scripture and to infer the mind of the authors of Scripture from it, by legitimate reasonings, as from certain data and principles" (7.7; 3/98). History in this sense is a systematic catalogue of the observed phenomena. In this case it must (a) contain the nature and properties of the language of the books of Scripture and their authors (7.15; 3/99); (b) collect the sayings of each book and organize them under main headings (7.16); (c) note those sayings that are ambiguous, obscure, or inconsistent (7.16); (d) describe the life, character, and concerns of the author of each book (7.23; 3/101); and (e) record the fate of each book, i.e., its reception, interpretation, and editions (7.23). When Spinoza examines a biblical narrative that has been taken by tradition to have a single author and then shows that it is composed of several narratives, each of which does not neatly cohere with the other, then he undercuts the traditional interpretative practice of assuming coherence and seeking devices to demonstrate it.

Nonetheless, the purpose of this enterprise is not to deny any meaning or value to Scripture. On the contrary, Spinoza emphasizes that the purpose of the method is to discover "what is most universal, what is the foundation of the whole of Scripture, and finally, what all the prophets commend in it as an eternal teaching, most useful for all mortals" (7.27; 3/ 102). From these universal principles, which I would call "metanarratives" and that have been arrived at through induction (i.e., the Baconian method of classification, etc.), we can then deduce more particular teachings that can guide us in the constantly changing circumstances of life (7.29; 3/103).[15] Spinoza is always careful to note that the moral principles are only inductively established and gain certitude through their practice and not through any internal epistemological criterion, as a truth of reason would. They function well to the extent that they emulate the rational truth. Thus, the purpose of the historical method is to discover teachings

---

14. The influence of Bacon has been noted by several commentators, including Curley and Smith.

15. Here I have in mind any casuistry, such as rabbinic literature in places.

that stand at the very limit of history, in the sense that they are supposed to endure through the vicissitudes of that within which they are found. Still, the principles or teachings do not transcend history itself and remain subject themselves to further investigation following the same method by which they were discovered. The lessons gained from history are employed within concrete historical circumstances in order to control them, though they are constantly affected by those same circumstances.

Spinoza's use of history in the TTP, like Bacon's, remains tied to a humanist idea of deliberative rhetoric, in which examples are used to persuade an audience of a particular good or course of action. The goal is not to eliminate the authority of the sacred texts but rather to find a new basis for it outside of rational theology and within the texts themselves.[16] The art of the rhetorician is to accommodate the principles he wishes to teach to the understanding and experience of the audience. Spinoza is no longer trying to accommodate the transcendent principles of reason to the mutable minds of man, as a theologian would, but historically contingent principles of action to the mutable minds of his readers.[17]

Spinoza's project was revolutionary in principle but not always in practice. We know that Spinoza did not convince most of the readers of the TTP in the seventeenth century with his interpretations of Scripture. It is a more open question whether he managed to remain faithful to the interpretative principles underlying his case. In other words, it seems as if Spinoza does have recourse to rational principles, especially when he moves to the metanarrative level of history, both in the understanding of the text, and in the understanding of the people whom he is attempting to persuade. It seems necessary that Spinoza, like the biblical prophets and historiographers he discusses, must employ an idea whose origin is outside the text in order to instill coherence in the fractured landscape he has uncovered through his criticism of the sources.

Spinoza and the Theory of History

Although the tools of this enterprise have subsequently been adopted by modern historiographers, Spinoza uses them for quite different ends. When Spinoza rejects the path taken by Maimonides and Lodewijk Meyer, in which reason is the principle of scriptural interpretation, he replaces

16. Whether Spinoza is successful in this—i.e., whether he does not surreptitiously have recourse to some rational principles that guide his interpretation—is open to question.

17. On accommodation as a principle of scriptural interpretation in Spinoza and others, see Amos Funkenstein, *Theology and the Scientific Imagination* (Princeton, 1986), sec. 4.B, 214–71.

ahistorical reason with a thoroughly historical method in which the patterns of association within the imagination are the basis of judging the validity and use of Scripture.[18] Some commentators have claimed that Spinoza does not exhibit any sense of historicity, at least in the TTP. What that means is that he apparently does not offer any explicit reflection on the shape of history itself and the relation of the historian to the shaping of that history, as, for example, in the Hegelian notion of increasing historical self-awareness of a subject as a cause in the fulfillment of history itself.[19]

Other writers have thought otherwise. Henri Laux argues that although Spinoza does not use modern language like "historicity" in his work, the concept itself has a very real meaning within his system.[20] To paraphrase: The idea of history is not an external category but belongs to the logic of the system itself, what Laux calls "une ontologie de la puissance" (291). Likewise, Pierre Macherey argues that there is a non-Hegelian theory of history in Spinoza, a nonidealistic form of dialectic, in which, at the same time as the material changes occur, the conditions of their intelligibility do as well.[21] Warren Montag describes this as the "dialectic of the positive."[22] For Etienne Balibar Spinoza's radical naturalism does not render history meaningless but rather gives it a new meaning based on the interpretive procedure of explaining events by their causes (36).[23] The interpretation of scriptural narratives in the TTP in terms of Spinoza's theory of passions and human interaction, as described in parts 3 and 4 of the *Ethics*, desacralizes them and gives them new meaning as part of a science of human nature. As we understand the causes of these narrative events, we are then able to act more efficaciously within analogous circumstances. Divine will is no longer acting on us but through us in the course of a history in which we, through our understanding, have become agents.

---

18. For a discussion of the context of such arguments, such as Van Velthuysen's principle of "historical cognition," see J. Samuel Preus, *Spinoza and the Irrelevance of Biblical Authority* (Cambridge, 2001), 126.

19. For a discussion and citations, see ibid., 182.

20. Henri Laux, *Imagination et religion chez Spinoza* (Paris, 1993), 291: "Si la notion d'historicité n'appartient pas au langage du Spinoza, elle acquiert toutefois chez lui un statut réel."

21. Pierre Macherey, *Hegel ou Spinoza* (Paris, 1979), 259.

22. Warren Montag, introduction to *Spinoza and Politics*, by Etienne Balibar, trans. Peter Snowden (London, 1998), xiv.

23. Balibar, *Spinoza and Politics*.

There is much compelling in these accounts offered by some of the very best French expositors of Spinoza's thought. However, as Balibar himself notes, a historical theory of human social passions does not itself amount to a philosophy of history, because it does not offer a "single, unambiguous explanatory schema" of that history (38). And, while it seems to be a commonplace among several of these thinkers to claim that there is an internal forward dynamic to history, they offer little evidence to support it beyond noting that the *conatus* found in individuals express-es itself also in institutions, whose course can be predicted. Why this implies historical progress is somewhat mysterious to me.[24] At most Spinoza seems committed, especially in the TP, to some theory of *anacyclosis*, in which one institutional form tends to turn into another, related one, through predictable internal causes and external pressures.

In any case, let me briefly sketch in the remainder of this section a somewhat different view of Spinoza's philosophy of history, influenced by these thinkers, yet differing from them in some key points. In order to find the explicit grounds of a philosophy of history proper we must look at the *Ethics*, and there we find three points that can serve as the basis for such a claim. (Let me note as an aside that for the first and third points I have, for brevity's sake, resorted to their statement in what Deleuze would call the "other *Ethics*," namely the appendix and preface, rather than a detailed exposition of their basis in the propositions and demon-strations.)[25]

First, Spinoza makes the negative claim that there is no teleology in nature. He argues for this point most vehemently in the appendix to part 1. God does not create or direct the world out of his own free nature; rath-er, the world is eternal and all things follow from God necessarily. Because men are for the most part ignorant of the causes of things, they imagine that nature works as they believe themselves to act, that is, on account of some end or advantage. Whatever in nature works to their advantage they believe must have been planned by some divine will to that end. But all such ends or final causes "are nothing but human fiction," and the attribution of such ends "turns Nature completely upside down," for God's perfection determines all things and he does not act for the sake of something (i.e., some end) that he lacks (2/80). This does not mean that

24. This question is also discussed in André Tosel, "Y-a-t-il une philosophie du progress historique chez Spinoza?" in *Spinoza: Issues and Directions*, ed. Moreau and Curley (Leiden, 1990), 306–26.

25. In *Spinoza: Philosophie practique* (Paris, 1981), Deleuze writes about the different "speeds" (*vitesses*) of the different parts of the *Ethics*: "les propositions et les scolies ne vont pas à la même allure" (170).

events are random and do not have a cause. History in the sense of a perfectly determined order of events exists, but the intelligibility of such events belongs only to God. There is no beginning, middle, or end to divine history, and, therefore, it cannot have any narrative structure. Human beings can use glimpses of this knowledge (as found in common notions, for instance) not to replace their conception of history—that is, as an account of action toward some end—but to understand better the causes of events within their inadequately conceived narrative structure.

Second, Spinoza argues that, because all individuals strive to persist in their nature and because nature as a whole is always more powerful than any individual *conatus*, each individual's striving to persist will often be expressed as a striving to increase the individual's power through the control of external things. The only true individual is substance, or God, but substance internally differentiates itself through the causal production of finite modes, which are, in a strict metaphysical sense, only relative individuals. (Here it is important to note that by individual Spinoza does not only mean human beings. Any organized collection of modes that has a rationally discernible principle of organization might be defined as an individual. So an ecosystem or institution might also have a *conatus*.) Each finite mode acts as a causal agent in a determined causal chain and that action expresses its essence as a finite mode of being. Spinoza calls this principle of activity in each finite thing a striving to persist in its existence, or *conatus* (E3p6). Seen in isolation, each striving would persist indefinitely. However, since each finite mode is part of a least one causal chain, it must be acted upon by other finite modes, some of which might harm it or even destroy it. Because each finite mode is infinitely surpassed by the totality of other modes in nature, the duration of its existence understood in relation to the power of external things on it, which Spinoza calls *fortuna*, is limited.[26] Thus the striving of an individual to persevere in its existence varies in intensity and duration according to influence of *fortuna*.

Third, Spinoza claims that the desire to persist is aided when individuals devise fictional models of either a future or past state that guide their action. In the preface to part 4 of the *Ethics*, he describes the process through which the models and ideals are constructed. The model—a perfect house, for instance—is based in some account of the construction of one. A builder has a plan, gathers material for it, and builds the house. The builder judges the perfection of the completed model in relation to his ideal and perhaps the ideals of others he knows or surmises. The inadequately conceived universal ideal of a house is then used to judge the works of others and the diachronic origin of the ideal—that is, its origin in

---

26. Spinoza defines *fortuna* in E2p49s (2/136) and also in TTP, 3.11 (3/46).

a narrative with a specific beginning and an end—is perhaps necessarily forgotten. Necessarily forgotten because it could not function as a universal if it were deconstructed into the many specific narratives (e.g., of particular houses) that have been elided into one.[27] Spinoza thinks that although these models are only "modes of thinking," kinds of fictions not found in nature itself, but only comparisons relative to particular individuals and situations, and potentially misleading, they are nonetheless useful as a guide to action. Because humans inevitably act with ends in view, in the constant struggle against *fortuna*, we require intellectual means to select and refine those ends. The model in question need not be solely synchronic, as some ideal of human nature. The historical narrative itself may be one such exemplary model, whether the life of Christ or the history of the Israelite nation.

Together these elements constitute a theory of history. Individuals inevitably tell the story of their actions in reference to such models in terms of a narration with a past, present, and future goal. That is, the structure of human action within nature is perceived by those actors as a diachronic narrative, though it can be informed by synchronic factors; and the use of historical rhetoric, as in the TTP, to influence the deliberations of others is the most effective means to spur action. The content of the rhetoric—the superchronicles, as I have named them above—is an effective aid in the deliberation of those it aims to affect, to the extent that it is able to modify the models that the members of the audience use to guide their actions, and modify them in ways that will benefit those who use them.

The histories individuals tell are natural expressions of their *conatus*, which are designed to aid it but also could hinder it, if the models are inadequately conceived. There is a fictional narrative structure within the striving of any individual, not as God sees it (adequately), but as we see it

---

27. Interestingly enough, in chap. 5 of the *Metaphysical Thoughts* appended to Spinoza's presentation of Descartes' philosophy, he talks about the origin of the truth and falsity of ideas in relation to narratives: "The first meaning of *true* and *false* seems to have had its origin in stories: a story was called true when it was of a deed that had really happened, and false when it was of a deed that had never happened. Afterwards the Philosophers used this meaning to denote the agreement of an idea with its object and conversely. So an idea is called true when it shows us the thing as it is in itself, and false when it shows us the thing otherwise than it really is. For ideas are nothing but narratives, *or mental histories of nature*. But later this usage was transferred metaphorically to mute things, as when we call gold true or false, as if the gold which is presented to us were to tell something of itself that either was or was not in it" (Curley 312; G1/246). This obviously requires more comment.

inadequately. It seems at times in the fifth part of the *Ethics* that the individual's goal is to approach a purely synchronic grasp of oneself but that would be only in terms of the laws that shape our actions. Any finite mode is also known by God in terms of its causal history, that is, the train of causes adequately perceived. So the purely synchronic view would be inadequate, and a diachronic grasp of our nature in terms of its causal history may be conceptually possible. Perhaps the goal of rational reconstruction of history—such as Spinoza's metanarrative reconstruction of Scripture with the Baconian tools of philology and classification—is to reform continually the naturally inadequate and imaginative diachronic grasp of our place in things, to replace imaginative narrative with a pure rational narrative of causal history. To achieve this, or even strive for it, would be to become to some degree (the more the better) other than human, no longer finite but quasi infinite and godlike, strange to all others. Our goal is to become released from the travails of *fortuna* and become immortal. This Spinoza calls beatitude or salvation. To the extent that critical history aids us in struggle, even the project of the modern historian has its messianic dimension.

Two Kinds of Messianism

Now let us return to Spinoza's letter to Oldenburg with which we began. Perhaps Spinoza could not have answered Oldenburg, because to judge whether Sabbatai Zevi was the messiah or not would have required not a miracle but a patient accumulation of the facts of his existence, including what produced him, what sustained him, and what effects he produced. But I think it not too far fetched to speculate that he certainly would not have been swayed by the current theologies of messianism, whether grounded in Kabbalah or anything else that pretended to transcend the realms of history.

There is little doubt that Spinoza would have been critical of the eschatological scheme of Sabbatai Zevi's messianic movement, both on account of the flawed historical narrative it offered and its false metaphysical basis. He exhibits little sympathy with the historical traditions of established churches. In the TTP, as many Jewish commentators have noted, Spinoza is overtly hostile to much of rabbinic literature and uses his historical method (the Baconian history of Scripture) to debunk its narrative claims. In his letter to Burgh, Spinoza argues that both rabbinic and Catholic historical arguments to support their oral traditions of testimony have been falsified by the "histories of the Church" of which his correspondent remains ignorant (Ep76, 344). Spinoza most likely would have been very critical of any narrative justification of the messianic movement. In the same way, he has no truck with the mystical metaphysics that were current in his time. In chapter 9 of the TTP, he attacks the interpretative practices of mystics who deny that the letters themselves of the Torah have been preserved uncorrupted and contain hidden mysteries, and writes: "Indeed, they claim that great secrets are contained in the very accent marks of the letters. Whether they have said these things out of foolishness and credulous devotion, or out of arrogance and malice, so that they alone would be believed to possess God's secrets, I do not know. I do know this: that in their writings I have read nothing which had the air of a secret, but only childish thoughts. I have also read, and for that matter, known personally, certain kabbalistic triflers, whose insanity always taxed my capacity for amazement" (9.33–34; 3/135–36).

Nonetheless, even if Spinoza were to reject the messianism of Sabbatai Zevi, it would not necessarily mean that he rejects all forms of messianism. Indeed, if my reconstruction of Spinoza's philosophy of history in the previous section is correct, then there may be a reading of Spinoza's work that is not hostile to some forms of messianic pretensions. If we take human action to be structured (or perceived to be structured by the agent) diachronically in narrative terms, and if it is necessary to posit a relatively synchronic model (or at least a narrative model that has been emended through the aid of synchronic reason, i.e., common notions) as a guide to that action, then the realization of that model, itself forever on the horizon of any particular train of actions, would appear to end or at least radically transform history as it becomes perfected. That is the messianic promise of salvation.

When we add the narrative content to this form of historical thought and action, then the case for messianism is further strengthened. On one level is the dialectic between the actual state (let us say the Dutch) and the perfect state (let us say Spinoza's model of the ancient Israelite state), which the former strives to emulate. On another level, we have the dialectic between the actual person (let us say, Jan) and the model of the perfect person whom Jan strives to emulate. Spinoza calls this model Christ, but he also calls it "God," who is "the exemplar of true life" (14.30; 3/177). (I think Christ is simply the natural messianic figure for his mainly Christian audience, but nothing depends on the details of the historical Christ here for the role the exemplar plays.) Spinoza postulates these two levels, the political and the personal, as distinct and irreducible to one another, but he also thinks that they are interrelated in some ways. The exemplar of moral life can indirectly affect the exemplar of political life and vice versa. If Spinoza does maintain a semblance and structure of messianism in his thought, then it would not be misleading to say that, while Christ certainly does not vitiate political life, and indeed requires it, the messianic exemplar nonetheless requires the Mosaic political life to serve it as an instrument, as the TTP serves the *Ethics*. To illustrate the theoretical point with our example: Jan requires the ideal of Christ to perfect himself. Yet he cannot embark on this ethical quest without a stable political constitution, which requires that the Dutch state emulate the rationally reconstructed narrative of the ancient Israelite state.[28] Finally the state does not exist as an end in itself, but serves the individual, Jan, who can be free only if the state allows him (and as many like him as possible) to pursue the messianic dream of salvation in the unfettered contemplation of nature and his place within it.

Here I think it is very useful to introduce a distinction made by Amos Funkenstein between realistic and utopian messianism.[29] Although he uses this distinction as an aid in the interpretation of Maimonides, I would not be surprised, though I have not yet found explicit mention of it, if Funkenstein has a debt to Spinoza here. For, as is well known, in the opening sections of the *Tractatus Politicus*, Spinoza distinguishes between the utopian dreams of philosophers who have no political experience and those realistic ends envisaged by experienced statesmen. (Indeed, to recall our earlier discussion, Spinoza employs the word "fabula" in section 5 of chapter 1 to underline the difference between the utopian claims of moralists, which he likens to the golden lands imagined by poets, and the realistic view of experienced political reformers.) Utopian messianism relies upon a specious metaphysics and postulates salvation as the consequence of a divine intervention, in which human history is transformed from without. Mankind is a mere passive subject in this divine drama, in which history is eventually overcome. Such a utopian messianism is a useful tool of political manipulation and can be dangerously subversive, as the case of Sabbatai Zevi shows.[30] Realistic messianism, in contrast, relies upon a naturalistic metaphysics and requires human beings to act within history through their use of reason (which, at least in part, is itself historically derived) for some historical end. Realistic messianism does not aim to eliminate history as such but rather to transform it into a process that better attunes it with the historical unfolding of the divine nature. God is not outside of history but in history, properly conceived, and is realized within its structures and causal paths. Christ, the messianic exemplar in the TTP, could just as well stand as an ideal for any divine person who

---

28. This leads the state to maintain religious life for the masses and enough freedom of speech so that religion can be emended as needed for the sake of society and the individual. Some of the individuals may then adopt rationally reconstructed narratives and engage in the intellectual pursuit of salvation.

29. Amos Funkenstein, *Maimonides: Nature, History and Messianic Beliefs*, trans. Shmuel Himmelstein (Tel Aviv, 1997).

30. Another example might be the case of the Anabaptists and their leader, John of Leyden, at Münster in 1534–35.

appears within history and yet whose moral conduct appears to transcend (but never actually does transcend) its vicissitudes. Christ never stands outside of history in Spinoza. As he mentions in several key passages, Christ does not, as the later Christian tradition held, abrogate the laws of Moses.[31] So the figure of a messiah must be realized within (and sometimes against) a system of law as defined by tradition and practice. It is the moral ideal as projected (and embodied) within the historical and political realm

As a footnote, it should be no surprise that, much like Maimonides, Spinoza imagines the possibility of a return to Zion.[32] If the Jewish people manage to reform themselves on the basis of the knowledge God has given all human beings and not wait passively for divine intervention on their behalf, then the reconstruction of a nation might be possible, and the conditions of the possibility of a true messianic age, in which the moral perfection of individuals is made possible by the stable, well-designed political institutions of the state, might be realized.

Spinoza and Jewish Modernity: A Possible Answer

So now we arrive at the end that brings us back to our original question concerning Spinoza's place within Jewish modernity. I hope I have presented enough evidence to question the view of those who insist on reading Spinoza anachronistically through the lens of the later Enlightenment and its critics.

Spinoza does not offer a theory of historical progress in which reason triumphs over the imagination. He is not committed to the corollary thesis either, that is, the idea of secularization of political and personal life. The importance of the imagination and its narrative structure in human life, along with Spinoza's deep commitment to an idea of God as the principle of intelligibility of all things, rules out the possibility of the total dissolution of religion. The state may acquire a new and different role, but that does not require the elimination of religion, only its reconfiguration with-

---

31. See TTP, 5; 3/71, for instance: "Christ by no means abrogated the law of Moses."

32. See TTP, 3.55; 3/57. On this particular point, see Y. Yovel, *Spinoza and Other Heretics: The Marrano of Reason* (Princeton, 1989), 190–93. On the relationship between Spinoza and Maimonides, see Heidi Ravven's recent articles in the *Journal of the History of Philosophy*, "Some Thoughts on What Spinoza Learned from Maimonides about the Prophetic Imagination": "Part 1. Maimonides on Prophecy and the Imagination" 39, no. 2 (April 2001), 193–214, and "Part 2. Spinoza's Maimonideanism," 39, no. 3 (July 2001), 385–406, as well as Warren Zev Harvey, "A Portrait of Spinoza as a Maimonidean," *Journal of the History of Philosophy*, 19, no. 2 (April 1981): 151–72.

in new political bounds, just as Judaism has done many times over the course of its history. As Spinoza points out with the English and their mistaken revolution against the monarchy, the bounds of tradition are meaningful and useful constraints on human action.[33] Just because Spinoza uses a metahistorical narrative to articulate that point does not mean that he thinks the historical narratives themselves have been rendered obsolete in a tradition. The upshot is that assimilation to the secular nation state need not be the goal or inevitable fate of Jews in modernity.

On a more positive note, Spinoza's work in the TTP and the *Ethics* offers a possible program for the reformation of Jewish theology and practice through the systematic translation of key concepts, such as providence and messianism, into naturalistic terms. As the parallel with Maimonides shows, there are a variety of possible metaphysical bases for Jewish theology, and one of the strengths of Judaism throughout its history has been to discover ways to incorporate the philosophical practices of other civilizations into its own. It is often claimed that only a metaphysics of absolute transcendence can preserve Judaism. But perhaps Spinoza shows that the demand for absolute transcendence need not be essential to Judaism, that is, if we can "save the phenomena" of Jewish life without this metaphysical grounding. As Spinoza himself points out, there are other voices within the Jewish tradition, including biblical and possibly rabbinic sources, that cleave to a theology of immanence rather than absolute transcendence.[34] To argue otherwise is to refuse the implications of

---

33. See TTP, 18.33 (3/227).

34. In the scholium to the crucial proposition in the *Ethics* in which he establishes the doctrine of parallelism, in which "The order and connection of ideas is the same as the order and connection of things" (E2p7), he writes that "some of the Hebrews seem to have seen this, as if through a cloud, when they maintained that God, God's intellect, and the things understood by him are one and the same." Who these Hebrews were is itself unclear, though various conjectures have been advanced. In a letter to Henry Oldenburg he makes an even more sweeping claim that his view that God is the immanent cause of all things not the transitive cause is found in Paul, perhaps the ancient philosophers, and "I would even venture to say, together with the ancient Hebrews, as far as may be conjectured from certain traditions, though these have suffered much corruption" (Epistle 73). On this point, see many of the essays in Ravven and Goodman, *Jewish Themes in Spinoza's Philosophy*, perhaps especially that by Warren Montag, and my own contribution to the cause, "Spinoza's Monism and Jewish Philosophy," provisionally forthcoming in *Light Against Darkness: Dualism in Ancient Mediterranean Religion and the Contemporary World* the proceedings of *Light Against Dark: Dualism in the Ancient and Modern World*, eds. Armin Lange and Randall Styers (Leiden: Brill, forthcoming).

the insights of modern historical criticism and cling to an essentialized Judaism that disregards dissenting voices. Or perhaps we might take Spinoza's strenuous efforts in the TTP to separate theology from philosophy as support for Menachem Kellner's recent provocative argument that Judaism does not require—indeed, is better off without—such philosophical dogmas at all.[35]

Finally, if Spinoza is traditionally viewed as a kind of icon of modernity itself, and if, as I have tried to point out, the traditional reading of his work as an Enlightenment thinker is at least questionable, then perhaps we need to take a closer look at the concept of modernity itself, and see how it can be reconfigured.[36] Spinoza shows us we can read the Bible and find new ways to make our history.

35. Menachem Kellner, *Must a Jew Believe Anything?* (Portland, 1999).

36. I have been influenced on this general point by Talal Asad, *Formations of the Secular: Christianity, Islam, Modernity* (Stanford, 2003).

PART II

CONTEMPORARY PERSPECTIVES

WHAT MAIMONIDES CAN TEACH US ABOUT READING THE BIBLE

Kenneth Seeskin
Northwestern University

LET ME BEGIN by getting right to the problem. For Maimonides the Bible is a repository of truth. Although it may seem to assert things that we know to be false, this impression is easily dispelled if we interpret it correctly. Should the literal meaning of a passage conflict with what reason can establish on its own, we have no choice but to interpret the passage in a way that resolves the conflict in favor of reason. The reason for this is clear. The Bible is a sacred text, the product of a divine revelation given to Moses and a series of succeeding revelations designed to shed additional light on the first one. If it contains opinions that are demonstrably false, its status as a sacred text would be compromised.

When I talk about opinions that are demonstrably false or "what reason can establish on its own," I mean, in the first instance, opinions that undermine the existence and incorporeality of God, and in the second, opinions that support them. If the Bible says that God has emotions and occupies space, Maimonides argues we must interpret these passages in a way that removes any trace of anthropomorphism. In fact, chapters 1–49 of Part One of the *Guide* are devoted to just this purpose.

As Spinoza points out, this strategy opens Maimonides to the charge of giving a projective interpretation.[1] Rather than ask what the Bible is trying to say on its own, Maimonides asks how to read it in a way that preserves its philosophical integrity. The danger is that *our* conception of truth reflects assumptions of which the original audience may have known nothing. If that happens, Spinoza argues, we distort the text when we try to preserve its truth. For example, Maimonides argues (*Guide* 2.29) that once we take the time to understand it correctly, we will see that the

---

1. Spinoza, *Theological-Political Treatise,* trans. R. H. M. Elwes (New York, 1951), 114–18.

structure of the world as described in the first chapter of Genesis is consistent with the principles of Aristotelian physics. To a modern scholar, this
sounds ridiculous. To suppose that the original audience would have
been familiar with natural science as Aristotle conceived it is to engage in
fantasy.

According to Spinoza, the problem is that Maimonides failed to distinguish meaning from truth. As Spinoza puts it:[2]

> ... although the literal meaning is repugnant to the natural light of reason,
> nevertheless, if it cannot be clearly overruled on grounds and principles
> derived from its scriptural "history," it, that is, the literal meaning, must
> be the one retained: and contrariwise if these passages literally interpreted
> are found to clash with principles derived from Scripture, though such
> literal interpretation were in absolute harmony with reason, they must be
> interpreted in a different manner, i.e., metaphorically.

Though I may have excellent grounds for believing that the Copernican
account of the solar system is true, that does not give me the right to say
that the Bible is committed to it. It follows that when Maimonides is finished reading the Bible, what we have is not so much an interpretation as
an idealization. From the standpoint of generations of scholars who have
accepted Spinoza's criticism, rather than say "Here is what the Bible actually means," it is as if Maimonides is saying "Here is what it is possible to
get out of it."

To this objection, Maimonides has three replies. (1) Nothing compels
us to interpret the Bible in its simple or external sense. (2) While Aristotle
himself had nothing to do with the opening verses of Genesis, Moses and
the patriarchs were scientists and philosophers in their own right. (3)
Unless we make a conscious effort to preserve the truth of the Bible, it will
lose its status as a sacred text and become just another ancient narrative.
From our standpoint, (1) is obviously true, (2) obviously false, and (3)
worth discussing. According to Maimonides, the job of the interpreter is
to find the level at which the text makes the most sense given everything
we know about the world. It is well known that at one point (*Guide* 2.25),
he goes so far as to say that if someone could demonstrate that the world is
eternal, he would have no choice but to interpret Genesis accordingly.

It is not my purpose to argue that we should return to a medieval conception of text criticism. Not only is there no evidence that Moses and the
patriarchs were philosophers, there is no independent evidence that they
existed. My purpose is rather to argue that despite the problems of Maimonides' approach, it still has something to teach us; that by its very
nature the Bible demands an interpretation that is in part an idealization.

---

2. Ibid., 102.

It may well be that given the length and historical significance of the text, it is misleading to talk about *the* proper way of understanding it. If so, the historical approach suggested by Spinoza also has difficulties.

Surely it is a mistake to view the Bible as nothing but a static document describing a world that has long since passed. Despite the apparently simple narration with which it sometimes proceeds, it is, in addition, a document that puts the reader on a trajectory, that points beyond the historical significance of the written word to something that is true for all time. I suggest, therefore, that the Spinozistic approach—"Apart from the question of its truth, what does the text actually mean?"—is not enough and must always be supplemented by the question "What message can we take from it?"

Consider the book of Deuteronomy. In one respect it is what we would expect (*Mishneh Torah*, Deut 17:18) implies: a copy or repetition of the Torah. In another respect it is much more than a repetition; to use the word I introduced earlier, it is an idealization. Moses, who began his mission as a political leader and transformed himself into a lawgiver, now becomes a teacher.[3] Not surprisingly much of Deuteronomy asks the people to look back and reflect on what happened prior to their reaching the outskirts of the Promised Land. To be sure, Moses' speeches do not constitute history in our sense of the term, because, in addition to a recitation of the narrative, there is a fair amount of reproach.

Beyond reproach, there is also a generous amount of what can only be called interpretation. The commandments revealed at Sinai are not just commandments anymore but a body of wisdom of which all the peoples of the earth are to take note (Deut 4:6–7). The validity of this wisdom exists for all times and cannot be amended. In connection with the giving of universal wisdom the people are told that they saw no form of God at Sinai (Deut 4:12), even though, as we will see later, the book of Exodus indicates otherwise. The covenant is no longer an agreement binding a specific people to its God, but a pledge that extends indefinitely and includes even "those not here today" (Deut 29:15). In sum, the giving of Torah, a historical event that took place in the desert, now becomes an eternally renewable event that transcends space and time and binds all future generations.

What the Moses of Deuteronomy is saying is that this is how we have to view the events that took place at Sinai if we are to understand their full significance. It is not just something that happened to a previous generation but the beginning of an open-ended spiritual narrative. To the objec-

---

3. This point is made by Hermann Cohen, *Religion of Reason: Out of the Sources of Judaism* (Atlanta/New York, 1995), 76.

tion that Moses's account of Sinai goes well beyond the original version of
the story, he would no doubt reply that a purely historical account would
miss the point: the laws given in the desert are not just commandments
issued by a particular ruler but a model for all people to study and emulate.

In view of this, we should not be bothered if certain parts of the narrative are emphasized and other parts ignored—selectivity is a normal part
of the process of idealization, which surveys a wide range of facts or
events and tries to distill their essence. Along these lines, Aristotle (*Poetics*
1451b) tells us that the difference between history and poetry is not the
mode of presentation, because if Herodotus had expressed himself in
verse, the result would still be history. Rather the difference is that history
describes "the thing that has been" whereas poetry describes "a kind of
thing that might be." The result is that poetry is more philosophical and of
graver import than history, because it deals with universals rather than
singulars. Aristotle is not saying that we can replace history with poetry in
all cases. A good empiricist, he was well aware that there are times when
an accurate account of singulars is needed. His point is that when we want
to understand the whole meaning of what happened, singulars are not
enough.

To stay with the Greeks a bit longer, Thucydides' concept of history
was much more like Aristotle's account of poetry. It is well known that
much of his account of the Peloponnesian War consists of conversations
that did not actually take place but in Thucydides' view were "demanded
by the circumstances." No modern historian could get away with this. The
fact is, however, that after we read Thucydides, we feel we know the characters and their motivations firsthand. By presenting idealized versions of
what they said ("what circumstances demanded"), he provides an insight
into the causes of the war that no simple recitation of facts could match.
The same could be said of Plato's portrayal of Socrates. Though it would
be interesting to know the facts of Socrates' life, they would not hold our
attention very long were it not for Plato's idealized presentation of him in
the dialogues.

That takes us back to Maimonides. Although the Torah does not rank
commandments by virtue of importance, Maimonides thinks he is on safe
ground in saying that all are means to the fulfillment of the first two:
acceptance of monotheism and rejection of idolatry.[4] Already there is a
problem because it is not clear what it means to say that God is one. Does
belief in a single pagan deity like Zeus qualify or belief in a god who cannot be seen but can still be located in space? Or what about a god who is

---

4. *Guide* 3.28, 3.32.

not in space but who possesses multiple attributes? If we stick with the plain sense of the text, we will not find answers.

Although the second commandment prohibits one from making an image of God, it does not say whether that is because God has no image or because God does not want to be worshipped by means of one. The picture gets more complicated at Exod 24:10, when we learn that Moses, Aaron, and the elders of Israel did see God. According to Abraham ibn Ezra, the passage means that they saw God as one sees something in a vision.[5] According to Saadia Gaon, all they saw was the glory (*kavod*) of God: a special light that emanates from God to the prophets.[6] By contrast, Maimonides (*Guide* 1.4) holds that the seeing involved is an imperfect intellectual vision brought on by thinking about God in too hasty a fashion.

Or consider Exodus 33, the famous passage in which Moses asks to see the face of God but is denied on the grounds that "no one can see me and live." Strictly speaking, the passage does not say that no one can see God, but that dire consequences will result if one does. Again Saadia takes the passage to be referring to the special light, which is so intense that a person who looks directly at it will die. And again, Maimonides takes vision as a metaphor for intellectual apprehension so that the passage is telling us that no one can know the essence of God. It may be that Num 12:8, which maintains that only Moses was permitted to look upon the form or figure (*temunah*) of God, is an allusion to Exodus 33, but it is hard to be sure. Lest the passage be taken as ascribing physical shape to God, Maimonides (*Guide* 1.4–5) says it means that only Moses was allowed to grasp the truth about God.

The strategy of these interpretations is clear. The passages in question must be interpreted in such a way that we preserve the monotheistic character of the text. Keep in mind that Ibn Ezra, Saadia, and Maimonides were heirs to a tradition that was comfortable with parables, metaphors, and other forms of elliptical expression. For them literal expression is not always desirable and, when dealing with subjects like God and prophetic experience, may not be possible. Recognizing this, Spinoza objected that when it comes to projecting one's own views onto the biblical text, the rabbis are as guilty as Maimonides. Why should we believe that the original audience would have gone to such lengths to remove any trace of anthro-

---

5. See *Ibn Ezra's Commentary on the Pentateuch: Exodus*, trans. H. Norman Strickman and Arthur M. Silver (New York, 1988), 524. Ibn Ezra compares this passage to 1Kgs 22:19 and 2Chr 18:18.

6. Saadia Gaon, *The Book of Beliefs and Opinions*, trans. Samuel Rosenblatt (New Haven, 1948), 130.

pomorphism? The truth is that we have no idea what the original audience thought or whether they even saw these passages as problematic. In all likelihood they did not. The Bible is not a work of theology. There is no word for monotheism in Biblical Hebrew and no passage where it is discussed in a straightforward way.

By the same token, why should we assume that these commentators were engaged in biblical scholarship as *we* understand it? The scholarship that Spinoza envisioned, which is to say scholarship that makes a radical distinction between meaning and truth, is a secular subject that applies the same critical methods to the Bible that it applies to other literary documents. If asked about these methods, traditional commentators would have replied that they were doing something more important: passing on a sacred doctrine of which they are the present custodians. For them there is no question that the text is monotheistic because the religion founded on it would make no sense unless it were. The fact that the original audience knew little or nothing of what shape that religion would take is not a valid objection. The truth of the religion transcends the opinions of any individual practitioner. To return to a concept I introduced earlier, the traditional commentators engaged in a kind of idealization. By that I mean that their interpretation was part explanation, part reconstruction, part extrapolation. In addition to what the text says, they wanted to call our attention to where it is trying to take us. Does this constitute abuse?

If monotheism is too abstract a subject with which to answer this question, let us consider issues of a more practical nature. As every reader of the Bible knows, one does not have to look far to find passages that condone, and, in some cases, glorify hatred, vengeance, and mass murder, including that of women and children. The books of Joshua and Judges supply ample evidence, but they are hardly alone. In some cases, e.g., 1 Samuel 15, the violence amounts to genocide. There are also passages that condone or glorify rape, incest, and human sacrifice. It is from these passages and others like them that we get the idea of the "Old Testament God," the jealous, vengeful ruler whose anger is so fierce that not even he can control it and who must be adored and appeased at every turn. The traditional commentators thought that despite the number and graphic nature of these passages, they don't tell us what the Bible is really about, which is love, repentance, and forgiveness. Told that the original audience may have paid more attention to sex and violence than it did to forgiveness, traditional commentators would insist again that that is beside the point. Though there are times when violence may be necessary, forgiveness is always necessary and is one of the qualities that God reveals to Moses at Exodus 34.

In a similar way, Maimonides argues in *Perek Helek* that the many passages that promise material rewards for obedience to God are not the true story either. Even passages promising health or strength miss the point if we are not careful how we interpret them. The true story is the path to intellectual love of God, a state that replaces attachment to material things with awe, humility, and reverence. In some ways even Spinoza would agree—despite the fact that, like monotheism, intellectual love is nowhere mentioned in the text. Though I have invoked the concept of idealization several times, we should keep in mind that Maimonides would not have been comfortable with this term. Rather than present an idealized version of the text, he thought he was uncovering secrets buried in it by people who realized that the true message was too controversial to be put on the surface (*Guide* 1, Introduction).

There is a good measure of elitism in this view. But before we criticize Maimonides, consider the following. Suppose we told people that by studying the Torah and observing the commandments they will not necessarily improve the material quality of their life. Suppose we said that however simple it may look, the text is deep and requires years of training before one can grasp its true meaning. Suppose we added that the text repudiates any form of magic or superstition so that we should not expect miracles to happen and must rely on our own resources. Thus the only respect in which the messianic age will differ from this one is that we will not have to fear political persecution and will be able to devote more of our time to study.[7] Suppose we finished by saying that the entire religion culminates in worship of a God we cannot see, control, or even comprehend.

No doubt some people would be happy with this message; Maimonides' point is that not enough would. The result is that Judaism must counteract powerful forces in the human psyche if it is to have any chance of success. That is why it begins by promising material rewards, describing miraculous exploits, and promoting belief in a god whose decisions can be influenced by flattery or entreaty. All these things are necessary if people are going to take the first steps along the way to love of God. At a superficial level, they are the stuff of biblical narrative and make up the passages that would have left a lasting impression on the original audience. If they are necessary, in Maimonides' opinion, they are also deplorable, for if this is all Judaism stands for, it would not be worth preserving.

The only way to make Judaism something that is worth preserving is to convince people that however simple they may look at first, the texts on

---

7. *Mishneh Torah* 14, Kings and Wars, 12.1. For the naturalistic character of Maimonides' view of the Messiah, see Amos Funkenstein, "Maimonides' Political Theory and Realistic Messianism," *Miscellanea Mediaevalia* 11 (1977): 81–103 as well as Menachem Kellner, *Maimonides on the "Decline of the Generations" and the Nature of Rabbinic Authority* (Albany, 1996), chap. 5.

which it is based go deeper. That is why interpretation is so important. Unless we make a conscious effort to turn people's minds from material things to spiritual, they will remain at the material level and ignore the lessons Judaism tries to teach. For Maimonides, philosophy is more than an academic discipline; by diverting our attention from the imagination, which can only conceive of material things, to reason, it is a necessary part of the process of spiritualization. The need to think in material terms is what is responsible for the lure of idolatry, a temptation that affects Jews and Gentiles alike. At one point (*Guide* 2.12), he goes so far as to say that that imagination is identical to the evil impulse and is responsible for "every deficiency of reason or character."

Without the corrective that philosophy brings to study of the Bible, we would have little hope of getting beyond a God who grants favors and succumbs to flattery. If one believes that Moses, the other prophets, and the rabbis who followed them got beyond this conception of God, then in Maimonides' opinion, they were doing philosophy even if they had never heard of Plato and Aristotle. So far from an abuse of the text, he would argue that philosophy is the only way of coming to grips with it.

In addition to relieving us of the need to think in material terms, philosophy relieves us of the conceit of thinking that everything in the universe was created for our sake. Although there are some things Maimonides thinks philosophy can demonstrate—mainly that God is neither a body nor a force in a body—it is well to remember that Maimonides never claims—on the contrary he repeatedly denies—that it can demonstrate everything we need to know. In fact, Maimonides emphasizes that if we pursue it far enough, philosophy will get us to the point where we become conscious of the limits of human knowledge and the need to stay within them (*Guide* 1.33). It is in this sense that he praises R. Akiva for not fooling himself into thinking he has demonstrated something when in fact he has not, for not pronouncing as false things that have not been refuted, and not aspiring to apprehend what is beyond human comprehension.

Simply put: philosophy brings us face to face with something vastly greater than ourselves. In the *Mishneh Torah* (*MT* 1, Basic Principles of the Torah, 4.12), he describes it this way:

> When a man reflects on these things, studies all these created beings, from the angels and spheres down to human beings and so on, and realizes the divine wisdom manifested in them all, his love for God will increase, his soul will thirst, his very flesh will yearn to love God. He will be filled with fear and trembling, as he becomes conscious of his lowly condition, poverty, and insignificance, and compares himself with any of the great and holy bodies; still more when he compares himself with any one of the pure forms that are incorporeal and have never had association with any corporeal substance. He will then realize that he is a vessel full of shame, dishonor, and reproach, empty and deficient.

According to him, this is the point where the Bible is trying to take us, and any interpretation that leads in a different direction needs to be rethought.

His conviction raises two questions: (1) Is there a point where the Bible is trying to take us? and (2) Did Maimonides identify it correctly? I do not presume to know the answers to these questions, but I am willing to say where my intuitions lie.

With respect to (1), I think Maimonides goes too far. The text is too complicated for us to say that it has a single view of human perfection. We saw that even the characterization of Moses changes when we move from Exodus, Leviticus, and Numbers to Deuteronomy. Once we include the great literary prophets, Maimonides' view begins to seem like the sort of generalization one would expect from a thinker of genius: brilliant but too restrictive.

With respect to (2), I suggest the answer is partly "yes." Maimonides did identify one view of perfection to which the Bible is committed. Here one thinks of the end of the book of Job, when God speaks to the title character out of the whirlwind and Job begins to see himself as a vessel filled with shame, dishonor, and reproach. In fact, Maimonides may well have had Job in mind when he wrote the passage cited above. But he could also have had in mind Moses hiding his face at the Burning Bush or Moses being told that he could not see the face of God and live. Though infused with philosophical convictions, his interpretation of these passages is so compelling it is hard to read them any other way. Simply put, the passages cry out for some sort of philosophical midrash.

What then can Maimonides teach us about reading the Bible? If I had to summarize the lesson on one foot, it would be that we should not treat the Bible like any other book for the simple fact is that the Bible makes a claim on our attention no other book can make. To read it in the way one reads other literary documents is to do it an injustice. Under the circumstances, it should not surprise us that its meaning is sometimes hidden and may not have been understood by the original audience. On the contrary, it should make us happy because it indicates that we are dealing with something of infinite depth. So let us put away the old objection that says philosophy is a Greek invention that has nothing to contribute to the interpretation of the Hebrew Bible. When a book that purports to be *from* God raises questions *about* God, it demands every bit of philosophical insight we can bring to bear.

JACOB AND ISAAC
A TALE OF DECEPTION AND SELF-DECEPTION

Charlotte Katzoff
Bar Ilan University

A PROFOUNDLY PUZZLING EPISODE in the patriarchal narratives of the book of Genesis is Jacob's deception of Isaac and his winning the blessing thereby. That Jacob's moral standing in this story is very problematic is widely acknowledged. Many have noted that in the ensuing chapters of his life Jacob is repeatedly made to suffer in ways that suggest that he is being visited by the wages of this sin.[1] One wonders how someone who deceives his father and cheats his brother could then be granted a divine blessing and go on to become the father of a great nation. I shall be putting this moral issue aside, however. And, although Jacob's character and conduct will play a part in my analysis, it is on the figure of Isaac that I will be focusing.

On the face of it, Isaac's role in this story is that of the hapless victim of a carefully thought out ruse. This view of him fits in with what we know about him from earlier on. Of the three patriarchs in Genesis, Isaac is marked by his passive nature. He lives in the shadow of his father, Abraham, in part retracing his steps.[2] In the most striking scene of his lifetime, Isaac's role is to be led unresistingly, perhaps uncomprehendingly, to the sacrifice.[3] And as opposed to both his sons, who choose their own wives,

---

1. On Jacob's choice of language in his complaint to his father-in-law, Laban, for having deceived him, which echoes Isaac's complaint about Jacob's having deceived him, see Martin Buber and Franz Rosenzweig, *Scripture and Translation*, trans. Lawrence Rosenwald with Everett Fox (Bloomington, 1994), 120–22, 136. I am indebted to William Hallo for this reference.

2. See Gen 26:12–19.

3. When he asks his father where the sheep is for the offering, Abraham answers him that "God will see to the sheep…" (Gen 22:8), a vague answer for such a fraught question, with which Isaac nevertheless makes do.

143

and especially in contrast to Jacob, who falls in love with Rachel in a dramatic scene at the well and then struggles to win her, Isaac's wife is chosen for him and delivered to him by his father's servant. We are tempted to see Isaac as a gullible old man, sensing that something is wrong, but unequal to the conspiracy hatched against him by his wife and son. As a result, he unwittingly grants the blessing to Rebecca's favorite rather than to his own.

This view of Isaac is difficult theologically. It raises questions about how God carries out his plans and how he relates to the heroes and heroines of the biblical narrative. What is at stake here is the future of the family of Abraham. The one who triumphs will not just be materially blessed, but will be designated to prevail over his brother and, ultimately, to be the heir to the Abrahamic blessing. Does God, who personally chose Abraham and made an everlasting covenant with him and his posterity, allow the succession to be determined by an act of deceit? Is the blessing here hostage to the opposing fancies of Isaac and Rebecca? To read this simply as an intrigue fueled by a conflict between a blind, credulous old man and his wily wife, in which the former is bested by the latter, is not only to discredit the patriarchal legacy, but also to undermine the providential view of Israelite history that the Bible promotes.

That this view of Isaac is out of focus can be seen also by comparing it to two other stories of deception in the Genesis narrative. One follows closely on this one: Jacob is fooled by Laban, who substitutes his older daughter, Leah, to be Jacob's bride, in place of Jacob's beloved, the younger daughter, Rachel. Jacob is an easy mark, a guileless victim of Laban's foul play. Jacob is again deceived, this time more brutally, by his sons, when they bring him Joseph's coat that has been dipped in the blood of a goat, tricking him into believing that his most cherished son was devoured by a wild animal. Jacob has no inkling of his sons' treachery, and their scheming against him meets no resistance. In neither of these instances does Jacob experience any epistemic tension, any doubts about the belief being foisted upon him. Isaac, on the other hand, in the story before us, is troubled. He resists, vacillates, struggles to penetrate the contradictions that beset him.

That this is not a story of a feeble old man mindlessly stumbling into a cleverly laid trap is attested also by the attitudes of Rebecca and Jacob. Neither Isaac's wife nor his son, who presumably know him intimately, take for granted their ability to deceive him. Rebecca's plan is carefully crafted. Jacob is to bring the food that Isaac had requested of Esau. Jacob must also swathe himself in goatskins, to simulate Esau's hairy skin. With all that, Jacob nevertheless fears that Isaac will see through the ruse and, instead of blessing, curse him. To exact his compliance, Rebecca must respond, "Let the curse be on me" (Gen 27:13).

This is, indeed, a tale of deception. I propose, however, that to do justice to the dynamics of the story, another, more contemporary, notion should be called into play, one that has been developed a great deal by analytic philosophers of late: the notion of self-deception. My thesis is that Rebecca's plot succeeds because Isaac cooperates in his own deception. A simple notion of self-deception would suggest that the subject comes to believe something he wants to believe. Because I see the motivation that generates Isaac's self-deception as being highly complex, I shall put forth a more complicated account. Support for my reading comes not only from the text before us but from the larger narrative of which it is a part. I shall further try to show how my understanding of this episode is consonant with the prevailing theological presuppositions and motifs of the Genesis narratives.

The Interrogation

Despite Rebecca's elaborate designs, the plan she devises falters from the very beginning. In Gen 27:18 Jacob approaches Isaac, bringing, as Rebecca has arranged, the offering Isaac requested from Esau. The flaw in Rebecca's scheme immediately comes to light. Jacob must signal his arrival; he must speak to Isaac. Neither he nor his mother has addressed this dimension of the encounter between the two. "Father," Jacob presents himself. Isaac is expecting Esau. Yet his response to Jacob's filial address is "Which of my sons are you?" Jacob's voice has sounded an alarm.

Jacob identifies himself as Esau, but Isaac plainly does not take Jacob at his word. His eyes are dull, but his ears are sharp and his mind is keen. He does not challenge his son directly, but there is no mistaking that he has misgivings. "How did you succeed so quickly?" he demands. Jacob's answer, "Because the Lord your God granted me good fortune," is designed to deflect his father's suspicions, and perhaps also to ingratiate himself with his father and thereby soften his defenses. Whether it is because Isaac finds this explanation implausible or that his hearing Jacob's voice once again stirs up his doubts, it is clear that he is not satisfied. By now he is so troubled that he does not conceal his suspicions. "Come closer that I may feel you, my son, whether you are really my son Esau or not."

The goatskins encasing Jacob's arms do not put Isaac at ease. The sound of Jacob's voice is vivid in his ears, and it does not match the feel of this son who stands before him. Isaac does not give way easily. He struggles with his conflicting evidence. We hear his anguish as he spells out his quandary: "The voice is the voice of Jacob, yet the hands are the hands of Esau!" More than skeptical, Isaac sounds incredulous. Although this son is carrying out the charge he just gave to Esau, although this son's skin feels like Esau's, what Isaac hears repeatedly—what he cannot fail to hear—is his son Jacob declaring that he is Esau.

How shall we characterize Isaac's doxastic state as he stands on the verge of giving the blessing? Both the objective features of the situation and his own protestations make clear his plight. Not only is the data in fact inconclusive, he is obviously aware that it is. Is it fair to say that he suspects this *may* be Jacob? Of course! Is it fair to say that he *strongly suspects* that this is Jacob? I think so.

At this point the text subtly signals a shift in Isaac's attitude. "And he did not recognize him, because his hands were hairy like his brother Esau's hands." The possibility that this is Jacob seems to be receding. Jacob's voice has lost its hold on Isaac; the goatskins appear to have won the day. Nevertheless, before he proceeds to the blessing, Isaac presses his son Jacob yet again. "Are you really my son Esau?" To which Jacob answers unequivocally, "I am."

The die is cast.[4] Isaac probes no more. He straightaway sends for the food and eats and drinks in preparation for the blessing. Then he asks Jacob to approach him so that he can kiss him. Jacob complies and the smell of his clothing reaches Isaac. Enraptured by the aroma, Isaac unquestioningly takes it as the smell of Esau himself—"the smell of the fields that the Lord has blessed." Isaac has transcended the conflict between his ears and his fingertips and now succumbs to his sense of smell. No longer grappling with the inconsistencies in his evidence, he pronounces the blessing.

Has Isaac simply changed his mind? People regularly reevaluate their evidence, reconsider their beliefs. People who change their minds in the usual way, however, have reasons for doing so. They can point to new evidence or to some aspect of the evidence that they had missed or misunderstood. Sometimes these reasons are what really caused the change; sometimes they are only rationalizations. In either case, however, such people can account for the reversal in rational terms. Isaac does not reject any of his evidence, however, nor does he reinterpret it. The paradoxical coupling of the voice of Jacob with the hands of Esau remains a mystery. For Isaac, the move from suspicion, or even belief, that this is Jacob to the conviction that it is Esau is a leap over, what Dion Scott-Kakures calls, a "cognitive fissure," a blind spot separating his earlier and later cognitive perspectives.[5] Isaac avails himself of neither rationale nor rationalization to bridge the gap.

---

4. I am indebted to Josh Berman for helping work out the timing in the progression.

5. See Dion Scott-Kakures, "Self-Deception and Internal Irrationality," *Philosophy and Phenomenological Research* 56 (1996): 48–56.

The Blessing

Although this blessing is not the blessing of Abraham, which Jacob will receive only later, its significance should not be underestimated. The occasion for the blessing is Isaac's perception that his death is approaching. In addition to the riches of the field, the blessing includes political supremacy: "May peoples serve you and nations bow down to you; may you be lord to your brother and may your mother's sons bow down to you." This is what was foretold to Rebecca by God when her sons were in her womb. It ends with an echo of the blessing that God originally bestowed upon Abraham, which ordained him as God's elected, "Cursed be they who curse you,/Blessed they who bless you" (Gen 27:28). Yet, despite the gravity of the deed, and although we see no grounds for laying his well-founded doubts to rest nor any signs that he thinks he has resolved them, Isaac bestows the blessing.

Before us here, as throughout most of the Genesis narratives, is a psychologically realistic human drama. Rebecca's urging her younger son to wrest the blessing from the older by deceiving his father may strike us as irregular, even bizarre and unethical, but it is not baffling. Given the message she received from God and her preference for Jacob, and assuming that she believed herself to have neither authority nor influence over her husband, Rebecca's decision to secure the blessing for Jacob by trickery is understandable. The same is true of Jacob's acquiescence to Rebecca's urging. Not so Isaac's behavior. How could Isaac have proceeded with this critical blessing, given his earlier suspicions and his palpable uncertainty until the very end? The mixed data certainly called for circumspection. Why did he not stall for time? Why did he not continue to probe—call in a third party or call for Jacob to be brought before him—to assure himself that this was really Esau?

Isaac investigates no further, I propose, out of fear of what he will discover. [6] He has more than a premonition that it would turn out that the petitioner is Jacob, and he would be obliged to denounce Jacob and take the steps required to assure that Esau receives the blessing. I argue that this is precisely what Isaac wants to avoid.

---

6. Christopher Hookway, "Epistemic *Akrasia* and Epistemic Virtue," in *Virtue Epistemology*, ed. Abrol Fairweather and Linda Zagzebski (Oxford, 2001), suggests that self-deception may be caused by a reluctance to acknowledge that more careful investigation may work counter to our goals or bring us face to face with unpleasant truths. Hookway attributes this observation (not explicit) to Mark Johnston, "Self-Deception and the Nature of the Mind," in *Perspectives on Self-Deception*. Ed. Brian P. McLaughlin and Amelie Rorty (Berkeley and Los Angeles, 1988), 63–92.

There is more that needs to be explained, however. How does it happen that Isaac, who clearly appreciates the conflicting nature of his evidence and is so suspicious from the outset, has a change of heart? He is now so certain of the very thing he has just persisted in doubting that he unreservedly gives the blessing. The aftermath of the blessing is no less a psychological mystery. When he realizes that it was not to Esau that he gave the blessing, Isaac trembles mightily. How could this discovery come to him as such a shock when, until the very last moment, he seemed unable to rid himself of the suspicion that he was giving the blessing to the wrong son? However, if Isaac is shocked to discover what he has done, he seems to recover quickly. It is clear to him that whoever preempted the blessing will remain blessed, yet he does not lament his mistake. There is no sign of anger or reproach toward the son who has duped him. In response to Esau's entreaties, Isaac, at first at a loss, in the end graces him with a distinctly second-class blessing, leaving him in principle subservient to his younger brother.[7]

There is, moreover, another, weightier blessing that Isaac is holding in store for his heir—the blessing of Abraham.[8] Isaac, this time in full cognizance of what he is doing and of his own accord, confers this blessing on Jacob, the son who has just deceived him, thereby confirming and enhancing the earlier, stolen, blessing. "May God bless you and make you fruitful, and multiply you...and give you the blessing of Abraham, to you and your descendants with you, to inherit the land you live in which God gave to Abraham." How do we explain Isaac's magnanimity?

What I am urging is that at the moment Isaac is poised to give the blessing he understands that Esau is not destined to receive it. At that moment, not only does he strongly suspect that he is blessing Jacob, he also believes that Jacob is the one for whom the blessing is intended. It is this double insight that underlies his decision to give the blessing when he does. However, given that these are the assumptions underlying his deci-

---

7. Like Esau's uncle, Ishmael, of whom the angel of the Lord had said, "his hand against everyone and everyone's hand against him" (Gen 16:12), Esau is destined, according to Isaac's blessing, to live by his sword.

8. According to some commentators, Isaac had been intending all along to give Esau only the former of the two blessings and to give Jacob the blessing of Abraham. See David Berger, "On the Morality of the Patriarchs in Jewish Polemic and Exegesis," in *Understanding Scripture: Explorations of Jewish Traditions of Interpretation*, ed. Clemens Thomas and Michael Wyschogrod (New York, 1987). This seems unlikely, however, because, given the content of the birthright blessing, the subservient brother would be the bearer of the Abrahamic blessing.

sion, the action Isaac is about to undertake is in stark opposition to his earlier commitments and intentions. Isaac resolves the opposition by "forgetting" his original assumptions, which conflict with the action he is about to take. By the time he actually confers the blessing, he believes that he is blessing Esau and he believes that Esau is the rightful recipient of the blessing. Isaac is engaging in self-deception.

Isaac's Self-deception

Alfred Mele stipulates the following conditions as jointly sufficient for entering self-deception in acquiring the belief that p:

1.   The belief that p, which S acquires, is false.
2.   S treats data relevant, or at least seemingly relevant, to the truth value of p in a motivationally biased way.
3.   The biased treatment is a nondeviant cause of S's acquiring the belief that p.
4.   The body of data possessed by S at the time provides greater warrant for $\sim p$ than p.[9]

Note that two of the requirements, 1 and 4, are logical. Requirement 1 is straightforwardly satisfied by Isaac's belief that he is conferring the blessing upon Esau. Requirement 4 may give some readers pause, however. They may not agree that Isaac's evidence provides greater warrant for its being Jacob than for its being Esau. Arguably, the evidence does not settle the matter.

According to one traditional version of evidentialism, if one's evidence for p is inconclusive, one is justified or permitted to either believe or disbelieve p.[10] So Isaac would be within his epistemic rights in believing that he is blessing Esau. A more stringent version of evidentialism, and one that is more faithful to the requirement that one's belief fit one's evidence, denies the subject such epistemic latitude. If one's evidence is inconclusive, as is the case with Isaac, the epistemically mandated doxastic state is suspension of belief. On this version of evidentialism, then, the gap between the inconclusiveness of Isaac's evidence and the certainty he displays by conferring the blessing is enough to satisfy requirement 4.[11]

---

9.   Alfred R. Mele, *Self-Deception Unmasked* (Princeton, 2001), 50.

10. Richard Feldman and Earl Conee, "Evidentialism," *Philosophical Studies* 48 (1985): 15–34.

11. There is also a view that someone might be counted as self-deceived who formed a true belief, provided it was on the basis of a biased interpretation of his evidence. See Scott-Kakures, "Self-Deception," 38. The emphasis, in this

Mele's requirements 2 and 3 are psychological. They call for a biased view of the evidence and for that biasing to cause the subject to adopt the faulty belief. How, then, may we establish what causes Isaac to believe that he is blessing Esau? Isaac, during the first part of the story, is completely rational; he goes where the evidence leads him. At the moment of the blessing he does not become delusional nor utterly irrational. He seems still to be moved by evidential concerns. His newfound confidence that he is about to bless Esau is, I propose, the result of his seeing his evidence in a different light, as justifying that confidence. Rather than assessing or interpreting his evidence objectively, as he did before, which resulted, at the very least, in skepticism on his part, Isaac's view of the evidence is now biased in favor of this belief.

Mele lists a number of ways in which biasing shapes people's beliefs.[12] Among them are selective focusing/attending, i.e., failing to focus attention on evidence that counts against p—in Isaac's case, the voice he hears—and focusing instead on evidence suggestive of p—in Isaac's case, the feel of the arms and the smell of the clothing. Another form of biasing is selective gathering of evidence, which includes overlooking evidence for p that is easily obtainable—in Isaac's case, his foregoing further opportunity to get to the bottom of the matter.

Requirement 2 specifies that the self-deceiver's biased treatment of the evidence be motivationally grounded. Not all biases meet this specification. Research into cognition supports the prevalence of "cold" biases, tendencies that are not accounted for by a particular subject's interest in systematically skewing his assessment of the evidence. These biases are regarded as cognitive shortcuts, taken more or less universally because they offer pragmatic benefits. It is clear, however, that the bias that causes Isaac's belief that he is blessing Esau is of the "hot" variety. It is motivated by Isaac's desire to believe that he is blessing Esau.

In analyzing what he calls "garden-variety straight self-deception," Mele stipulates that in self-deception that p, the desire that p is what motivates the biased treatment of the data.[13] Mark Johnston proposes that we understand biasing to be motivated by the desire that a belief be true,

---

view, then, is on the manipulation of the evidence. Similarly, it might not be essential to self-deception that the subject's belief fail to comply with what his evidence in fact indicates. It would be sufficient that the subject believe contrary to the way he views his evidence. Isaac clearly believes that the evidence is troubling, yet, in giving the blessing, expresses the conviction that he is blessing Esau.

12. Mele, *Unmasked*, 26.

13. Ibid., 25.

accompanied by anxiety that it is false.[14] On this model, Isaac would be motivated to believe that he is blessing Esau, because he wants it to be Esau but fears it is Jacob. We are arguing, however, that Isaac wants it to be Jacob that he is blessing. Why then does he self-deceive himself into believing that he is blessing Esau, rather than openly and explicitly bless Jacob?

Isaac's Mixed Motives

At the time we witness Esau being summoned by Isaac to receive the blessing, Esau is no stranger to us. We know that from before his birth, he is destined by God to serve his older brother. He grows up to become a skillful hunter, whereas Jacob "was a mild man and stayed in camp" (Gen 25:27). Isaac favors Esau because Isaac has a taste for game, we are told. No judgment is made in the text as to the worthiness of this motive, but the reader may have some reservations. We have seen Esau sell his birthright to Jacob for some bread and lentil stew, upon which the narrator comments, presumably disapprovingly, that Esau "spurned" the birthright (Gen 25:34).

What are we to make of Isaac's feelings toward his firstborn? He does not seem to know of God's communication to Rebecca or of the transaction between his two sons. His preparing to bless Esau shows that he takes him to be the rightful claimant. We know, however, that Isaac's feelings toward Esau are not unadulterated. Immediately preceding the present episode we read: "And Esau was forty years old and he took for a wife Judith the daughter of Beeri the Hittite and Basmath the daughter of Elon the Hittite. And they were a source of consternation to Isaac and Rebecca" (Gen 26:34–35). Yet Isaac does not renounce Esau, nor do we have reason to think that his affection for Esau flags.

To appreciate the complexity of Isaac's feelings, we need to widen our gaze beyond the bounds of this narrative. Isaac himself is the bearer of a contested birthright, the younger of his father's sons, whose supremacy was secured by the banishment of the older. Does his older son, the outdoorsman, remind him of his older, perhaps beloved, perhaps admired, brother, Ishmael, "the wild ass of a man" (Gen 16:12), who was lost to him? Does he see himself in the younger Jacob, the mild-mannered homebody? And if so, is it in Jacob's being a potential usurper that Isaac identifies with him or in his being the true heir of his father? Or both? Bear in mind also that Isaac has witnessed within his family, at very close range, estrangement and alienation—the rupture of both parental and fraternal ties—in the wake of a father's choosing the younger son over the older.

---

14. Johnston, "Self-Deception," 73.

Let us venture also to factor Isaac's relationship with his wife, Rebecca, into the complex of Isaac's emotions. Even assuming that she did not share God's tidings with Isaac, could Isaac have been unaware of her preference for Jacob? Was he determined to follow his own inclinations, no matter?[15] Or, was his love for Esau tempered by his knowledge that she did not share it?

Isaac is a man conflicted—between his love for and commitment to Esau and his intuition that Esau is not suited to inherit the father Abraham. Initially he summons Esau, but he has misgivings. As the interrogation proceeds, his suspicions that Esau is not the one standing before him grow. Perhaps being confronted by the likelihood that this is Jacob rather than Esau helps to jolt him into the recognition that this is as it should be. On the verge of giving the blessing, he understands that the one he should be blessing is Jacob. Why, then, does he not announce that he has changed his mind and proceed accordingly? Think of the cost to Isaac of such a move, of choosing one son and rejecting the other. Esau would know of this betrayal, would be pained and incensed by it. His rage would be directed against Isaac at least as much as against Jacob.

Given this picture of Isaac's motivational state, what should he do? One option that recommends itself, and that has been imputed to him by some commentators, is to simply feign credulity.[16] He can pretend that he believes he is blessing Esau, confident, or almost confident, that he is blessing Jacob. He would, indeed, be betraying Esau, but with relative impunity. He would have to bear the brunt of Esau's disappointment, but not his wrath. Esau would be furious with Jacob for stealing his blessing, but the fury would not be compounded by jealousy at Jacob's having stolen his father's affections as well. On this reading, the story is not one of deception and self-deception, but just of deception. The perpetrator is not Jacob, as we thought, however, since Jacob's attempt at deception failed, but rather the dissembler is Isaac.

Although viewing Isaac as performing a cynical charade makes sense of what he does from a pragmatic point of view, what appears to be his genuine delight in the smell of Esau's clothing and his mighty trembling upon learning of the deception do not support such a reading. Furthermore, there is little of what we know of Isaac from elsewhere to suggest that he would be inclined to compromise his integrity so severely, or that

---

15. These questions were suggested to me in conversation with Howard Wettstein.

16. See the medieval commentator Abrabanel on Gen 27:30 and the contemporary feminist critic Tikva Frymer-Kensky, *Reading the Women of the Bible* (New York, 2002), 20.

he would even be capable of doing so.[17] That he is simply lying is ruled out by an additional consideration. I postulate that it is not simply the outward repercussions of an open confrontation that Isaac fears. He shrinks from the inner emotional upheaval attending his betrayal of his older son, the one he had favored, whom he had led to expect the blessing. Perhaps also he dreads the humiliation of acknowledging that his wife loved more wisely than he. Isaac wishes to negotiate the present situation in a way that will compromise him least in his own eyes and in the eyes of others.

Isaac's Strategy

Although we do not regard Isaac as simply putting on an act, the fact that we are tempted to do so advances my argument. If Isaac's pretending to believe that he is blessing Esau could serve his interests, then his self-deceiving himself that he is doing so will work even better. Indeed, it has been suggested that self-deception evolved as a strategy for more effective lying. A person who believes the tale he is telling will be less likely to emit the signs of stress and self-consciousness that accompany conscious lying and are apt to give him away.[18]

Isaac is motivated to bias his evidence by the belief-desire complex I have outlined above. He believes that he is blessing Esau because he wants to believe it. He does not want the belief, for the sake of which he biases his evidence, to be true, however. Although he wants to *believe* that he is blessing Esau, he wants it to be the case that he is blessing Jacob. Thus, Isaac's self-deception does not conform to the simple model.

David Pears considers instances of self-deception in which people form unfounded beliefs that they do not want to be true, which are intrinsically unpleasant or even painful to them.[19] These are often cases in which the self-deception is motivated by emotions such as fear or jealousy. A husband who has no evidence that his wife is being unfaithful may nevertheless form the belief that she is, even though he is grieved by the thought and does not want it to be true. According to Pears, this kind of conduct can often be explained by the person's having an ulterior goal,

---

17. One might point to Isaac's presenting Rebecca to the men of Gerar as his sister rather than his wife as an instance of deception on his part (Gen 26:6–11). Isaac is lying here to foreigners out of fear for his life, rather than to his son. Furthermore, he fails to carry off the deception. He gives himself away by fondling Rebecca in the sight of the Philistine king.

18. R. Trivers, *Social Evolution* (Menlo Park, Calif., 1985), 415–17, quoted in Mele, *Unmasked*, 89.

19. David Pears, *Motivated Irrationality* (Oxford, 1984), 42–44. Mele accommodates such cases under the rubric of "twisted self-deception" (95).

toward which the unpleasant, counter-indicated belief is a means. In the case of the jealous husband, he forms the belief that his wife is unfaithful as a strategy for ensuring that he will be zealously on guard against any rivals for her affections. By exaggerating the danger, he increases the likelihood that he will take the steps required to thwart it.

Thinking of self-deception as a strategy preserves the principle that the subject's adoption of a biased view of his evidence is motivationally grounded in a desire for some sort of gain for himself. The gain, however, need not be that the unfounded belief be true. On my reading, Isaac wants to believe that he is blessing Esau as a means of achieving his ultimate goal, the principal component of which is to bless Jacob. Although the achievement of the latter, in itself, is compatible with his believing that he is blessing Jacob, Isaac's more complex goal, as I have laid it out above, is better advanced by the belief that he is blessing Esau.

Annette Barnes subscribes to Johnston's view that reducing anxiety is the root motivation for self-deception but allows that the anxiety may pertain to beliefs other than the one caused by the bias, thus accommodating Pears's more comprehensive approach.[20] According to Barnes, the belief caused by the bias may be desired for its presumed usefulness. The subject believes that his having the biased belief will help bring about the truth of the belief about which he is anxious, the belief he wants to be true but fears is not.

Barnes's expansive view is congenial to the story of Isaac, but her notion of anxiety does not do justice to Isaac's mental state. As she sees it, the motivational state of the self-deceiver is clear-cut; what provokes his anxiety is the gap between what he wants to believe and what he finds himself believing. Isaac's anxiety is, indeed, in part epistemically grounded—he is, at least at times, uncertain about the facts. Were he wholeheartedly behind his choice of Esau, however, or alternatively, were he not conflicted over giving the blessing to Jacob, he might have taken direct action to ascertain the identity of the person petitioning him. Torn as he is, however, he resorts to self-deception. I am suggesting that the anxiety at the root of his self-deception is also fueled, perhaps fueled primarily, by his ambivalence about which of his children he wants to receive the blessing and his lack of confidence in his ability to resolve his discordant desires.

It seems, then, that the source of the anxiety that motivates the self-deceiver may also be motivational. The anxiety may be caused not only by one's fear that the facts are not as one would like to believe, but also by one's conflicts about what one wants them to be and one's uncertainties about how to resolve one's conflicts. The unreasonably jealous husband,

---

20. Annette Barnes, *Seeing through Self-deception* (Cambridge, 1997), 39.

for example, although he finds the thought of his wife's unfaithfulness painful, may at the same time want an excuse for being angry at her or for treating her poorly. This might also color his reading of the evidence.[21]

A model that takes into account the subject's motivational state and makes sense of the particulars of the strategy I have attributed to Isaac is recommended by Alfred Mele. Mele cites James Friedrich's "primary error detection and minimization" analysis of lay hypothesis testing.[22] According to Friedrich's analysis, the principle governing the testing of a hypothesis is the avoidance or minimization of "costly errors," errors the subject sees as having painful consequences. The subject considers hypotheses that he perceives as furthering that goal and tests them in a biased fashion so that he can more easily adopt them. Since Isaac strongly suspects that he is dealing with Jacob and also has a strong intuition that Jacob is the one who should receive the blessing, and yet at the same time loves Esau and is loathe to betray him, for him the "primary error" would be to take direct action, halt the blessing and investigate further. The belief that he is blessing Esau protects him from committing that error. To secure that belief, he engages in self-deception.

Bela Szabados observes that a person feeling called upon to give up deeply held commitments is pained by the prospect. He may perceive such a concession as profoundly threatening to his sense of self. It may be difficult for him to abandon his former commitments at once; he may need time for retrenchment and adjustment. According to Szabados, in such circumstances self-deception may provide an occasion for self-transformation.[23] Isaac's commitment to Esau is a function, not simply of his taste in food, but also of his childhood experiences and family history. It is anchored in his perceptions of his own identity. That it is ultimately overturned, that Isaac, so shortly after having been deceived into blessing Jacob, gives Jacob another blessing of his own volition, is in line with Szabados's observation that self-deception may make possible a reversal of

---

21. Barnes treats such a case as a possible counterexample to her claim that there are instances of self-deception in which the subject does not desire the belief he forms to be true. It could be that, rather than not wanting the belief to be true, he is simply ambivalent (48). Barnes does not point to ambivalence as a possible source of anxiety.

22. James Friedrich, "Primary Error Detection and Minimization (PEDMIN) Strategies in Social Cognition: A Reinterpretation of Confirmation Bias Phenomena," *Psychological Review* 100 (1993): 298–319, quoted in Mele, *Unmasked*, 31.

23. Bela Szabados, "The Self, Its Passions and Self-Deception," in *Self-Deception and Self-Understanding: New Essays in Philosophy and Psychology*, ed. Mike W. Martin (Kansas, 1985), 160.

one's deeply held attitudes and commitments—a radical change of heart
that could not be effected by a direct or self-conscious reappraisal.

Is Isaac Morally at Fault?

Two of the characters in our drama perpetrate a deception, as a result
of which their moral standing is compromised. Although there is no
explicit disapproval of Jacob's conduct in this episode, as we noted earlier,
his life thereafter is beset with misfortune. He seems to be receiving his
just desserts. Similarly, although there is no explicit condemnation of
Rebecca in the text, perhaps the fact that she must send away her beloved
Jacob never to see him again counts as her punishment.

Isaac, in my account, is "guilty" of self-deception. Does this diminish
his moral stature? Self-deception figures as part of the standard array of
coping mechanisms we avail ourselves of in times of stress. Often it is to
be lamented because it is counterproductive. Acting on false or unwarranted beliefs is not, on the whole, an effective way to achieve one's goals,
and even if the self-deception achieves its goal, other very important goals
may be forfeited thereby. Many instances of self-deception are deplored
because of the pain they cause others. Sometimes, however, we commend
an instance of self-deception as the best or only way of achieving a welcome end.

If we regard subsequent developments in the story as keyed, at least
in part, to the characters' moral desserts, then Isaac's conferral of the blessing upon Jacob clearly does not discredit him. Not only does it serve
Isaac's own purposes, but the reader too must applaud its results. Esau is
displaced by the worthier Jacob but is not made to suffer the humiliation
he would have experienced had he been openly rejected by his father.
Isaac is spared the pain that his deliberately and knowingly doing what
he is doing would have caused him. He is not compromised by his deceiving his son and depriving him of his due, because he does so unwittingly.[24] He emerges from the ordeal in Esau's good graces and with his self-
respect intact. It is against Jacob that Esau bears his grudge; his trust in his
father is not shaken. Isaac's strategy is further vindicated by the ultimate
reconciliation between Esau and Jacob.

What interpretation of self-deception allows for so sympathetic an
attitude toward Isaac? The favorable results that ensue from the blessing
are compatible with either of the following: Isaac's conduct is not subject

---

24. Herbert Fingarette suggests that the self-deceiver is motivated by a concern for
     his own authentic inner dignity and that it is our perception of this that moves
     us to feel compassion toward him rather than regard him as a mere cheat. See
     his *Self-Deception* (California, 2000), 139.

to moral censure because in engaging in self-deception Isaac did nothing intentional; the happy results of the blessing are the natural playing out of a successful strategy, but are not to be seen as Isaac's reward for having acted well. Alternatively, Isaac intentionally engaged in self-deception and is morally praiseworthy for doing so, and the favorable outcome is Isaac's reward. I shall begin with the second possibility.

A natural way of incorporating intentionality into the notion of self-deception is to understand it on the model of other-deception.[25] We do not count a person who inadvertently—unintentionally or unknowingly—misleads someone as deceiving him. To qualify as a full-fledged deceiver he would not only have to know or believe that he was causing his victim to believe a falsehood but also be deliberately taking steps to convince him of it.[26] Correspondingly, a person who simply misinterprets his evidence, even if it is due to his own negligence and even if as a result he comes to believe what he wishes to believe, is not self-deceived. By analogy with the deceiver of others, the self-deceiver, on this model, intentionally biases his evidence in order to cause himself to form a belief he takes to be false and intentionally conceals this from himself.

If the self-deceiver intentionally induces in himself a false or unwarranted belief in order to achieve a goal that, presumably, he desires not to acknowledge, he may well be subject to moral censure. Ignorance, as a rule, exculpates, but if someone intentionally brings it on himself in order to use it as an excuse, how can he then hide behind it? If Isaac were deliberately concealing from himself that he was blessing Jacob in order to escape responsibility for betraying Esau, he would be derivatively responsible, not only for blessing Jacob and betraying Esau, but also for doing so underhandedly.

Aside from the general philosophical difficulties inherent in the intentionalist view of self-deception,[27] no intention on Isaac's part to engage in self-deception is apparent.[28] Although his deciding to give the blessing

---

25. For a discussion of this view of self-deception, see Harold A. Sackheim and Ruben C. Gur, "Self-Deception, Self-Confrontation, and Consciousness," in *Consciousness and Self-Regulation*, vol. 2, ed. Gary E. Schwartz and David Shapiro (New York and London, 1978), 139–97; see also, Mele, *Unmasked*, 59ff.

26. Perhaps, however, I could deceive you into believing what I took to be a true proposition, if I caused you to believe it by manipulating the evidence.

27. For a discussion of these problems see Barnes, *Seeing*, chap. 5.

28. Should we posit "hidden intentions" to account for the phenomenon of self-deception? Mele argues that we should introduce hidden intentions into the account only if there is data that cannot be explained without them. Mele insists that there is no such data. See Mele, *Unmasked*, chap. 3.

when he does is deliberate, and as a result his view of his evidence is partial, and therefore biased, there is no evidence that he decides to confer the blessing at that point in order to secure a biased view of the evidence.

Freer of paradox and more in tune with the episode we are studying is a nonintentionalist rendering of self-deception, positing the operation of unconscious biasing processes automatically triggered and sustained by a person's desires and beliefs.[29] Unaware of these processes, the subject would also be unaware of the beliefs and desires that prompt them. In certain kinds of stressful situations skewing one's belief-forming processes may typically be the "default response."[30] These processes can be purposive—their function may be to reduce anxiety—even though they are not intentional.

An example of such an automatic process, posited by Yaacov Trope and Akiva Liberman, is cited by Mele.[31] According to Trope and Liberman we tacitly assign a "confidence threshold" to each of the hypotheses we test; we unconsciously and unintentionally fix the weight of the evidence required for its acceptance. The lower the threshold, the sparser the evidence required to reach it. Faced with two opposing hypotheses, we can skew the weighting of the evidence for each by manipulating their confidence thresholds. This constitutes a bias toward the hypothesis for which the lower level has been fixed. It will triumph over its rival even though the evidence supporting it is weaker. As Mele points out, our desires can influence what we come to believe simply by influencing our acceptance and rejection levels. Although the manipulation of the thresholds is motivated by the self-deceiver's goals, this is not say that he is consciously or even unconsciously trying to further those goals.

The notion of a "confidence threshold" fills out the error minimization account of biasing we introduced earlier. It helps us account for Isaac's "transformation." As we noted before, what Isaac wanted most to avoid was truly believing that Jacob stood before him asking to be blessed. Isaac established the thresholds for the two hypotheses—that he is about to bless Esau and that he is about to bless Jacob—on the basis of the relative costs of believing each of the two, given his antecedent assessment as to the likelihood of each of them being true. At the time he sets the

---

29. See Barnes, *Seeing*, chap. 5. Also, Johnston, "Self-Deception," 73ff., and Mele, *Unmasked*, chap. 2.

30. Barnes, *Seeing*, 164n20.

31. Yaacov Trope and Akiva Liberman, "Social Hypothesis Testing: Cognitive and Motivational Mechanisms" in *Social Psychology: Handbook of Basic Principles*, ed. E. Higgins and A Kruglanski (New York, 1996), 239–70, quoted in Mele, *Unmasked*, 34.

thresholds so as to cause himself to believe that he is blessing Esau, he strongly suspects that if he proceeds with the blessing he will be blessing Jacob. The latter belief had taken hold in the course of his interrogations prior to his self-deception, when his confidence thresholds were evenly balanced. But in the end his goals and concerns unconsciously bias him in favor of the former hypothesis.

Does a nonintentionalist account remove all responsibility from the self-deceiver? One juncture at which it may be possible to take the unintentional self-deceiver to task is suggested by Scott-Kakures. He focuses on the self-deceiver's cognitive state after he has adopted the desired belief. [32] Given the cognitive fissure that separates his present perspective from his former one, the self-deceiver cannot explain to himself how he came to believe what he now believes. Upon reflection, he understands that without any reason for having rejected his former beliefs, he is, in a sense, still committed to them, and nevertheless he is currently holding a set of contrary beliefs. This thought should make him uneasy and tend to undermine his current beliefs. That there is an unaccounted for epistemic gap in his cognitive history should give him pause. If he is to persist in his self-deception, he must turn his eyes away from his epistemic predicament. For doing so, rather than confronting his irrationality and attempting to set matters right, the self-deceiver may be held responsible.

Given that at the time of the blessing Isaac was lodged at the far end of the fissure, did he not remember that he had started out on the other side? Could he explain to himself how he came to abandon his doubts so completely? Did he try? And if not, given the importance of what he was about to do, perhaps, from a moral point of view, he should have tried. In Isaac's defense, however, it must be pointed out that the possibility of recognizing that one is being irrational in the sense defined by Scott-Kakures arises only after the transition has been negotiated, in the self-deceiver's look over his shoulder, so to speak. In Isaac's case this possibility lasts for only a brief interval, for immediately after he finishes blessing Jacob, Esau appears and the hoax is discovered. Isaac has little time to reflect upon his newly acquired doxastic state or puzzle at how he came to it.

There is a more general responsibility, however, that a self-deceiver may bear, even in a nonintentionalist account. Although he does nothing to initiate the processes that afford him the beliefs he desires, he may be guilty of not taking sufficient steps to block or curtail those processes. Indeed, there may be circumstances in which one cannot keep oneself from yielding to the cognitive mechanisms that bring relief from anxiety. Perhaps, however, at other times one may be able to resist giving way, and

---

32. Scott-Kakures, "Self-Deception," 51.

if so, one may be blameworthy for failing to do so.

If Isaac is capable of resisting his inclination to believe as he wishes, rather than as his evidence dictates, not to do so when the issue is of such major importance might be morally questionable. If he were motivated simply by his aversion to domestic strife, we might deem him a coward. On my reading, however, Isaac's goal is more comprehensive. It is to cause the blessing to be given to the worthy recipient while inflicting minimum collateral damage to the relationships within his family. If we are sympathetic to this goal, even though we cannot credit Isaac for engaging in self-deception in order to achieve it, since, by hypothesis, he does not do so intentionally, we do not censure him for failing to foil the cognitive mechanisms that come to his aid.

The Theological Import of Isaac's Self-deception

The stealing of the blessing is part of a larger saga of the patriarchal family that culminates in the establishment of the House of Israel as God's chosen people. Abraham, the founder of the line, is chosen by God, who promises to make him the father of a great nation. The need to provide for an heir to continue Abraham's line is at the heart of the drama of Genesis. Childlessness, on the one hand, and sibling rivalry, on the other, repeatedly cast their shadows over God's promise. While the story line is moved along by the feelings and actions of the actors in the drama, the narrative, taken as a whole, testifies to God's providence and especially to his steering the course of the children of Abraham.

There is no contest for Abraham's place. In this he is unique, however. Throughout the patriarchal narratives succession is a subject of tension and strife. It standardly calls for the rejection of aspiring contenders. The contests between Isaac and Ishmael, Jacob and Esau, and Joseph and his brothers occupy center stage, but the record also includes the ascendancy of Joseph's younger son, Ephraim, over the older, Manasseh, as well as the reversal of the birth order of the twins Peretz and Zerach, born to Tamar and Judah.

God explicitly decrees the election of both Abraham and Isaac. If we skip forward to the elevation of Ephraim over Manasseh, we find Jacob making the determination as a prelude to his prophetic blessing of his sons. It is clear that God stands behind that determination as well. That the transmission of the Abrahamic line from Isaac to Jacob is embedded in this providential account argues for its similarly bearing God's imprint. Indeed, before our story begins, we hear God's prophetic announcement to Rebecca, which foreshadows the story's resolution. Perhaps this is what inclines Rebecca to favor Jacob, as a result of which she contrives to secure him the blessing. If so, the divine pronouncement not only foretells the future, but is also a link in the causal chain that shapes it.

I see God's role in the birthright story as more pervasive, however. And, as I read the Genesis narrative, it does not simply establish God's control over the unfolding events; it also inscribes a pattern of divine involvement and tracks a progression. The parameters of the latter are the roles of God and the patriarchs and, derivatively, the roles of the matriarchs. As the story proceeds there is a successive lessening of God's overt intervention. The stamp of God's authorship is unmistakable throughout the story, but over the course of the narrative it becomes more covert, more subtle. Concomitantly, as the Abrahamic legacy is transmitted from generation to generation, each succeeding patriarch enjoys a fuller understanding of the steps he is implementing and he carries out his mission more autonomously. As the patriarch comes more into his own, the divine presence recedes into the wings, and we see the role also of the matriarch declining.

Sarah, the first matriarch, defiantly stakes out a claim for her son. Her struggle on Isaac's behalf is motivated, not by a divine utterance, but by her maternal love and anxiety for Isaac's future. When Sarah demands of Abraham that he cast off Ishmael, his firstborn, the thought of sending away his son "distressed Abraham greatly" (Gen 21:12). To secure the banishment of Ishmael, thereby establishing the younger, Isaac, as Abraham's sole heir, God openly addresses Abraham, ordering him to do Sarah's bidding. God endorses Sarah's initiative. As a result, Sarah's son triumphs and God's design is realized.

In the struggle among the sons of Jacob, the last of the patriarchs, Judah gains ascendancy over his brothers by dint of the lapses of the latter and his own virtues. Joseph has a privileged position because Jacob loves him best of all his sons. Although in the background of Jacob's favoring Joseph is his love for Rachel, the role of Rachel in Joseph's rise is muted. So is the role of God.

Jacob exercises his patriarchal prerogatives into the generation of his grandchildren. In the last of the succession dramas in Genesis, Jacob's favoring of Ephraim over Manasseh, there is no maternal involvement at all. At this juncture, Jacob, whose eyes, like his father's when he conferred the blessing, are "dim with age" (Gen 48:10), and of whom it is said that "he could not see," nevertheless crosses his hands when he blesses his grandsons in order to give the greater blessing to the younger. When Joseph points out his error and tries to reposition his hands, Jacob objects, saying: "I know, my son, I know." Although Jacob cannot see his grandchildren, he knows that he has demoted the older son and he knows that the younger one will be greater. Joseph is silenced; Jacob speaks with authority.

We do not suspect that Jacob is simply acting out of personal preference or favoritism. His being the grandfather rather than the father of
Manasseh and Ephraim distances him from the emotional entanglements
that complicated the earlier patriarchs' involvement in their sons' destinies.[33] We are not told that God imparted any privileged knowledge to
Jacob, but it is clear that Jacob is already speaking here, as he will in the
forthcoming blessings, with a prophetic voice. Yet Jacob makes no mention of God. He takes full responsibility for his departure from the natural
birth order. Jacob professes to be acting out of knowledge, and he claims
the knowledge as his own.

Theologically the Isaac episode must be positioned somewhere between Abraham's heteronomous expulsion of Ishmael and Jacob's autonomous election of Ephraim. And Rebecca's role must be interpreted
against the background of Sarah's instigating Ishmael's expulsion and the
absence of any maternal involvement in Ephraim's election. Like the triumph of Isaac over Ishmael, the triumph of Jacob over Esau was brought
about by the efforts of the matriarch. However, whereas Sarah spoke out
boldly on behalf of her son and, with God's support, won her husband's
submission, Rebecca manipulates history from behind the scenes. She too
champions the divinely ordained heir in the face of her husband's opposition, but in her case the divine plan requires only that her son, not her husband, do her bidding.

What, then, is God's role in this story? My thesis is that it is not
restricted to the prophecy granted Rebecca before our story begins. God
openly decrees Abraham's choice of Isaac and grants Jacob prophetic and
explicit knowledge of the ascendancy of Ephraim. It is inconceivable that
he simply leaves Isaac "in the dark."

Isaac's Self-deception and Divine Revelation

Prior to his conferring the blessing upon Jacob, I have argued, Isaac
knows or strongly suspects both that the son he is about to bless is Jacob
and that Jacob is the one destined to receive the blessing. He suspects that
it is Jacob because he repeatedly hears Jacob's voice. What makes him
think that Jacob rather than Esau is the one who should receive the blessing, however? Earlier I pointed to Isaac's dismay at Esau's taking Hittite
wives as a factor that might undermine his loyalty to Esau. I now want to
bolster my argument by speculating that perhaps Isaac's distress at Esau's
marital choices was not simply a contingent emotional reaction, but that
his consternation was a divinely ordained state. As God did to Isaac's

---

33. See Devora Steinmetz, *From Father to Son: Kinship, Conflict and Continuity in
Genesis* (Louisville, Ky., 1991), 123ff.

father before him and as he would do to his son after him, God revealed to Isaac the destinies of his children.

We think of divine revelation most commonly as an immediate communication, such as God's command to Abraham to heed Sarah's bidding. Such revelation is assertoric, open and explicit. Jacob knows that Ephraim will be greater than Manasseh, however, although God never tells him as much. Rather, God directly plants the knowledge in Jacob's consciousness. That is the way we picture much of prophetic knowledge. God's revelation to Isaac is not by means of assertion, however, nor does he directly introduce into Isaac's consciousness knowledge of which of his sons should receive the blessing.

Philosophers of religion offer us accounts of revelation according to which truths may be disclosed in indirect ways. Nicholas Wolterstorff sees the essence of revelation to be the dispelling of ignorance. For revelation to occur, however, according to Wolterstorff, ignorance need not be actually dispelled. It is enough that "something is done which *would* dispel ignorance if attention and interpretative skills were adequate."[34] An example of how this may happen is provided by George Mavrodes, who suggests that God may "program" someone or cause him to have a natural cognitive disposition that is activated or triggered by certain stimuli.[35] These stimuli take the form of data or evidence for a particular conclusion. The person responding to the stimuli may not merely draw the conclusions that are logically called for by the data, but may go beyond the information contained in the stimuli. This might count as an instance of divine revelation, God having endowed the recipient with the relevant cognitive disposition, and perhaps also provided for the requisite stimuli, in order to transmit a particular truth.

In our story Esau's taking foreign wives causes Isaac and Rebecca grave displeasure.[36] In doing this Esau does not violate any explicit divine injunction. We do not hear Isaac and Rebecca reflecting on the significance of Esau's marital offenses. Their reaction is visceral rather than cerebral. How do they come to feel so deeply about this? Central to Isaac's identity is that he is the son of Sarah, whose country of birth is the same as that of Abraham, and who, some say, was Abraham's half sister. He secures his status as Abraham's heir by prevailing over Ishmael, whose mother is

---

34. Nicholas Wolterstorff, *Divine Discourse* (Cambridge, 1995), 23.

35. George Mavrodes, *Revelation in Religious Belief* (Philadelphia, 1988), chap. 2. Mavrodes dubs this the "causation model" of revelation and identifies it as the Calvin-Wolterstorff view, 63ff.

36. I am not arguing, however, that God engineered Esau's marriages.

Egyptian. Isaac's father charges his servant to travel to the land of his birth to find him a wife. The servant is enjoined, above all, not to bring back a Canaanite woman. In the city of Nahor, when he discovers that the young girl he has encountered is from Abraham's family, the servant thanks God for the special favor he has awarded his master.[37] In his eyes and in those of Rebecca's family, the match was made in heaven.

Upon being presented with his bride, Isaac takes her into his mother's tent and is comforted for her loss. Both Rebecca and Isaac see in their union the extension of the earlier generation, from whom they are inheriting their divine calling. It is no wonder, then, that they see Esau's marital choices as a breach of their family ethos. It negates the meaning of their marriage and the raison d'être of their life together: that Abraham's line be perpetuated to carry forth God's covenant. For this purpose, Abraham's lineage must remain pure, unalloyed by the offspring of the strange and idolatrous nations from whom Abraham's children are singled out. It is not an incidental feature of the story that, after the blessing, the ruse to which Rebecca resorts for removing Jacob from Esau's vengeful reach is to send Jacob back to her ancestral home so that he not take a wife from the daughters of Canaan. Nor is it accidental that Esau, at the conclusion of the present episode, once again proves his ineptitude by taking a wife from the daughters of Ishmael in the hopes of appeasing his parents.

With Mavrodes' model of indirect revelation it becomes possible to integrate Isaac's blessing of Jacob more tightly into the patriarchal saga. We may assume that it is part of God's design that the overwhelming and abiding importance of endogamous alliances be impressed upon Isaac's soul. We may speculate as to whether God achieved this by shaping Isaac's sensibilities or whether God let Isaac be naturally educated under the tutelage of Abraham and Sarah. To the extent that Isaac is "programmed" to be pained by the threat of his line being contaminated, however, the effect of Esau's taking foreign wives is, ultimately, to dispel his ignorance about Esau's true nature, to cause Isaac to know which of his sons is worthy of the blessing.

Note that throughout this episode there is no suggestion that Isaac's affection for Esau has waned. God does not interfere with Isaac's love for his son; he allows Isaac's natural emotions to be pitted against his Abrahamic commitments. Whereas Abraham's love for Ishmael brought him up against God's clear-cut directive to send him off, Isaac subordinates his

---

37. Note that Rebecca's grandfather, Nahor, is also the uncle of her grandmother, Milkah. Thus, she is both Abraham's great-niece, as she is the granddaughter of Nahor, Abraham's brother, and also his great-great-niece, as she is the great-granddaughter of Haran, Abraham's other brother.

love for his firstborn to an inner call, which, I am suggesting, also emanated, implicitly, from God. Abraham is ordered to submit; Isaac is left to come around on his own. Depicting Isaac as choosing his successor with the help of divine revelation places him more squarely in the patriarchal tradition. Having internalized God's directive as Abraham had not, but having implemented it unawares—in contrast to Jacob, who knew exactly what he was doing—Isaac occupies the transitional position marked out for him in the patriarchal saga.

On my reading, Isaac is not simply a vessel through which the blessing is transmitted. The authority for the succession remains vested in him, and the choice is made, ultimately, according to his own lights. The integrity of the Abrahamic line is preserved. Although Jacob wrested the blessing by deceit, his place in the Abrahamic succession is affirmed. Not because of Isaac's blindness does he receive his blessing, but because of Isaac's vision.[38]

---

38. I would like to thank the Philosophy Department of Yale University for its hospitality during my sabbatical stay there. I would also like to thank Josh Berman, Yehuda Gelman, and George Mavrodes for reading and providing helpful comments on earlier versions of this paper. Richard Swinburne and Howard Wettstein were kind enough to discuss some aspects of my interpretation with me, and their suggestions enriched my work. Especially do I want to thank Nicholas Wolterstorff for the many delightful conversations we had about the patriarchs and matriarchs and for his encouragement for my project.

GOD'S PROJECT

Jerome M. Segal
University of Maryland

IN THE FOURTH CENTURY BCE, the Greek philosopher Epicurus wrote that "the blessed and immortal nature knows no trouble itself nor causes trouble to any other, so that it is never constrained by anger or favor." God is neither moved nor moves in relation to the affairs of humankind. Such a conception of God, as a creative power behind the world, but not engaged within it, has had numerous adherents during the last two thousand years. But a God of that sort bears no relationship to the God we find in the biblical narrative.

Above all else, God in the Hebrew Bible is emotional. Indeed, he is hyper-emotional in relation to humankind; so much so, as we have seen with the story of the Flood, that he himself recognizes a need to control his emotions—thus he binds himself with a promise to never again destroy the world with a flood, and he places the rainbow in the sky to remind himself of this commitment.

The only time that God is remotely calm is in the very beginning of Genesis, before he has fully engaged with humankind. With utter majesty he creates the heavens and the earth. He separates light from dark, and the land from the sea. He creates the plants and the animals and then humankind. At each step along the way, we are told that God saw that what he had created was good. In the end, "God saw all that he had made, and found it very good."

Even in this calm, we have a basic pattern of interaction. Something has been created and is there to be seen. God sees it, and he reacts to it. At this early stage, he is pleased, very pleased. These are the first emotions, as

A shorter version of this paper appears as chapter 3 in *Joseph's Bones: Understanding the Struggle Between God and Mankind in the Bible Story* (Riverhead, 2007).

God is enlivened by his own project. Thus, we are immediately introduced to a God who feels things. And here at the very beginning, just
before God creates humankind, he announces his intention: "I will make
man in my image, after my likeness." And then the narrator tells us that he
did so: "And God created man in his image, in the image of God he created him; male and female he created them."

Never again will God possess the tranquility that is exhibited in these
first pages. He is about to become an emotional whirlwind. But if the God
of the Bible is a god of surging emotions, what are they about? And why is
God so engaged in the affairs of humankind? What is the meaning for him
of this project? And why does he want a being in his image?

These are fundamental questions, and no literary interpretation of the
Bible story can be viewed as adequate unless it provides answers to them.
The importance of answering these questions is so obvious that it should
hardly need to be stated. After all, God is the central character in the story;
how is it possible to understand the story unless we understand his motivation?

There is always the default option that God is ultimately a mystery to
humankind, that we are not capable of fathoming his purposes. Even in
literature, this is not impossible. One could construct a story in which the
central character makes no sense at all. He would not fall into patterns that
suggest motivation, and there would be no clues and certainly no direct
explanation by the character of his own purpose. While we can imagine
such a story, it would be distinctly unlike the Bible. In the Bible, we are
given clues; we can find patterns and critical events that enable us to penetrate God's purposes and understand his intensity; and, on occasion,
God provides a specific explanation of why he has acted as he has. It is not
just that God is portrayed anthropomorphically in the Bible—as if he has
human traits—he is portrayed as a very specific person. Viewed in relation to other works of literature, the Bible gives us more material to understand his character than we often find. Our task as readers is to pull this
together into an overriding construct that makes the best sense of it all,
makes the deepest sense out of the broadest possible features of the story.

The Creation of Humanity

The most important clues as to the nature of God's project come from
a passage I have already considered, the Garden of Eden episode. Here
are the elements:

1. Morality is portrayed as objective, being the subject of a higher
    form of knowledge.
2. The knowledge that comes from eating the forbidden fruit is not
    moral wisdom but rather the capacity to use moral categories.

3. God most definitely does not want humanity to be possessed of both moral knowledge and immortality.

4. In saying "Now that the man has become like one of us, knowing good and bad, what if he should stretch out his hand and take also from the tree of life and eat, and live forever!" God makes clear that with the gap between humankind and the divine beings now considerably narrowed, he does not want to see it closed. Maintaining a distinct realm of advanced humanity—beings with moral categories, but without immortality—is central to God's purpose.

In reflecting on the garden scene we might ponder why, if God did not want humankind to have moral knowledge, he placed the tree of such knowledge in the garden in the first place? Or to put it slightly differently, why did he create humankind as beings with the potential to use moral categories, and why did he make Eve someone who would be motivated to eat the fruit because she perceived it as a source of wisdom?

A standard answer is that God has created humankind as free to choose, that while God did not want humankind to choose to violate his first command, this choice had to be possible for that freedom to be real. Some go further and say that in so disobeying God, humankind revealed its propensity for evil (or disobedience) and thereby became responsible for what befell it (mortality).

In part this seems to me sound. God has created humankind as free to obey or disobey his commands. To create humankind with this ability (we can call it freedom) was indeed God's choice, and an essential part of his project. This, however, leads to another question: Why does God want the existence of a free being?[1] In creating Adam and Eve, God has created a unique form of animal, yet still an animal. But he wants something beyond this. He wants humanity—that distinct mix: humankind in possession of moral categories but without immortality. Moreover, he wants humankind to live out its terrible fatedness, its knowledge of its ultimate death, in full awareness that it brought this on itself through disobedience to God. Thus, mortal humans with moral categories are not part of the original creation. They are the result of the interaction between human-

---

1. Before expanding on this, let me note that I believe the "standard answer" may err in saying that God did not want humankind to eat of the tree of knowledge of good and evil. Another possible reading is that God wants humankind both to choose and to choose to disobey, thus becoming morally conscious. Indeed, one can go further and say that by placing the two trees in the garden and by making the tree of knowledge alluring, perhaps even by putting the snake in the garden, God established an elaborate setup.

kind and God, and they are made aware that they have brought mortality upon themselves. In sum, God wants humankind to be free, to be morally conscious, to be mortal, and to recognize itself as both responsible for its own fate yet dependent upon God. We will understand much about God and his project if we can understand why he wants this kind of being to exist.

Babel

The Tower of Babel story is strikingly brief, consisting of only ten sentences. Yet it serves as a pivotal point in the overall narrative. It comes just after the story of the Flood, and just before the opening of the long story of Abraham. Structurally, it moves God's attention and that of the reader from humankind as a whole to a single family, that of Abraham. And from Abraham will emerge his grandson Jacob, also known as Israel, thus the Israelites—the single people whose history is the focal point of the Hebrew Bible.

A central feature of the Babel story is God's creation of distinct peoples out of a previously undifferentiated humankind. God does this by creating different languages "so that they shall not understand one another's speech." We are told, "That is why it is called Babel, because there the Lord confounded the speech of the whole earth; and from there the Lord scattered them over the face of the whole earth" (Gen 11:9).

It should be emphasized that God's intent is not merely to create diversity or a multiplicity of languages and cultures. This is not about God's love for his creatures and his delight in the multitude of different patterns that human life can take. One could imagine such a story. One could imagine a god delighted by his own creatures, fascinated by their comings and goings. We can imagine that such a god would view each culture as a unique treasure and a unique source of interest and amazement. He might say, "Why restrict the mode of being human to one cultural form, when one can have hundreds, each with its own inherent value!"

While we can imagine such a story, this, of course, is not what we are told in the Babel story. Rather we are told that God "confounded their speech there, so that they shall not understand one another's speech." And twice we are told that he "scattered" humankind. Thus, God wants humankind to be not only diverse, but to be foreign and incomprehensible to one another. He wants an absence of understanding, and, I would argue, misunderstanding and distrust. Indeed, we can see the Babel story as suggesting that God wants there to be enmity and even war between these varied nations.

That this is no overinterpretation is supported by the opening of the Abraham story that immediately follows Babel. In the story's second verse

God makes a promise to Abraham that can be read with an eye to how the covenant is premised upon the dispersion and enmity between nations, set in motion at Babel (Babylon). God covenants with Abraham:

> I will make of you a great nation,
> And I will bless you;
> I will make your name great,
> And you shall be a blessing:
> I will bless those who bless you,
> And curse him that curses you;
> All the families of the earth
> Shall bless themselves by you. (Gen 12:2–3)

This structuring of humanity into nations, some greater than others, some blessed and some cursed, this is the basis for the covenant with the Israelites, and it presupposes the diversity and enmity initiated at Babel. Without a context in which there is a hierarchy of nations and a fierce competition among them, this commitment to Abraham, and through him to the Israelites, would lack both meaning and value. Thus, it is through the actions at Babel that God makes himself instrumentally important to the future Israelites. He is setting the stage for what he will become: a god of war.

More generally, we can say that God, through the imposition of human mortality, has made humankind vulnerable, and now through the creation of nations that cannot comprehend each other, he has situated humankind into groups that threaten and fear each other. Within this newly structured human condition, in which we are by birth part of this grouping and foreign to that one, he has made himself indispensable.

The motivational question remains. If this is a correct description of what God has done at Babel, why has he done so? Broadly speaking, there are three types of answers. The first is that he does it for his own amusement. The second is that he acts out of some purpose, itself rooted in some need. And third, that his motivation and plan are beyond our comprehension. This last, though most in tune with religious readings, is a default option. Moreover, it is undermined by the text itself. In the Babel story we are given an account of what it was that triggered God's decision to confound humankind's speech and to scatter humankind across the earth:

> All the earth had the same language and the same words.... And they said, "Come, let us build us a city, and a tower with its top in the sky, to make a name for ourselves; else we shall be scattered all over the world." The Lord came down to look at the city and tower that man had built, and the Lord said, "If, as one people with one language for all, this is how they have begun to act, then nothing that they propose to do will be out of their reach." (Gen 11:1–6)

Immediately upon saying this, God "confounded the speech of the whole earth." The passage above gives us some degree of comprehension of God's action. It is not done out of amusement. It is not done out of malevolence. Nor is it done as punishment for some violation of a commandment. It is done out of some anxiety, the exact nature of which has yet to be uncovered. When God says, "If ... this is how they have begun to act," we have the same strange note in his voice that we heard when he expelled Adam and Eve from the garden saying, "Now that humankind has become like one of us ... what if he should stretch out his hand and take also from the tree of life...." In both cases there is a note of fear, and it is a fear of what the next step might be. In Babel the fear is that "nothing that they propose to do will be out of their reach."

At Babel we are told that the humans said to one another, "Come let us make bricks and burn them hard." And we are told that "brick served them as stone, and bitumen served them as mortar." With this as their base they were able to build their city and their tower. What we are given here is a twofold picture. First, there is the introduction and discovery of technology. Very early on, human beings discover how to fashion bricks and make them hard, as hard a stone—a man-made stone that substitutes for God's creation (natural stone). Further, they discover how to use the minerals of the earth to connect those bricks, one to another, into walls and structures. Secondly, there is cooperation. Humankind, with "the same language and the same words," has found it possible to work together for a common purpose, with a common idea, in this case "to make a name for ourselves, else we shall be scattered all over the world." Humankind has an awareness of danger, senses the importance of being unified, and successfully carries out a breakthrough project of technological and social accomplishment.

God takes note, and experiences the power it represents. He projects it forward, saying that if this is what they can do at this early stage, then ultimately nothing "will be out of their reach." While this might be an exaggerated implication, it is not unlike what many believed three centuries ago, when scientific and technological discoveries began to unveil the secrets of nature. There are many today who still believe something of this sort, that if humankind does not blow itself up first, through science, ultimately we will be able to conquer every constraint.

In the Babel story God expresses a fear of a growing, ever-expanding human power and capability, a fear of infinite human reach. He envisions that humans will develop powers that would make them godlike, able to achieve whatever they desire. In the aftermath of the Flood, that world-traumatic demonstration of human mortality, the immediate concern of humankind is its vulnerability, and if one thinks in terms of drowning, the

construction of an edifice that reaches to the heavens is, at least in symbolic terms, understandable.

   On a more fundamental level, God appears to think that the range of
human ambition extends to a desire to overcome mortality itself. It is this
unstated, but perhaps not unthought, possibility that humankind might
find a way to overcome death that specifically links God's decision to
expel humankind from the garden and God's decision to confound
human speech. At bottom the fear is the same, that humankind, now that
it has gained the moral categories and "become like one of us," shall find a
way to take from the tree of life and with the aid of future technologies
further close the gap between God and humankind.

   One cautionary note: in speaking of God's fear of an all-powerful
humanity, one must be crystal clear that what is involved here is not a
physical fear. There is nothing in the text to suggest that humankind could
ever endanger God in a direct physical (if one can use that word) contest.
There is no reason to imagine that when God says that nothing would be
beyond the reach of humankind, he believes that humankind might some-
day develop powers that are more powerful than his own—a God who
can create the universe in six days could instantaneously snuff out all
human life and all human technologies, no matter how advanced.

   This fact of the story, that in a straightforward sense God cannot be
endangered by humanity, helps to define and expand the puzzle. How
can a God who cannot be endangered somehow be in danger? What is
there to be afraid of? What is at stake for God? What negative outcome
could he possibly suffer at the hands of a god-like humankind?

Pharaoh's Heart

   The fullest statement of God's project emerges in the book of Exodus.
The setting is the confrontation between Moses and Pharaoh. The reader
has been told in advance that extracting the Israelites from the power of
Pharaoh will not be easy. But God has made clear to Moses that this will
be done. At the scene of the burning bush, God tells Moses:

> I have marked well the plight of my people in Egypt and have heeded their
> outcry because of their taskmasters; yes, I am mindful of their sufferings.
> I have come down to rescue them from the Egyptians and to bring them
> out of that land to a good and spacious land, a land flowing with milk and
> honey ... I will send you to Pharaoh, and you shall free my people, the
> Israelites from Egypt. (Exod 3:7–10)

   Moses, of course, does not have to be told that it will not suffice to
merely demand the freedom of the Israelites. And God is explicit on this
point, saying, "I know that the king of Egypt will not let you go except by

force. So I will stretch out my hand and smite Egypt with various wonders that I will work upon them; after that he shall let you go." (Exod 3:19–20)

In Moses's first encounter with Pharaoh things go as might be expected. Moses chooses not to speak in his own name, but rather to quote to Pharaoh the words of God. He tells Pharaoh, "Thus says the Lord [Yahweh], the God of Israel: Let my people go...." Here I should note that Pharaoh is not being asked to free the Israelites, but only to let them go for a few days "that they may celebrate a festival for me in the wilderness." Moses asks Pharaoh for permission for the Israelites to go a distance of three days into the wilderness to perform a sacrifice. Yet even this modest request is turned down. Pharaoh has never heard of this god, and he is not impressed. He says, "Who is Yahweh that I should listen to him and let Israel go? I know nothing of Yahweh...." (Exod 5:2)[2]

Not only does Pharaoh not permit the Israelites to depart so they may make their sacrifice, he makes it more difficult for them to fulfill their quotas of bricks. Whereas previously Pharaoh's agents provided the Israelites with the straw that goes into the mud bricks, they are now told to gather it themselves. As a result they are unable to meet their quotas and the Israelite foremen are beaten by the Egyptians. In turn the foremen criticize Moses for "making us objectionable to the Pharaoh." And Moses, with a critical voice, questions God, saying:

> O Lord, why did you bring harm upon this people? Why did you send me? Ever since I came to Pharaoh to speak in your name, it has gone worse with this people; yet you have not delivered your people at all. (Exod 5:22–23)

God responds, "You shall soon see what I will do to Pharaoh." God then makes clear that it is no accident that the Israelites have not been quickly liberated. He tells Moses that he will make him "an oracle to Pharaoh," using his brother Aaron as his spokesman. They are to repeat to Pharaoh all that God will instruct Moses to say. Yet this will be of no avail, for we now learn that God will prevent Pharaoh from being responsive. God tells Moses:

> But I will harden Pharaoh's heart, that I may multiply my signs and marvels in the land of Egypt. When Pharaoh does not heed you, I will lay my hand upon Egypt and deliver my people the Israelites, from the land of Egypt with extraordinary chastisements. And the Egyptians shall know

---

2. Here I am quoting from *The Jerusalem Bible*, which uses the name Yahweh rather than substituting for God's name the term "the Lord." I find the story to be more comprehensible when Pharaoh attributes no particular status to Yahweh.

that I am the Lord, when I stretch out my hand over Egypt and bring out
the Israelites from their midst. (Exod 7:3–5)

The text does not tell us anything about Moses's reaction to this revelation. Perhaps it does not seem strange to him that God would deliberately harden Pharaoh's heart so that God would have this opportunity to
work his "marvels." On the other hand, perhaps Moses finds this astonishing. We are not told: God does not explain, and Moses does not ask. We
are told only: "the Egyptians shall know that I am the Lord [Yahweh]."
Whatever Moses's response, the reader might well wonder why it is
important to God to be able to work these terrible deeds and why it is
important that the Egyptians should come to know of God's power.

At this point in the story, something of a contextual explanation is
provided. Previously, when Moses quoted to Pharaoh the words of Yahweh, Pharaoh, as we have seen, responded contemptuously, saying,
"Who is this Yahweh … I know nothing of Yahweh." Now God will
ensure that Pharaoh will know indeed. The reader can here understand
the hardening of Pharaoh's heart as God's angry response to Pharaoh's
dismissiveness, and the "chastisements" God intends will ensure that in
the future other pharaohs will sit up and take notice upon hearing the
name Yahweh.

The story then progresses through a series of plagues that God inflicts
upon the Egyptians: blood, frogs, animal plague, boils, and so forth. Having sat through many a Passover seder, the Jewish reader may be somewhat inured to these calamities, but the text brings them to life. Egypt is a
country that lives by virtue of the Nile; water is everything. We are told
that the water was turned to blood, and the fish died, and the water was so
foul smelling that it could not be drunk. Frogs are then brought upon the
Egyptians. Not just a few, not just many, but a choking number. Frogs
filled not only the river, they were in the palace, in the royal bedroom, in
the pharaoh's bed, in the ovens, in the food.

What emerges is a symbolic contest between Yahweh and the sorcerers of Pharaoh, each causing amazing events. Pharaoh's men, however, do
not protect Egypt from the plagues brought through Moses. Nor do they
inflict parallel harm upon the Israelites. Rather, they demonstrate their
powers only by duplicating the plagues themselves. They show that they
too can turn water to blood and that they too can make frogs swarm all
over Egypt. This self-destruction of Egypt at the hands of Pharaoh's own
magicians is almost humorous. And while this duplication of plagues cannot be good for Egypt, Pharaoh and his advisers apparently believe that
responding to the challenge of a foreign god takes precedence. As amazing as the powers of Pharaoh's advisers are, turning water to blood and
summoning frogs is the outer edge of what the Egyptian magicians can

do. When Yahweh, through Moses, has man and beast attacked by lice, the Egyptian magicians fail in their attempt to duplicate the phenomenon. Thus the greater power of Yahweh is demonstrated.

Pharaoh, as one might expect, is not unmoved by these events. They are not mere annoyances but dangers that threaten the life of his kingdom. In response to the frogs, even though his magicians could also bring frogs, he agrees to let the Israelites go and do their sacrifices. Yet when the frogs are gone (at Pharaoh's request Moses pleads with God to remove them), Pharaoh refuses to keep his promise. As a result, more, and worse, plagues follow, but none is effective in freeing the Israelites. In one plague, all the livestock of Egypt are killed, yet we are told, "Pharaoh's heart hardened, and he would not let the people go." All this would seem impossibly foolish were it not for the fact that we have already been told that God would harden Pharaoh's heart, and, indeed, as the plagues progress we are told again that "the Lord stiffened the heart of Pharaoh, and he would not heed them." Thus it is underscored throughout the encounter that God is orchestrating these events.

Previously, God had explained to Moses that the purpose of hardening Pharaoh's heart was to provide God with the opportunity to demonstrate to the Egyptians his vast powers. But there is more to it than that, and in a remarkable passage God provides to Moses a fuller account of the nature of his project:

> Then the Lord said to Moses, "Go to Pharaoh. For I have hardened his heart and the hearts of his courtiers, in order that I may display these my signs among them, and that you may recount in the hearing of your sons' sons how I made a mockery of the Egyptians and how I displayed my signs among them—in order that you may know that I am the Lord. (Exod 10:1–2)

In the entire Bible, this passage is the most extensive revelation of God's motivation. It is important to remember that the events that are being explained here are, within the text, historical occurrences of a major order—nothing less than the step-by-step destruction of Egypt, the greatest power of its day.

The logic of God's motivation is complex:

1. He hardens Pharaoh's heart, in order that:
2. He may "display his signs among them," in order that:
3. The Israelites may recount among themselves, through the generations, this very story, in order that:
4. The Israelites, through the generations, may know "that I am the Lord" [in more direct translations, "that I am Yahweh"].

We are being told that history is pedagogy. It happens the way it happens, because it is God's way of teaching his chosen people. The vehicle for this teaching, except for the first generation, which experiences it directly, is the telling of this history. And the purpose of this telling, and thus of the events themselves, is that the future generations shall attain a certain kind of knowledge: "that I am Yahweh."

The Bible, of course, is itself the telling of the events in question. It follows then that, according to the Bible, when we today read of these events in the Bible (or hear a reading), this latter-day hearing in the twenty-first century is the reason why these events occurred several thousand years ago. And if we are thus brought to the knowledge referred to in the phrase "know that I am Yahweh," then God's purpose of thousands of years ago is fulfilled in the effect the Bible story has upon us. According to the story, shaping our reaction to the Bible as modern-day readers is the purpose behind the events that we are reading about; we are thus drawn into a direct role within the story. We, the off-stage readers, are central factors in the story itself. Were there no readers of the Bible story, the story itself would not be credible, for it posits the continued existence of its audience. What is beyond amazing is that a several-thousand-year-old story, which posits future readers as the explanation both for the events it portrays and for its existence as the portrayal of those events, should turn out to be the most widely and continuously read story in all history.

This is an extraordinary conception, both of literature and of history. It tells us that history (understood as the retelling of the past) is not merely a factual account of the past, but the intended cause of the past. Events occur so that there might be the retelling. In the Bible God does not explicitly say, "The Bible is my instrument"; yet the Bible is that telling of the story that God wants to be continually told. Thus the Bible self-referentially presents itself as the vehicle through which God's purpose, that we know that he is Yahweh, is to be achieved.

Two questions are in order. First, what exactly is this knowledge that God wants his people to have, this knowledge that "I am Yahweh"? And secondly, why is it so vital to God that the Israelites have this knowledge—what is the deeper motivation?

Knowing that "I Am Yahweh"

Today neither Christians nor Jews make substantial use of the term "Yahweh." It has a somewhat foreign sound. Yet in the Hebrew Bible, in ancient and modern Torah scrolls, and presumably in the text that both the ancient rabbis and Jesus read, the name of God is spelled out with four Hebrew characters that in the English alphabet are rendered as YHWH. When vowels, which are lacking in Hebrew, are added, this is typically rendered: Yahweh. In the Jewish tradition, when the Bible is read aloud, the reader does not pronounce this name, but rather substitutes the term

"Adonai," which itself translates as "the Lord." In some English translations, both Jewish and non-Jewish, this shift is also made in the written
text. Thus in some translations, the printed English text uses the phrase
"the Lord" rather than the term or name YHWH (which matches the
Hebrew) or Yahweh or even Jehovah.[3]

In the biblical text, in God's own words, he says he is acting so that
the Israelites may "know that I am Yahweh." Here, it will not do to substitute "the Lord" for Yahweh. Whatever is meant by "knowing that I am
Yahweh," it does not seem to be the same thing as "knowing that I am the
Lord." When a character says, "I am the Lord," this sounds very much like
saying, "I am God." By contrast, the term "Yahweh" functions as a name.
This makes a difference. Thus, in this critical passage, when we read God
saying that he wants humankind to know that "I am the Lord," we are led
to think either that God is asserting his status, saying that he, not others
(e.g., the gods of Egypt), is the Lord, or alternatively, we may think that
God is stating his desire that humankind know that God exists, that
humankind "believe in God." But if we shift to "I am Yahweh," then
God's effort to have the Israelites know that he is Yahweh is harder to
grasp.

While the term "Yahweh" does function as a name, something more is
involved. Of course, the character in the Bible who says "I am Yahweh" is
Yahweh; he has told us that this is his name and there is no reason not to
believe him. There is no context to assume possible deception or pretense
(that he is really someone else, yet goes around pretending to be Yahweh).
This, however, makes clear that when God says that he wants humankind,
or the Israelites, to know that he is Yahweh, he is not saying that he wants
them to know that he is named Yahweh. They already know that.

The perplexing question, however, is: What beyond this does he want
them to know? One possible answer is that we are on the wrong track
when we say that God wants the Israelites to know that he is Yahweh. Perhaps what he wants is for them to "know Yahweh," that is, to be familiar
with Yahweh, to have Yahweh known to them, rather than to know any
specific thing about Yahweh. This seems a promising avenue to consider,
but it is incomplete. The Israelites and the Egyptians could have become
"familiar" with Yahweh through any of a variety of experiences. It is clear

3. This is the case in the Jewish Publication Society translation, which I have
relied upon predominantly. Often enough this works quite well for understanding the narrative, but not always; on occasion, when it helps in grasping
the story, I have quoted from other translations that retain the term "Yahweh."

from the text, however, that God thinks of himself in a certain way and that for him, to know Yahweh involves more that vague familiarity.

Knowing Yahweh among the Gods?

Some of this is less mind bending if we think in terms of multiple gods. Imagine a story, be it Greek or Hindu or from some other polytheistic tradition, in which there are many different characters, all of whom are gods. Within that imagined story, there are several understandable interpretations of what it would be for one of these gods to assert himself before a specific population and say to them, "You shall know Yahweh!" This would not be a demand that they believe in God, nor a demand that the population be merely familiar with the god Yahweh. Rather, in the context of a specific story, this might be understood to mean (1) that the population was to adopt this god, and not others, as its special deity, or (2) that the population react to him in a certain way, for instance, that they be terrified of him. Thus, we can envision a god saying something of this sort just as he sets out to so thoroughly traumatize a population that they and their descendants will never be without a powerful ongoing consciousness of the presence of Yahweh, having him more fully in mind than other gods.

Can we understand the biblical Yahweh in these ways, as asserting himself in relation to other gods? This leads to a very fundamental question about the biblical text. Is the Bible story itself a story of one god among many? This may sound a strange question because we so thoroughly identify Judaism and Christianity with monotheism. Yet the strangeness of the question emerges not from the biblical text, but from our inability to read the text freely, to read it on its face, rather than through the lens of what we believe it must say. Indeed, this specific orientation, reading the text on the assumption that it posits a monotheistic world, is probably the most difficult to relinquish of all our background assumptions about the Bible.

When we let ourselves read the Bible freely, however, no question is more natural than whether there are one or many gods in the world of the biblical narrative.

Biblical scholars have given particular attention to the fact that the Bible contains different names for God. This feature of the Hebrew text, that in some passages the name Yahweh is used and in other passages Elohim is used, was central to their conclusion that the biblical text was edited from several different documents. Scholars have sought to separate out these various texts, identifying, with some disagreement, which passages came from the J text (the Yahweh text) and which from the E text.

When I say that it is most natural to wonder whether the biblical narrative takes place in a universe of one or of many gods, this has nothing to do with these matters of the multiplicity of God's names. Even if the J and E documents were written hundreds of years apart, and even if historically Yahweh and Elohim were, at one point, different deities, this has no bearing on the question at hand. In the Bible story there is no doubt that they are one. The question is whether or not, within the story, other gods are taken to exist, not just by the Israelites or the Egyptians, but as part of the background "reality" posited in the story.

The naturalness of the question "One god or many?" comes from an entirely different factor, one that stares us in the face: the biblical narrative is completely ambiguous about this matter. On the one hand, it can be argued that many gods are posited:

1. The Bible nowhere has God clearly assert, I am the only god that exists.[4]
2. There is no commandment that makes it a crime to assert that other gods exist; the crime is always to worship them.
3. The Ten Commandments open with "I am Yahweh your God who brought you out of the land of Egypt, out of the house of slavery. You shall have no gods except me." It does not say, "There are no other gods than me."
4. When God instructs Moses to go to Pharaoh, he says to tell him, "Yahweh the God of the Hebrews, has sent me...." Thus, God himself speaks in a way that suggests that he is one god among many.

In short, the text is such that it is totally natural to conclude that other gods exist. If this is the belief of God, as well as the belief of the human characters, and if the narrator never contradicts this belief, then one can reasonably conclude that the narrative space is one in which other gods do exist. On the other hand, one can reasonably argue that this is jumping to a conclusion that is not warranted:

1. Most importantly, no other god ever appears in the text; if they exist, they are always off stage.
2. No events ever occur that are unambiguously attributed to these other gods. Even when Yahweh, through Moses, duels with Pharaoh's sorcerers and when they succeed in also turning water into

---

4. In Deuteronomy 32 is a poem in which God asserts "There is no God beside me," but in the context of the poem as whole, this remains ambiguous.

blood and summoning frogs, these events are attributed to the magicians themselves, not to their gods.

3. God, in the Bible, is presented as having created all that exists. Though there are other divine beings, presumably angels, and though no account of their creation is ever given, the scope of God's creative power is so vast that it is hard to understand what powers could be left over for other gods to exercise.

The beliefs of the biblical humans that there are other gods, therefore, may be just that, beliefs not "facts." God, for whatever reason, does not choose to disabuse them of these beliefs. He may want the Israelites to take him as their god within a context in which they believe, falsely, that there are other gods.

Such arguments, on both sides, could be strengthened were the argument extended. The point, however, is that the reasoning is strong on both sides. Clearly, the biblical narrative leaves open the question of whether or not there are other gods. Moreover, this must be seen as a deliberate decision by the author, because it would have been remarkably simple to resolve the matter, either by having another god appear or by having the narrator explain that there was only one God, with God explicitly teaching the same thing. None of these potentially decisive actions was taken. Instead, the matter was left open, at least until Moses' last address to the Israelites in Deuteronomy. In the main, we are not supposed to know for sure whether there are other gods or not. We are allowed to read the story with one belief or the other, so long as we recognize that the two understandings are not resolved.

Though the alternative choice is possible, I have decided to approach the story as one in which there is only one god, Yahweh. Given that the text is ambiguous on these matters, this aspect of my interpretation doesn't rest on the text itself, but on methodological grounds.

Suppose we read the Bible story as one in which there are multiple gods. This has the virtue of suggesting a coherent account of God's motivation. If God is one among many, then we can assimilate his actions within a larger picture of competition between the gods. Exactly what that competition is about we can't say with certainty, but it can be fit into the patterns of human competitions over status, power, and prestige. From this perspective, what God really cares about is his place among the gods themselves. His engagement with humankind and with the Israelites is an arena within which he seeks to triumph in his god-to-god relations. For instance, he seeks to have his people triumph over the peoples of other gods. Further, he seeks to demonstrate the commitment to him of his own people, that they will be faithful to him and to him alone. Of course, there is no direct textual evidence for this competition among the gods, but if we accept that there are other gods, then such hypotheses are not far-fetched and they do enable us to understand why God is passionate about the Israelites.

Indeed, in the Bible, something similar to this is detailed in the book of Job, where the unjust afflictions God bestows upon Job are explicitly explained as God's response to a challenge that Satan makes to him. Here Satan is not another god, but a rather powerful divine being. This may seem, to some, to be no difference at all; among the Greek gods, some were more powerful than others. And Satan is no mere servant of God's will. God's relationship to Satan emerges as of sufficient importance to God, that it motivates him toward injustice to Job. If such independent, powerful, immortal divine beings exist, it is no great stretch to simply posit other gods, to envision the entire narrative within some such god-to-god relations.

The problem with all this is not that it is speculative (which it is, but not unreasonably so) but that it gives us such a disappointing book. It diminishes everything. If God is primarily competing among the pantheon of gods, how shallow a story. How absurd a conception of human existence. How mundane a divine being.

With the alternative, that there is only one god, and further, that God knows he is the only god, we have no easy answers, but we have a story that is worth trying to penetrate. What is it that is driving this god who is aware of himself as the only god? Why does he want a free, morally conscious, mortal, and dependent humanity to know him? Why does he care? These are puzzling but powerful questions, ones that lead us deep into the heart of being. Methodologically, it is the better option.

God's Motivation

The question of God's name and God's titles is somehow central to the entire biblical tale, both when Abraham and God discuss Sodom and when God himself tells us that having the Israelites know that he is Yahweh is his central purpose. This issue of "Who is God?" emerges in radically different ways in Genesis and in Exodus. When Abraham argues with God, his fundamental project is to bring God under the constraints of morality. He does this in dialogue with God when he speaks of God as "the judge of all the earth," saying "Shall not the judge of all the earth deal justly?" In this conversation Abraham is seeking to have God take on a certain self-identity, to see himself as the just judge of all the earth. Were God to fully embrace that self-identity, however, he would not experience the constraints of morality as constraints. Rather, as one seeing himself as the just judge, acting justly would be experienced as acting from himself, acting freely.

Because it is God's self-identity that is at issue, the stakes could not be higher. God ultimately determines all that befalls the world. Thus, Abraham's quest is to transform the universe, to make justice a fundamental principle of all that happens. Given what we know of the world in the Bible, we can conclude that, at best, Abraham was only partially successful.

In Exodus, in the encounter with Pharaoh, we see that God is seized with the project of having the Israelites know him. But here the issue of "Who is God?" seems strikingly devoid of content. God is not intent on having the Israelites know his justness as a judge or any other substantive aspect of his identity.

One might think that there are two distinctly different issues here, one having to do with descriptions of what someone is like (e.g., is he kind; is he just; is he forgiving?) and one having to do with someone's name (e.g., Is he Yahweh?). But these are intricately linked. In the Bible names are repeatedly given or taken because of their meaning. They are often enough not mere names, but descriptive or commemorative phrases. And often enough, a person is renamed to mark some transformation in his being or the meaning of his existence. We saw previously how Joseph named his son Manasseh "meaning 'God has made me forget completely my hardship and my parental home.'" At a critical juncture God says to Abram, "this is my covenant with you: You shall be the father of a multitude of nations. And you shall no longer be called Abram, but your name shall be Abraham, for I make you the father of a multitude of nations." (Gen 17:4–6) And at another point, when Jacob wrestles through the night with a divine being (some say it is God, some an angel), he is told "Your name shall no longer be Jacob, but Israel, for you have striven with beings divine and human, and have prevailed." (Gen 32:29) Indeed, in that very episode Jacob says to this being, "Pray tell me your name." But he is told, "You must not ask my name!" We are not told why Jacob is denied this knowledge, but it seems as if the divine being is fearful to reveal it. Thus names and knowledge of names are of great importance. At least some of the time a name involves a description of a person, and having that person (and others) think of himself in terms of that description is part of a process of transformation, of internalizing a new self-identity.

When God first appears to Moses and tells him of his mission to free the Israelites, Moses immediately wants to know God's name. He says: "When I come to the Israelites and say to them, 'The God of your fathers has sent me to you,' and they ask me, 'What is his name? what shall I say to them?'" (Exod 3:13) Exactly what is going on here is not clear. Moses may well be anticipating problems that he will have with the Israelites, or he may be citing this as an indirect way of attaining knowledge of God's name. Implicit in Moses's query is the notion that knowing God's name will, to some extent, make the Israelites more likely to be responsive to what Moses will say to them.

It is thus quite interesting to see how God responds to Moses's request for his name:

> And God said to Moses, "Ehyeh-Asher-Ehyeh." He continued, "Thus shall you say to the Israelites, 'Ehyeh sent me to you.'" And God said further to Moses, "Thus shall you speak to the Israelites: The Lord ["Yahweh" in direct translations] the God of your fathers, the God of Abraham, the God of Isaac, and the God of Jacob, has sent me to you:
> This shall be my name forever,
> This my appellation for all eternity (Exod 3:14–15).

There are three responses here: (1) Ehyeh-Asher-Ehyeh; (2) Yahweh; (3) God of Abraham, Isaac, and Jacob.

"Yahweh" we are familiar with. It is a name that is used several thousand times in the Bible. The phrase "the God of Abraham, Isaac, and Jacob" is also something we have heard before. Moreover, this might be viewed less as a name of God than as a descriptive phrase that helps to explain to the Israelites who Yahweh is. Later on, I will argue that more is involved here, but for now, I want to focus on the first of these three responses, the name Ehyeh-Asher-Ehyeh.

This is the first and only time this name appears in the Bible. Yet it comes at a key moment. It is revealed not only to Moses, but he is told to use it when explaining who God is to the Israelites. A great deal has been written about this name, yet it remains enigmatic. Scholars are unsure even of how to translate it. The Jewish Publication Society translation used above is merely a transliteration of the Hebrew, not a translation. A footnote is provided saying "Meaning of Hebrew uncertain; variously translated: 'I Am That I Am'; 'I Am Who I Am'; 'I Will Be Who I Will Be,' etc." Yet even as scholars disagree on the precise meaning, the consensus is that the phrase means something. As a name, of course, it need not. Names such as Thomas, or Richard, or Phillip don't have meanings; they are just names. Moreover, even if an etymological inquiry were to reveal that such common names once did have meanings, the way Smith, and Carter, and Fisher once did, they no longer function as such. Neither the speaker nor the listener attributes meaning to such names. While names needn't have meanings, the point, however, is that the name "Ehyeh-Asher-Ehyeh" is generally thought to be meaningful. In the narrative it seems to be telling us something important about God. More exactly, God seems to be telling us something important about his nature when he tells us this name.

Consider the translations sometimes given, "I Am Who I Am"; "I Am That I Am"; "I Will Be Who I Will Be." Let us assume that one of these is correct. What exactly could this be telling us about God? The first and the third of these actually are meaningful sentences; indeed, they are logical truths, tautologies that are true of all persons. I am who I am, and you are who you are. I will be who I will be, and you will be who you will be. All this seems to tell us nothing of substance, quite unlike saying, "You are the judge of the earth." Moreover, and this is paradoxical, since they are true of all beings, they do not distinguish God from anyone else. While the first and the third possible translations are true sentences, the second of these, "I Am That I Am," while structurally similar to "I Am Who I Am," remains odd, and it is not clear that it even represents a grammatical sentence.

If we want to understand the real meaning of "Ehyeh-Asher-Ehyeh" in the story perhaps we should consider what God is doing when he responds to Moses in this manner. What is he conveying either about himself or to Moses? Suppose some stranger asks you to convey a message to a third person, and you ask, "Who should I say you are?" and the response is "I am who I am." While the phrase "I am who I am" is, at least in one sense, true of all persons, to actually respond to a request for a name in this way is to do something of significance. One possibility: it could be a way of saying "don't ask." It could be a way of deflecting the question. It could be a way of giving an answer, yet not taking any risks. Alternatively, it could be a joke, or an insult, or a warning. It could simply be a deliberate attempt to be enigmatic.

I noted earlier that after Jacob wrestles with a divine being, he asks its name and is told "Don't ask." If we assume that something similar is at work here, then when God tells Moses that he is "I Am that I Am," God is using a name that doesn't yield power over him. It is as if God is now saying, "I am what I am, you shall know me in virtue of what I do, and what I do is what I choose to do, for I am unconstrained." Thus, God may be engaged in an assertion of freedom, refusing not only to be bound as Abraham sought to bind him, as the just judge, but to be bound by any characteristic at all. That said, we are still left to wonder about the possible significance of the specific words God chooses in both instances. After all, there are many ways of conveying the "Don't Ask" message, and many different ways of being enigmatic, if this is what is involved. Why say, "I Am Who I Am" or "I Am That I Am"? What, if anything, is conveyed by the use of such terms?

In the Exodus text, there is a second sentence that follows. God says, "Say to the Israelites, 'Ehyeh sent me to you.'" This is a shorter version of the name, often translated as "I Am," and seen as a variant of Yahweh. Thus, God is telling Moses to simply refer to him as "I Am" when addressing the Israelites. Generally we use the phrase "I am" as the beginning of a sentence that will attribute some property or characteristic or action to the speaker, as in "I am unhappy" or "I am forgetful" or "I am running." Some of these attributes are important and others are not; some of them are central to the identity of the person and others not. But to refer to oneself as simply "I Am" or to call oneself "I Am That I Am" or "I Am Who I Am" pulls away from any specific property or attribute and toward the issue of being itself. It suggests that God is saying that his nature, his way of being, is somehow different from that of humans. What is conveyed then is a kind of self-sufficiency or independence of being. And, of course, as noted earlier, this is just how many philosophers have thought of God, as Epicurus did, for example, when he taught that God is not moved by us. What is strange, however, is that we know that the God of the Hebrew Bible is exactly the opposite. In his interaction with humankind he is passionately engaged and passionately moved, even enraged and carried away. Not only is the God of the Bible anthropomorphized, he has a very distinct and explosive personality. So why is he presenting himself so differently, as such a different kind of being, as if he were like the divine immortal Epicurus envisioned?

Sartre's Insights into Consciousness

The issue that has emerged, God's mode of being, falls into areas philosophers have called ontology and metaphysics. They are overwhelmingly perplexing, and from time to time other philosophers, such as David Hume in the eighteenth century and the logical positivists and ordinary language philosophers in the twentieth century, have come along and denounced much of such inquiry as either confused or as nonsensical and meaningless gibbering. At the very least, metaphysics and ontology are extremely difficult matters to even talk about, and often those philosophers who pursue such matters, somewhat like poets struggling against the constraints of existing language, have felt a need to invent a new vocabulary just to express themselves satisfactorily. This, of course, makes it all the more difficult to grasp what, if anything, is being said.

In 1943 the French philosopher Jean Paul Sartre published his most important work, *Being and Nothingness,* and established himself as the leading existentialist philosopher of the twentieth century. His central area of concern was the nature of consciousness, in particular self-conscious beings and their interactions. Whether or not he succeeded in uncovering truths about the very nature of being, I will not judge. But viewed from a nonmetaphysical point of view, Sartre had astonishing insight into the nature of human psychology. It will serve our inquiry well to take a short excursion into his thought. My concern here is not with Sartre's ideas *per se*; rather I shall try to present a Sartrean perspective that strikes me as sound and as relevant to the issue at hand, even if it might stray from full fidelity to Sartre.

Sartre's central focus is on the nature of human existence. A living human being is a being with consciousness, but it is not a disembodied consciousness. We are lived, embodied physical objects. Thus, we are not fully outside the physical universe; we are subject to the physical laws that regulate objects in time and space. Yet unlike many other living creatures, human consciousness goes beyond having sensations and perceptions. As we develop, we become conscious of ourselves, that is, we ourselves are the objects of our own consciousness.

It is thus possible to speak of two different modes of being, the In-itself and the For-itself. The existence of a totally inanimate object, say a stone, is existence in the mode of the In-itself. It simply is what it is. The nature of existence in the mode of the For-itself is radically different. Because it is self-aware, and because, except in rare cases, we are not paralyzed consciousnesses trapped inside our bodies, we are able to self-determine ourselves. For Sartre, the hallmark of the For-itself is that it is free. This extends not just to bodily actions, but to elements of consciousness as well. Thus, Sartre has a radical theory of the emotions, in which, contrary to the common sense way of speaking, they are not truly "passions" that befall us, and with respect to which we are passive; for Sartre, they are aspects of consciousness with respect to which we are active. Even if we do not fully bestow our emotions upon ourselves, we choose to either hold ourselves within our emotional states or step outside of them. We are free to be otherwise. While we have a past that in some sense defines who we are, a self-conscious being is never purely what it has been. At every moment, it creates itself anew. Thus, we both are what we are, and in some sense, are not what we are. Or to put it differently, the way in which we are what we are is fundamentally different from the way the In-itself (e.g., the stone) simply is what it is.

Our world is not just the world of objects and the self-conscious self. It is populated also by other self-conscious beings. And those beings constitute the Other, a developed consciousness that is not mine. The Other takes as the object of its consciousness not just itself, but me. And I, in turn, take the Other as my object. In this taking of the Other as an object, we see the Other as having certain characteristics. These we experience as properties of the Other, not as freely self-imposed qualities, held in place from moment to moment. Thus, for example, we see the Other as having a specific personality, and we perceive the being of the Other as in continuity with what the other has been in its past. Thus, our perceptions of each other tend to diminish or deny the degree of transcendence in the being of the Other. In short, we tend to make objects out of each other.

It should not be thought that this objectifying is something that the self must react against, as though it revels in its freedom and resists the constraints imposed by the other's perception of itself. Indeed, much the opposite is true. Just because the self is aware of its freedom, it is aware of the fact of its own emptiness, that it never just flows from past into future, and that it never truly has properties or characteristics the way an object does. Thus, the For-itself is aware of its own ultimate inner emptiness, its nonbeing. Freedom becomes something to be escaped from, something that we experience in anguish. Thus, we may run to and embrace the Other's objectifying perception of ourselves, just because it fills us up and gives us a reality and stability and existence that we lack.

Sartre's most penetrating discussion is of what he terms *"mauvais foi"* or bad faith. It is sometimes translated as self-deception. The central issue concerns the different ways in which a person might think of himself. Given that we are beings that exist both in the mode of the In-itself and the For-itself, how should we think of ourselves and of each other? That is, how do we experience ourselves and others if we are fully honest, fully authentic?

Sartre asks us to consider a waiter in a café. "His movement is quick and forward, a little too precise, and a little too rapid. He comes toward patrons with a step a little too quick....All his behavior seems to us a game....But what is he playing? We need not watch long before we can explain it: he is playing at being a waiter in a café...." Similarly, "There is the dance of the grocer, of the tailor, of the auctioneer, by which they endeavor to persuade their clientele that they are nothing but a grocer, an auctioneer, a tailor...."

But this is the outward presentation; the inner perception is different: "From within, the waiter in the café cannot be immediately a café waiter in the sense that this inkwell is an inkwell, or the glass is a glass...." The waiter knows there is another reality outside the role. Yet to the public he represents himself falsely, as if we did not sustain himself in his role. Yet it is not that he is not a waiter: "there is no doubt that I am in a sense a café waiter—otherwise could I not just as well call myself a diplomat or a reporter? But if I am one, this cannot be in the mode of being-in-itself. I am a waiter in the mode of being what I am not." [5]

This, for Sartre, is not a special case of a particular role or mask that someone puts on; rather the exploration of "bad faith" reveals something general about consciousness. He asserts, "The condition of the possibility

---

5. Jean Paul Sartre, *Being and Nothingness* (city, date), 60.

for bad faith is that human reality, in its most immediate being ... must be what it is not and not be what it is."[6]

Let us return to the Bible, to God's statement of his name, understood as "I Am That I Am" or "I Am Who I Am." A Sartrean orientation enables us to fathom God's strange name. If one wanted to emphasize the fundamental gap that exists between humankind and an infinite God, one would want to go beyond mere differences in degree, for instance, beyond saying humankind is knowledgeable, but God knows more, or even God knows everything. One would want to go beyond saying, humankind may on occasion be good, but God is always good, even beyond God is perfect. Rather, one would say that God's mode of existence is fundamentally incommensurate with human existence. And thus no predicate affirmed of a human being can ever properly be asserted or denied of God. All one can say of God, and all we finite beings can truly know of God, is that he exists, that He Is. Being beyond language, he can, in truth, tell us nothing of himself except that his name is "I Am."

So far, so good. This formulation works for many a conception of God. There is only one problem: as noted above, this conception is radically foreign to the god who is presented in the biblical narrative. Though God says his name is "I Am That I Am," the god we find in the story is a god with a consistent character, a god who has his personality just as we have ours. This is a god who has passions and has regrets and, most centrally, has insecurities.

The interpretive problem is one of trying to understand exactly how it is that humankind could in any sense be threatening to God. Why does a god who creates us in his image and allows us, through eating of the Tree of Knowledge, to become more like him, fear that we should become too much so? And why, I have asked, does this God so fear unified humankind acting as one at Babel that he fractures humankind into mutually incomprehensible cultures?

We must not be misled by God's name. What we must ask is this: If the God in the Bible is fundamentally like humankind rather than fundamentally unknowable, then what are we to make of his encounter with Moses, of his stating his name as "I Am That I Am"? The answer, I believe, is that God is posturing. In this self-presentation to Moses, God is like the waiter in the café; he is affecting a role that he cannot truly be. He is playing the role of being God, and moreover, he does this not in full awareness of the deception, but in bad faith, in self-deception. He wants us to see him as one who does not depend for his being on how we see him, but in his very concern with how we see him, he is revealed as dependent.

---

6. Ibid., 67.

At one point, Sartre says that God is impossible, that the very idea of God involves a contradiction. To understand the Bible story, however, we do not have to accept this metaphysical thesis; nor do we have to deny it. We are not engaged in the search for metaphysical truth. Rather, what we need to see is that the God in the biblical narrative presents himself to Moses, and to himself, as being God in a way that, for him, is simply untrue. He is not an Epicurean god who just is. The Epicurean god might appropriately be named "I Am," but this cannot be said of Yahweh as portrayed in the Bible.

The Motive

Immediately after saying that Moses should tell the Israelites "Ehyeh [I Am] sent me to you," God tells Moses to say to the Israelites, "The Lord [Yahweh] the God of your fathers, the God of Abraham, the God of Isaac, and the God of Jacob, has sent me to you." As already noted, there is a practical reason for telling the Israelites that it is the God of Abraham, the God of Isaac, and the God of Jacob that has sent Moses. Presumably these three patriarchs are important figures to the Israelites, and presumably the Israelites know some of the stories of their encounter with God, perhaps even of God's covenant with Abraham. Thus, by so identifying himself, God establishes his bone fides with the Israelites. (It is interesting that he does not further say that he is the God of Joseph, but that is another matter.)

While there is this practical reason for God to call to mind Abraham, Isaac, and Jacob, there is still a question. Why does this occur to God? After all, there are innumerable ways of impressing the Israelites. Is there something more at work here? I suggest that there is. God does not just suggest to Moses that Moses identify Yahweh in terms of the patriarchs, God also so identifies himself. He sees himself as the God of Abraham, Isaac, and Jacob. This is his name, or appellation, for himself.

Being the God of Abraham, Isaac, and Jacob, is, for God, no little thing. He has invested a great deal of time and energy in becoming the God of Abraham, Isaac, and Jacob. And much of the book of Genesis is devoted to detailing this. With Jacob in particular, this was not automatic. Of note is the encounter at a site Jacob names "Bethel," the house of God. There Jacob has a dream in which "the Lord was standing beside him and he said, 'I am the Lord, the God of your father Abraham and the God of Isaac: the ground on which you are lying I will give to you and to your offspring.'" Here it seems almost as if God is recruiting. He already is the God of Abraham and Isaac and now he wants Jacob; he is making an offer. And Jacob responds contractually. We are told, "Jacob then made a vow, saying, 'If God remains with me, if he protects me on this journey that I am making, and gives me bread to eat and clothing to wear, and if I return safe to my father's house—the Lord shall be my God' (or, Yahweh shall be my God)." (Gen 28:20–21)

This is Jacob's own covenant, and it does not have to do with becoming the father of nations. It is very here and now. He wants protection, food, clothing, and a safe return on a perilous journey. If he gets it, then Yahweh shall be his god. This is not a matter of believing in God, not a matter of seeking some demonstration that God exists, not a matter of countering atheism. Rather, it has to do with the establishment of a relationship between Jacob and Yahweh. Jacob lays down his conditions for taking Yahweh unto himself as his God.

For God, this binding to himself of Abraham, Isaac, and Jacob is just the beginning. His larger project, as we have seen, is for the Israelites, through the generations, to know that he is Yahweh. And indeed, as mentioned above, God is also interested, in a secondary kind of way, that the "Egyptians shall know that I am the Lord." The question remains: Why is this project God's project? Why is it so important to him that he become the God of the Israelites, or alternatively, that they know that he is the Lord, that he is Yahweh?

The answer, I believe, is that it is only through this that God can know that he is God. Alternatively, this can be put not as a matter of knowledge, but as a matter of being. It is only by virtue of being the God of a people that God can be God. What is at stake for God, and here I mean from the very beginning of the story, when he creates man in his image, is the question of his own reality. God's fundamental project is To Be and for this he needs humankind, and ultimately he decides that he needs a specific people, the Israelites.[7]

This proposition, that God needs humankind in order to be God, can be taken on two levels, first as ontology, and second as psychology. With respect to both, it should be clear that my concern remains that of offering a literary interpretation of the text. I am not meaning to stray into metaphysics for its own sake. Rather I am saying that the Bible story as we find it presents a god who can only Be if he has humans for whom he is God (or who know him). The validity of this interpretation does not depend upon the independent metaphysical question of whether or not God can exist without believers. That thesis could be false, but the interpretation sound, so long as that is the perspective of the book itself. And whether or not it is the perspective of the book can be determined only by considering wheth-

---

7. God's need for humankind is an important theme in the writings of Rabbi Abraham Joshua Heschel.

er that interpretation makes fuller, deeper sense of the text than any other interpretation.

As I have suggested, this account of God's motivation, that he seeks to exist, does provide us with a powerful answer to a very fundamental question: Why is God so engaged in the process of being known to the Israelites? What is it to him? If we see God as himself in a quest for being, we can understand the stakes, for they are ultimate. There is no more fundamental motivation of any living thing than to be. And there is no more fundamental process of nature than the transition of living things from mere potential to fulfillment or actualization. So if we see the biblical text as positing a god who needs humanity in order to know himself as God, or in order to be God, then God's emotional stake becomes self-evident. Indeed, it becomes very human; it is that quest that motivates our lives as well, the quest for identity, the quest to come more fully into being truly oneself.

In ontological terms, this is a thesis about what it is to be a god. Consider for a moment the Greek pantheon. What exactly is it that makes Zeus, Aphrodite, Neptune, Mercury, and all the others gods? They have several features that human beings do not have: The have superlative levels of powers and immortality. These, we should note, are just the capabilities that God seeks to keep from humankind. Human power is to be limited by scattering humankind into nations that are incomprehensible to each other, and immortality is prevented by forcing humankind out of the Garden of Eden. But are great powers and immortality sufficient to be a god? Suppose that the universe contains only such figures and no humans. The first result is that the very notion of great power tends to dissolve. Against what standard is a power great? If there are multiple gods, then the power of one limits the power of another. True, they may all be vastly more powerful than the humans, but what if there are no humans? Remove humankind from the story and all you have are a group of immortal beings with certain capabilities. Does that make them gods? For them to be gods, it seems there must be those beings who are non-gods.

Suppose that there are two sets of beings, those that are human and those that are like the humans but are immortal and have greater powers. Are these latter beings gods or just other creatures? Perhaps being a god involves having a certain position in a relationship, just as being a master or a slave requires the existence of the other. Perhaps a being is a god only if it is recognized as such, only if it is prayed to, only if it is seen as a god by a non-god.

Since I am not engaged in this ontological question for its own sake, I needn't try to answer these questions. For interpretive purposes, as an explanation of God's motivation in the biblical text, it is sufficient that this

is a meaningful thesis and that it is textually plausible that God experiences himself as most fully being God only when he experiences himself as so
perceived by an appropriate Other, one whose look can confer a sense of
being.

Thus, my claim is only about the Hebrew Bible, only that the central
character, Yahweh is portrayed as having an existential insecurity, as
being fundamentally unsure of who he is, of needing to have a realm of
humankind that sees him as God in order for him to know himself as God.

So understood, the Hebrew Bible is telling us a very particular story,
the story of what it is to be a people thrown into a world that is ruled by
that kind of god-personality. It is a story that operates at the intersection of
philosophy and psychology, concerned with how an infinitely powerful
deity comes to have an identity through his awareness of others' knowledge of him. The story turns on his investment in humankind. We are said
to have been created in his image, but it is we who provide him with his
image. Human eyes function as the mirror that enables him to see himself.
It is this role that, on the one hand, opens possibilities for the human to
gain power over the infinite power and, on the other, gives rise to fear and
hostility on the part of the infinite.

An Existential Novel

When Abraham confronts God over the constraints of morality, he
does not say, "It is wrong to punish the innocent along with the guilty,
and you should not do so." Rather, he says:

> "Far be it from You to do such a thing"

> "Far be it from You!"

> "Shall not the judge of all the earth deal justly?"

In the use of "Far be it from You!" Abraham presents himself as the Other
who knows God's true nature. Implicitly, he claims that God has a certain
kind of character, and that it would be inconsistent with the essence of
that character for God to act unjustly. And by bestowing upon God the
appellation "the judge of all the earth," Abraham offers to God a self-identity that requires just action as that which comes from God's true being.[8]

---

8. A judge, of course, might in any given instance act unjustly, but without some
   commitment to justice the power that dispenses punishment cannot be said to
   be engaged in judging. Indeed, the very concept of punishment implies that
   there is a connection between the pain dispensed and some prior deed viewed
   as the reason why the pain was inflicted.

In response to Abraham, one could imagine that God would say:

> You presume too much when you presume to know me.
> I am that I am.
> If I will, there is nothing that is far from me.
> And I will what I will.

But God does not make a response of this sort at all. Rather, we see that Abraham's stance as the knowing Other has an impact. God, at least initially, moves toward living out this identity that Abraham has pronounced. Given the Flood narrative, it is hard to attribute to God, prior to his interaction with Abraham, a self-identity that does not allow for the punishment of the innocent. What is displayed in the scene of Abraham pleading for Sodom is the fluctuating being of God's self-identity under the gaze of Abraham. In Sartre's words, "I recognize that I am as the Other sees me." And further, "for me the Other is first the being for whom I am an object; that is, the being through whom I gain my objectness."[9]

It is not only Abraham who recognizes that God can be affected by this kind of appeal; Moses too realizes that God's self-identity is in question. While Moses is upon Mount Sinai receiving the Ten Commandments, the Israelites construct for themselves the golden calf. God is enraged and says to Moses, "I see that this is a stiff-necked people. Now, let me be that my anger may blaze forth against them and that I may destroy them, and make of you a great nation." (Exod 32:10)

Moses quickly responds to try to save the Israelites. He urges God to recall his promises to Abraham, Isaac, and Jacob that he will make their offspring "as numerous as the stars" and that he will give the Promised Land to those offspring. But in addition to this "keep your promises" argument, Moses tries another tack as well. He says: "Let not the Egyptians say, 'It was with evil intent that he delivered them, only to kill them off in the mountains and to annihilate them from the face of the earth.'" (Exod 32:12) We are told that "the Lord renounced the punishment he had planned to bring upon his people." We are not told whether he changed his mind in response to the first of these arguments or the second, or in response to the combined weight of the two. But it seems sound to conclude that the appeal to how the Egyptians would think of God had some weight. This is further supported by what we saw earlier, that God wanted to impress not just the Israelites but the Egyptians with his power. Finally, it must be remembered that Moses is at this point no stranger to God. He is closer to him than anyone, and if Moses' automatic response is

---

9. Sartre, *Being and Nothingness*, 222, 270.

to call to God's attention what the Egyptians might say of him, this suggests that God is indeed mightily concerned with his image.

After this success in turning God's wrath, and perhaps hoping to further enhance his power over God, Moses asks to see God. He says, "Oh, let me behold your Presence!" This is parallel to, but a step beyond, his earlier request for God's name. God, however, will not allow this. He says, "You cannot see my face, for man may not see me and live." (Exod 33:20) God is setting limits here to the amount of Otherness he will allow humankind to attain.

In Sartre's words, "To be looked at is to apprehend oneself as the unknown object of unknowable appraisals—in particular, of value judgments.... Thus, being-seen constitutes me as a defenseless being for a freedom that is not my freedom. It is in this sense that we can consider ourselves as "slaves" in so far as we appear to the Other."[10] Subsequently Sartre says that in relation to the Other, "I am in danger. This danger is not an accident but the permanent structure of my being-for-others."[11] Sartre, above, calls attention to the danger that comes because the other is capable of value judgments; a being that can make value judgments has the power to bestow upon oneself either a negative or a positive self-identity. This capacity for value judgments or, more generally, appraisals is the outcome of having the categories of good and evil, or more widely, good and bad, as the tree in the garden is sometimes identified.

It should not be thought that sensitivity to this power dynamic between the judging self and other was a discovery of the nineteenth or twentieth century.[12] Such issues were also matters of concern in the ancient world. Consider the following passage from the Roman Stoic philosopher Epictetus:

> If any person was intending to put your body in the power of any man whom you fell in with on the way, you would be vexed; but that you put your understanding [better translated as identity or sense of self] in the power of any man whom you meet, so that if he should revile you, it is disturbed and troubled, are you not ashamed at this? (*The Manual*, 28)

Here, the Stoic philosopher is saying that the danger posed by the Other is simply one that we permit it to pose when we worry about being reviled. It is a matter of psychology, not a permanent structure of the ontology of being. Sartre would disagree, but, whatever its root, the phenomenon of a person falling under the power of others because of the way the judgment

---

10. Ibid., 267.

11. Ibid., 268.

12. The nineteenth-century philosopher Hegel strongly influenced Sartre.

of the Other may affect one's sense of self was as familiar to the ancients as it is today.

In the biblical narrative, God deliberately brings into being this conscious Other, humankind. In order for there to be an Other that can see God as he wants to be seen, this Other must be created in God's image. That is, it must have the higher level of judgmental consciousness that comes from the possession of moral categories and is thereby able to make judgments on the level that God seeks to internalize. One cannot experience oneself as worthy of esteem by internalizing the gaze of an animal that lacks the categories of worthiness. For this reason, the tree of knowledge of good and evil is placed in the garden. At the same time, the morally conscious Other cannot be allowed to become another god, for then God would not be known as God. So humankind must be driven from the garden. Even so, the conscious Other that can give God his being as God represents a danger in virtue of this very power. Abraham demonstrates this when his invocation of a moral identity for God is experienced by God as constraint. In response, God moves to control this very power that he brings into being. Yet the control cannot be too complete lest the very freedom of the Other, that which allows it to bestow being, be lost. God needs humankind to have the very powers that make humankind dangerous.

Let us take a second look at that key moment in the Garden of Eden after the fruit has been eaten. We are told, "Then the eyes of both of them were opened and they perceived that they were naked; and they sewed together fig leaves and made themselves loin cloths." In the earlier discussion of this episode I put emphasis on the impact that coming to moral consciousness had on Adam and Eve: it enabled them to have the new emotion of shame. I also pointed out that in using the "eyes opened" metaphor, moral consciousness is portrayed as a kind of seeing, and the moral dimension, as an objective structure of reality.

We can consider this passage also from a Sartrean point of view, and here the emphasis would be on the phrase "they perceived that they were naked." What exactly is it that Adam and Eve saw? Presumably Adam saw both that he, Adam, was naked, and further that Eve was naked. Eve also had two perceptions, that she Eve was naked, and also that Adam was naked. Yet even this is incomplete, for Adam also saw that Eve saw that he was naked, and Eve, in turn, saw that Adam saw that she was naked. That is, each had a perception of themselves as naked in the eyes of the Other. And it was this recognition of themselves as seen in the eyes of the Other that gave rise to the shame that moved them to clothe themselves.

Interestingly, Sartre opens his discussion of what he calls "being-for-others" by asking his readers to consider the example of shame. Sartre tells us that

> [shame] in its primary structure is shame before somebody. I have just made an awkward or vulgar gesture. This gesture clings to me. I neither judge it nor blame it. I simply live it.... But suddenly I raise my head. Somebody was there and has seen me. Suddenly I realize the vulgarity of my gesture, and I am ashamed. The Other is the indispensable mediator between myself and me. I am ashamed of myself as I appear to the Other.... Shame is by nature recognition. I recognize that I am as the Other sees me.[13]

In this analysis, had Adam been alone when he ate of the fruit, though he would have gained moral consciousness, he would not have experienced shame, for he would not have experienced himself as naked-in-front-of-the-other. Thus, for Adam and Eve to come into full awareness of themselves, they both have to exist. In their relationship they come to realize themselves both as the object of the look of the Other and as the one who looks at the Other. And I would suggest, coming to understand themselves both as one who sees and is seen by the Other, they come to be as God needs them, as beings that can know Yahweh.

What is remarkable in the text is that God seems to know that in order for the first human to come into full selfhood, there must be another. God first creates Adam and then he places him in the Garden of Eden, along with the two trees, the tree of knowledge of good and evil and the tree of life. God then warns Adam, telling him not to eat of the tree of knowledge of good and evil. But this in insufficient as a setting for the development of the human being. There is one missing element: the potential Other. Thus we are told, "The Lord God said, 'It is not good for man to be alone.'" (Gen 2:18) The next sentence is usually translated as some variant of "I will make a fitting helper for him." But consider how much more insight is gained by the alternative wording given in Richard Elliot Friedman's translation: "I'll make for him a strength corresponding to him."[14] Not only does this fit exactly with what is needed for their mutual self-emergence to occur, it also fits better with the portrayal of Eve. She is no helper or helpmate. She is a strength indeed.

For those who believe in an omniscient deity, it would be no surprise that God would know that Adam, to become himself, needs an Other, that

---

13. Sartre, *Being and Nothingness*, 221–22.

14. Gen 2:18 as translated by Richard Elliot Friedman in *Commentary on the Torah with A New English Translation and The Hebrew Text* (San Francisco, 2001).

it is "not good for man to be alone." But the story, as I read it, does not present an omniscient deity. Moreover, it presents God as being generally opaque and disinterested in the inner life and inner needs of humankind. But if this is how God is presented, then how is it that he knows this one very basic fact about man: that it is not good that he be alone. The answer, I suggest, is that this issue is very much on God's mind. It goes to the heart of his entire project of creation, and in particular it goes to the point of his creation of humankind in his image. God himself knows of aloneness. He knows that it is not good for God to be alone. Cast in a more existential vocabulary, he knows that he cannot be God if he is alone.

There are two senses of not-being, both of which involve not-being-seen by an Other. The first is a matter of the absence of the Other that could potentially see oneself. This is the existential reality for God before humankind is created, and it persists until the fruit is eaten, an act that constructs the full-fledged Other that can convey being. But with the existence of this Other, there comes into being the far more acute sense of not-being: to not be seen in the presence of the Other. This is what we mean when we speak of being "looked through," to not be noticed by the very Other one looks to for notice. Here not-being-seen projects upon the self its own nonexistence. This is the true danger that the human other constitutes for God. This threat is itself far more powerful than to be the object of a negative judgment. Thus, once God has set for himself the project of being seen as God by the Israelites, to not be seen by them, but to have them see other gods, is the greatest assault on his being. And not surprisingly, it is the cause of his greatest rage. Indeed, even when they are focused on him, God is aware of this dependence, and thus is always simmering. It is thus that he is a jealous God.

SAMSON AND SELF-DESTROYING EVIL

Eleonore Stump
St. Louis University

IN A RECENT EXCELLENT BOOK on the problem of evil, Marilyn Adams defines horrendous evils as "evils the participation in which (that is, the doing or suffering of which) constitutes prima facie reason to doubt whether the participant's life could (given their inclusion in it) be a great good" to the sufferer.[1] A large part of her book is given over to considering whether there are benefits to such unwilling innocent sufferers that could possibly redeem the suffering and turn the sufferer's life into a good for the sufferer. Many reflective people looking at cases of horrendous evil feel strongly that there is nothing, there could be nothing, which defeats the evil in such cases. No benefit is brought about by the suffering which could not be gotten without the suffering and which is worth the suffering. The efforts of theodicy to find such benefits strike them as shallow at best and obscene at worst. It must follow on such a view that a person whose life manifests horrendous evil is a person whose life was not a good for him; such a person would have been better off if he had died at birth or had never lived. Job gives voice to this sort of attitude when he curses the day he was born and complains with bitter passion, "Why did I not die from the womb? Why did I not emerge from the womb and perish?" (Job 3:11)

I think it is indisputable that sometimes the suffering a person endures breaks that person past healing. Sometimes a person's life is irremediably ruined, in the sense that it can no longer be made whole; its initial promise can no longer be fulfilled. The paradigm of such a person in the Greek world is Oedipus. Sophocles has Oedipus claim to be among the worst of the afflicted,[2] and it's not hard to see why. By the time he appears

---

1. Marilyn McCord Adams, *Horrendous Evils and the Goodness of God* (Ithaca, N.Y.: Cornell University Press, 1999), 26.

2. *Oedipus at Colonus*, ll.104–5.

in *Oedipus at Colonus,* he is a homeless, blind beggar, disfigured, bedeviled by fear, tormented by self-loathing, and shunned with horror by all who meet him. What is broken and ruined in Oedipus couldn't conceivably be restored to wholeness. Surely this is horrendous evil if anything is.

And yet Sophocles's Oedipus is pitiably anxious to make clear that his dreadful acts were in some important sense involuntary. "There is more of suffering than of violence in my deeds," he tells the Chorus.[3] It's not hard to see why this claim matters to him. Job suffers horrendously, but at least he suffers as a victim, not as a perpetrator. He is broken and his life is wrecked, but the responsibility for the horror does not lie with him; and so there remains this much beauty in him and in his life: he is innocent. It is also possible, however, to be broken and ruined and to know that one has brought the horror on oneself.[4]

---

3. *Oedipus at Colonus,* ll.266–67.

4. Because I am focusing on the brokenness and ruin of the life of a perpetrator of great evil, I am concerned with a somewhat different problem from that discussed by Ian Boyd in his excellent paper, "The Problem of Self-Destroying Sin in John Milton's *Samson Agonistes,*" *Faith and Philosophy* 13 (1996) 487–507. Boyd puts the problem that concerns him this way: "Self-destroying sin is evil, the doing of which gives a Christian *prima facie* reason to doubt whether her life could be counted a great good to her on the whole. That is, most people would agree that her doing this sort of evil constitutes a *prima facie* reason to doubt whether, given the inclusion of such evil action, her life can be a great good to her on the whole." (p. 489) I am concerned not with the way in which the inclusion of a serious sin by itself mars a life; rather, I am concerned with the cases of broken and ruined lives, felt as broken and ruined by the sufferer, where the culpability for the suffering lies with the sufferer. Furthermore, as I now see the case of Samson, my evaluation of his case differs from Boyd's, which I at one time shared. Boyd says, "it would, of course, have been better if Samson could have attained all of the goods he did and fulfilled God's promise without sinning. But, given the choices Samson made, his suffering at his sin (and God's response to it) is sufficient for the attainment of the goods that defeat his evil." (p. 498) On Boyd's evaluation, although the combination of the evil of Samson's sinning and the subsequent good of Samson's heroism constitute a good life for Samson, it is not clear that there wouldn't have been a better life for Samson if God had brought about Samson's death before he began the process of wrecking his life by sinning. And so, on Boyd's evaluation the problem that concerns me here remains. There seems no answer to the question why an omniscient, omnipotent, perfectly good God would allow Samson to live long enough to engage in the serious sins that ruin his life. There is an answer to this question only in case there is some good for Samson which would not have been attainable without the sinning and the ruined life which it yields. That is, there has to be some Christian analogue to the view of

Another Version of the Problem of Evil

There is therefore another version of the problem of evil that also bears consideration, namely, that which focuses on the horrendous suffering of the lives of perpetrators, rather than victims, of great evil. This version of the problem has been largely left to one side, I think, because we tend to react without pity to the perpetrators. We take them to get what they deserve. And yet imagine that Goebbels failed to kill himself, after his wife had killed their six children and herself at his instigation; imagine that in the final fall of Berlin he had finally seen himself just as we see him today. It is not hard to put Job's lines in Goebbels's mouth: it would have been so much better for him if God had let him die at birth. And if that line is true, as it seems at first glance to be, then the problem of evil can surely also be raised about the horrendous evil of being a perpetrator, as well as a victim. Even if it were true that the suffering of the perpetrator were deserved, if both the evil and the deserved suffering could have been prevented, if the perpetrator would have been much better off dying young rather than living to perpetrate the evil, then why wouldn't an omniscient, omnipotent, perfectly good God provide for the death of the perpetrator before he does the evil?

The case of the perpetrators of horrendous evil is thus the hardest case for theodicy. If it can be shown that even a person whose own culpable acts have broken him and left him in horrendous suffering can have a life which is a good for him, then there is an a fortiori argument to other less disturbing cases. So, for these reasons, I want to explore one case of horrendous evil in which it is the sufferer's own doing that his life was wrecked as it is. I want to look carefully at the story of Samson.

It should be said here that I am not the first person to think that the case of Samson shows us the problem of evil in a particularly disconcerting form but that it also gives us deep insights useful for theodicy. Milton thought so, too, and wrote a play incorporating his understanding of the story of Samson. It is clear that Milton saw his own case as analogous to Samson's in many respects, and rightly so. When the Puritans fell from power, Milton, who had given so much of himself to their cause, was left blind, impoverished, and imperilled by his enemies. And he was a failure at what he himself saw as his vocation to poetry. Up to that time, his great gifts for literature had been prodigally spent on political pamphlets, and his announced plan to produce a great English epic poem looked more

the Greek tragedians that there is some great good which cannot be gotten without suffering. Nonetheless, Boyd's understanding of the problem of self-destroying sin and his reading of Milton have been helpful to me.

like bombast than promise.[5] So Milton's interest in the story of Samson was not abstract, but personal and anguished. He thought about the horrendous evil of Samson's life out of the ruin of his own life. And the thought is very good. In considering the biblical story of Samson, then, I will also be guided by Milton's understanding of it.[6]

Samson in Captivity

In introducing *Samson Agonistes*, Douglas Bush picks out *Oedipus at Colonus* as one of the preceding works of literature Milton's play most resembles,[7] and it is not hard to see why he thinks so. Milton's view of Samson is in many respects similar to Sophocles's view of Oedipus. Like *Oedipus at Colonus*, *Samson Agonistes* begins by calling attention to the panoply of the protagonist's sufferings, and there is considerable similarity between the two characters on this score. To begin with, like Oedipus, Samson is blind. The lament over the loss of sight that blind Milton puts in blind Samson's mouth is heart-rending, and it reminds us not to gloss over blindness as a small evil:

> Light, the prime work of God, to me is extinct,
> And all her various objects of delight
> Annulled, which might in part my grief have eased,
> Inferior to the vilest now become
> Of man or worm; the vilest here excel me,
> They creep, yet see; I, dark...
> ...exiled from light,
> As in the land of darkness, yet in light,
> ...
> Myself my sepulchre, a moving grave,
> Buried, not yet exempt
> By privilege of death and burial
> From worst of other evils, pains and wrongs... (ll.70–105)

For Samson, there are indeed many other evils. Oedipus is at least free to wander among his countrymen with his daughters. Samson is exiled, imprisoned, and set to work at hard and demeaning labor, grinding grain like a beast for his enemies. Like Oedipus, Samson is a pariah to the communities around him. But there is an extra measure of humiliation for

---

5. Horace, *Ars Poetica*, 137–39: "parturient montes, nascetur ridiculus mus." I am grateful to James Alexander Arieti for helping me with this reference.

6. For an excellent study of this work of Milton's and its relevance to theodicy, see Boyd 1996.

7. *The Complete Poetical Works of John Milton*, ed. Douglas Bush (Boston: Houghton Mifflin, 1965), 513.

Samson, because he is forced to use his strength, which was meant to be employed in the liberation of his people, to give food to their enemies; and his enemies exult over him in this condition.

For both Oedipus and Samson, the pain of their condition is made more bitter by the memory of the state from which they have fallen. But for Samson the reversal in fortunes is considerably more complicated than it is for Oedipus, however tangled Oedipus's story is.

To begin with, Samson was called to the state from which he fell. Rescuing his people from their oppressors was his vocation; it was, quite literally, what he was born for. The angel who announces Samson's birth to the hitherto barren woman who becomes his mother tells her to avoid wine, strong spirits, and unclean food and to make sure that no razor ever comes on the child's head, because the child to be born will be a Nazarite from the womb. This special son, the angel tells the woman, is destined to begin to deliver Israel from the Philistines.[8] Samson's downfall is thus not just a personal catastrophe; his failure to fulfill his vocation is also a national disaster. And this disaster is Samson's fault.

Milton sums up Samson's state succinctly by having Samson say,

> Now blind, disheartened, shamed, dishonored, quelled,
> To what can I be useful, wherein serve
> My nation, and the work from Heaven imposed...? (ll.563–565)

Samson's Relation to God

Heaven is, of course, the other problem for Samson. There is the problem of intolerable guilt, which Milton unaccountably left off the list of Samson's troubles in the preceding lines and which I will address a little later. But there is also Samson's relationship to God.

That there was such a relationship, that it was direct and powerful, and that Samson trusted in it as a regular part of his life is shown by the episode of the battle at Lehi. There, the story says, Samson single-handedly slaughtered a thousand of the enemy, and the Philistines were soundly defeated in the battle. But afterwards Samson was very thirsty. And so, the text says, "Samson called to Yahweh and said, 'It was you who gave this great deliverance by the hand of your servant. And now I am dying of thirst, and I will fall into the hands of the uncircumcised'." (Judges 15:18)

---

8. There is, of course, also a prophecy in Oedipus's story, namely, the prophecy that sets the tragedy in motion, that Oedipus will kill his father and marry his mother. But although this prophecy could be interpreted as an indication that the gods have ordained for Oedipus the course his life takes, it would take a particularly tendentious person to consider a destiny to parricide and matricide as a vocation.

And God provided water for Samson by breaking open a place in Lehi, from which water then flowed.

It is notable that Samson not only thought to call on God when he needed a drink but that he called on him in such a familiar way. There is not only no reverent address in Samson's prayer; there is in fact no address at all. Samson simply turns to God to speak to him directly, as if invocation of the Deity, to get his attention and call him to listen, were unnecessary for Samson.

None of the other common elements of prayer are present in Samson's speech either. There is no plea for God's help, not even a single 'please.' As far as that goes, Samson appears not to think it necessary even to make a petition. He asks nothing of God. He simply presents himself to God as thirsty and in want of water. The closest he comes to making a plea or a petition is to point to a danger to himself: unrelieved, the condition in which he is will lead to his being captured by his enemies. Samson points to this possible outcome as a sort of *reductio ad absurdum* of the idea that God could leave him thirsty. As the prayer shows, then, Samson expects that his want of water and the unquestioned unacceptability of his falling to the Philistines will be enough for God to provide, immediately and on the spot, what Samson needs. It's equally notable that in this story God seems to agree, at least to this extent: without comment, God provides the water.

The episodes recounting Samson's deeds and experiences also suggest some wild, strong connection between Samson and God. The story of Samson's exploits begins in this way: "the boy grew, and Yahweh blessed him; and the spirit of Yahweh began to move him in the camp of Dan...."(13:24–25)

Subsequently, when Samson engages in some feat of great strength, the story often (but not always) says that the spirit of the Lord came on him—or rushed into him, as the evocative Hebrew has it.[9]

But in the catastrophe at the end, the text explains, not only is Yahweh's spirit not coming on Samson, but in fact Yahweh has departed from Samson.[10]

What would it be like to find that the God who had only to see your need to satisfy it, who rushed into you and made you triumphant, was gone from you? Among the things Samson must long for—light, freedom, home—the absent love of the God who rushed into him, with whose strength he was great, must prompt the most painful pining.

---

9. See Judg 14:5–6, 19; 15:14–15.

10. Judg 16:20 says of Samson that he did not know that the Lord had departed from him.

If horrendous evils can be ranked, if they are not simply incommensurable, then, taken all in all, Samson's sufferings seem to me among the worst. However great Oedipus's misery, it lacks the torment of being abandoned for cause by a deity once intimately, gloriously, with you.

Abandoned for Cause

And it is indisputable that Samson was abandoned for cause; his fall is his fault. But what exactly is Samson culpable for?

Milton, like very many interpreters of the story, thinks that Samson's fault consists in having told Delilah his secret.[11] But here, I think, Milton has to have it wrong.

To see that this is so, consider how we would have to read the story about Samson's capture if Milton were right.

Delilah wants Samson to tell her the secret of his strength. Now Samson has some practice at the suffering of having his secrets betrayed by a woman he loves. Samson's marriage to the Philistine woman at Timnath ended abruptly at the wedding when his bride treacherously revealed the secret she had wheedled out of him. And so Samson, who is as capable of drawing inferences from bitter experience as other people, doesn't tell Delilah his secret but rather lies to her instead. The wisdom of his decision to lie is immediately apparent—to him as well as to us—because Delilah loses no time in betraying him by passing his lie on to the Philistines, who use what Delilah tells them to try to capture Samson.

One might suppose that Samson would react to Delilah's betrayal in the same way that he reacted to the betrayal of the woman of Timnath, by exploding into fury, leaving her, and killing Philistines. But, in fact, nothing of the sort happens: no fury, no leaving, no attacks on the Philistines. On the contrary, we simply get a repetition of the same scenario. How are we to account for the fact that hot-tempered Samson not only doesn't explode against her and the Philistines in league with her but instead tamely gives into Delilah's whining and wheedling a second time and pretends again to tell her his secret?

The answer to this question lies in effect in Samson's answer to Delilah's first request for his secret. Why is his response to her initial request a lie? Surely, because he does not trust her not to betray him to his enemies to be put to death. So he believes that the woman he loves, with whom he

---

11. Contemporary interpreters tend also to read the story in this way. So, for example, Robert Boling in his commentary in the Anchor Bible Judges (Garden City, N.Y.: Doubleday, 1975), 249: "[Samson's] treason is the betrayal of state secrets and the tragic squandering of his great strength...."

is sexually intimate, can't be trusted not to want him dead. That is a fairly stunning failure to trust, on his part.

And that is why Samson is not angry when he finds that Delilah is in league with his enemies. She doesn't betray his trust as his bride of Timnath did—he doesn't give her any trust to betray. He is prepared to take her and enjoy her; he is not prepared to give any of himself to her. And so he doesn't get angry when she tries to betray him to death. Because he has lied to her, she can't in fact harm him; and because he hasn't invested himself in her, he doesn't mind when she tries to do him in. She's like a cat one has carefully declawed; her attempts at attack may be occasions for amusement or annoyance, but they can't cause any serious reaction.

Now, on Milton's view, how will we have to read the story of Delilah's fourth and final attempt to betray Samson? After three occasions on *each* of which it has to be obvious even to the most obtuse that Delilah has betrayed him to his enemies, on Milton's reading of the fourth occasion Samson is so wearied by the endless importunities of the woman he is besotted with that he tells her the truth about the way in which his enemies can do him in.

But it can't be that Samson now believes Delilah is trustworthy,[12] and it's equally absurd to suppose that he tells Delilah his secret because he now desires to surrender to his enemies. It is true that the story says Delilah vexed him practically to death, so that in the end he told her all his heart. And he does in fact this time, for the first time, tell Delilah something which is true: he has been a Nazarite from the womb, and he has never been shaven. But the question remains whether in telling her this truth, Samson is telling her what he believes is the key to his capture by the Philistines. If he did believe it, then it is evident that he would have to think Delilah wouldn't use the information to do him in or that he wouldn't care much if she did.

If it isn't sufficiently clear that neither of these states for Samson is psychologically credible, the rest of the episode shows decisively that such an interpretation of the story is wrong. If Samson had resolved to let Delilah in on the way in which the Philistines could capture him, then when the Philistines did surround him, Samson would realize he was lost. Even if he had somehow supposed that after three times of betraying him to his destruction, Delilah had somehow turned trustworthy, he would know how wrong he had been when he found the Philistines around him. Or if he had anticipated such a result but didn't care, then he would sim-

---

12. Though this is how some contemporary interpreters read the story at this point. So, for example, Boling 1975, 249, says: "[Samson] could not believe, as in the wedding story, that the woman would betray him."

ply surrender tamely—or at least despairingly—when the Philistines attack him. But none of these things happens in the narrative. On the contrary, in the story, when Delilah wakes him with the cry that the Philistines are upon him, he responds by saying, "I will go out this time as before and shake myself free." (16:20) To suppose that Samson has this reaction after having given the manifestly treacherous Delilah what he himself believes is the key to his destruction is to make psychological gibberish of the story.

So although very many people read the narrative as Milton does here, Milton can't be reading the story correctly at this crucial point. But, then, how are we to understand this last episode with Delilah? What is it that Samson is culpable for?

Samson as Liberator of His People

To see the answer to this question, it is helpful to look at the episodes in which Samson demonstrates his great strength. Yahweh's spirit is said to come on Samson in only half of these episodes. In the interest of brevity, I want to look at just one of these.

In that episode, Samson seeks out a prostitute who is in Gaza, the Philistine territory to which he is taken when the Philistines finally capture him. Surely, there is a kind of complacency, if not arrogance, in Samson's taking the risk of visiting a prostitute in enemy territory; and, of course, in the story Samson's enemies do get wind of his presence, alone and unprotected, in their midst. Their plan for capturing him depends on the fact that the city's gates are barred at night; they feel sure that they've got him penned up in their city till the morning, when they mean to try to kill him. But the story suggests that Samson also has a plan and that it also involves the city's gates. The story says that Samson got up at midnight to leave through the barred gates. There is no suggestion that Samson knows his presence has been revealed to his enemies. As far as that goes, there is no suggestion that Samson is or needs to be worried about the Philistines even if they were to surround him in the morning. He has, after all, single-handedly defeated a small army of Philistines in the preceding battle. Nonetheless, Samson gets up in the night to leave the barred and gated town—and to make sure the Philistines know that the great Samson was in it.

Samson could leave the town in some simple way, by using his strength to get through the gates somehow. But getting away isn't what Samson wants, or at least not all he wants. And so he removes the gates themselves, to flaunt his strength and to manifest his disdain of his enemies to them. Samson will have the whore he wants when he wants her, without hindrance from the contemptible Philistines, just because he is the mighty Samson. If there is any doubt about this reading, it ought to be dispelled by what Samson does with those gates. It would have been a sufficient thumbing of his nose at the Philistines for Samson to uproot the gates and throw them down outside the city wall. What Samson actually does is to put them on his shoulders and lug them all the way up to the top of a hillside, to deposit them there, in view of the surrounding country. There is more than a little hubris in this. And Yahweh's spirit does not come on Samson for this stunt.

It is worth keeping this episode in mind as we look at the part of the story involving Delilah.

The episode involving Delilah occurs near the end of Samson's two decades of serving as judge of Israel. And what does the story suggest about this time? Certainly not that Samson has succeeded in liberating his people from the Philistines. The Philistines are still at least a force to be reckoned with seriously, as their capture of Samson himself makes plain. But there is also no sign that Samson is planning any great public exploits designed for the liberation of his people. On the contrary, the only thing recorded of him at this stage of his career is that he is busy dallying with Delilah. His miraculous birth, his earlier victories over the enemies of his people, his intimacy with God have come to this: after twenty years, his people are not liberated from the Philistines, and his strength is going into preserving a liaison with a woman from whom he knows he has to keep a careful psychic distance.

Furthermore, consider the way in which his great strength comes into play in the episode with Delilah. With the Gaza prostitute, Samson used his power as a means of evading and scorning his enemies. With Delilah, he no longer cares to evade the Philistines, and he even seems bored with scorning them. He knows that they can't beat him, and he no longer has much interest, apparently, in beating them. He's content just to let them surround him when they will and to brush them off like flies, as a nuisance not worth much notice, when they do. How glorious a flowering of his life and mission is this? The great gift of strength God gave him for the liberation of his people he is now using as a private means to keep his shabby and inadequate love life going.

Yahweh's spirit doesn't come on him when he does.

But this petty self-absorption is not the worst of the episode with Delilah.

On each of the first three times when Delilah presses Samson for his secret and he tells her a lie, the Philistines immediately afterwards do to Samson what Samson's lie leads them to expect will defeat Samson. At least after the first occasion, Samson can't be surprised at what happens; he must expect it. So, at least after the first time, when Samson tells Delilah a lie about what will defeat him, he must expect that the Philistines will do to him whatever he puts into their heads with his lie. It is clear, too, that he expects to shake free of their devices, as he himself puts it in the story. This is also what he expects when, on the fourth time of being betrayed, he finds himself surrounded by the Philistines and shaven. When he sees the Philistines around him after he has told Delilah about his Nazirite status, he supposes that he is going to experience nothing more than the fourth repeat of the same farce. And so he tells himself that he will shake himself free this time as before. It cannot be, then, that he himself really believed what he told Delilah, namely, that if he were shaven, he would be weak like other men.

And why would Samson believe a thing of that sort? It is so clearly false. Both from the narrator's point of view and from Samson's, there is just one correct explanation of the source of Samson's strength: it comes from God. The narrative drives home the point that Samson's strength comes from God by its comment on Samson's mistaken belief that he can shake the Philistines off this fourth time as in the preceding three. The text explains Samson's mistake *not* by saying that Samson didn't know he was shaven. The text says Samson didn't know that Yahweh had departed from him.

So the right way to understand Samson's fourth explanation to Delilah of the secret of his strength is as a mixture of truth and lies. Samson believes and says truly that he has never been shaven because he has been a Nazirite of God's from birth. But the next part of his speech isn't true and he doesn't believe it: it isn't the case that simply shaving him will destroy his strength. The lazy complacency that keeps him by Delilah lying and brushing off the Philistine attacks when they come leads to his revealing some deep and important truth to her; but it doesn't give her the secret of his strength, and Samson doesn't expect that it will. When he tells Delilah that cutting his hair will make him weak, he is again lying to her, at least in the sense that he is telling her as true what he himself believes to be false.

It is important to see one other implication of Samson's fourth explanation to Delilah of the secret of his strength. After the first three attacks by the Philistines, Samson has to know that his telling Delilah about his Nazirite status is tantamount to giving it up. If Delilah and the Philistines believe that Samson's strength is in his hair, then Delilah and the Philistines will shave him, and Samson must understand that they will.

In this light, consider the attitude that has to underlie Samson's telling Delilah about his Nazirite status. That status was given to him together with the mission to which his life is supposed to be dedicated. But Samson isn't taking that mission seriously here. In the episode with Delilah, Samson is fighting with the Philistines not for the sake of freeing his people but just as a way of continuing to sleep with Delilah. That in these circumstances Samson elects to tell Delilah about his Nazirite status is evidence that it doesn't mean much to him. Samson doesn't suppose that his strength depends on his hair. It depends on God, as Samson knows, and it is God's gift to Samson. But if strength is God's gift to Samson, Nazirite status is God's demand of Samson. To rely on having the gift and to be willing to dispense oneself from the demand is to treat God as if he were in Samson's service. Explaining his Nazirite status to Delilah as a means of placating his Philistine concubine and continuing to hang around in enemy territory enjoying her is thus a little like a Dominican's using his habit as a make-shift sheet for his mistress. The purpose for which the symbol is being used shows a disdain for the thing symbolized. It therefore also shows a disdain for God, to whom respect for the symbol and what it symbolizes is owed.

The worrisome element in Samson's attitude towards God after the battle at Lehi thus finds its full-blown awfulness here. Here, with Delilah, Samson takes it for granted that since he is the champion of his people, God will have to continue to bestow the gift of strength on him, but that it doesn't matter much what Samson himself does or how he treats God. As Samson sees it, dispensing himself from his Nazirite status as a means of mollifying his mistress carries no cost for him, the mighty Samson. With unreflective complacency, he simply assumes that God will keep him mighty when the Philistines surround him after shaving his hair.

And so, in an odd sort of way, by his attitude towards his Nazirite status and by lying about it, Samson makes true what was false before he lied about it: cutting his hair deprives him of his strength. Samson's strength departs from him when his hair is cut, not because his strength is in his hair but because Yahweh departs from him when Samson doesn't care that his hair is cut. If Samson was contumelious towards the Philistines in the episode with the Gaza prostitute, he is contumelious towards God in this episode with Delilah.

This, then, is what Samson is culpable for.

The End of the Story

The part of the narrative that, in effect, constitutes the end of Samson's story begins with the text's comment that Samson did not know the Lord had departed from him. (16:20) Samson is culpable for the contumely that prompts God to depart from him; but God's departing is responsible for the catastrophe that follows, and it is worth noticing this fact. If God had stayed with Samson till after the Philistine attack, then Samson would not have been captured by the Philistines. He is captured, blinded, imprisoned, subjected to hard labor, and paraded as a trophy to an alien god because God chooses to leave Samson when he does. And so, as it turns out on my reading of this narrative, God has not only the sort of indirect responsibility for horrendous evil which I discussed at the outset of this paper; he also has direct responsibility for the suffering Samson undergoes at the hands of the Philistines. God could have waited till Samson was safe before leaving him, and at that point he could have let Samson know that he was bereft of the strength God gave him, so that Samson kept himself out of danger in consequence. Instead, in the story, God leaves just then when Samson must have his strength to avoid ruin. Although Samson brings the disaster on himself in the sense that his contumelious acts are responsible for God's leaving him, it is God's leaving Samson at that very time that lands Samson in the catastrophic condition he is in at the end. Why does God do this?

This question in effect returns us to the question with which this paper started, namely, whether the life of a person suffering horrendous evil brought on himself by his own evil actions can somehow be a good for that person. We will have an answer to the question about God's reason for leaving Samson when he does if we can see something that redeems the horrendous evil of Samson's life and makes it a good for Samson. But if there is anything of that sort in this narrative, it will have to come in the very last acts of Samson's life, when he is a captive among the Philistines.

In his captivity among the Philistines, Samson is plunged into the horrendous suffering I described at the outset of this paper, and the mission for which he was born looks like a decisive failure. The victorious Philistines are having a celebration to thank their God for letting them capture Samson, and Samson is the main entertainment for the celebration. By the time of this celebration, Samson has been a Philistine prisoner long enough for his hair to have begun to grow back, and also long enough for some change to have taken place in him.

The nature of the change can be seen in the prayer he makes to God in the Philistine temple. The regrowth of his hair is not the return of his strength; the restoration of his strength requires the return of his God to him, and Samson knows it. And so he prays to God for strength. But this prayer is significantly different from that other recorded prayer of his, after his victory at Lehi when he needed water.

When he was dying of thirst, he prayed to God in this way: "It was you who gave this great deliverance by the hand of your servant. And now I am dying of thirst, and I will fall into the hands of the uncircumcised". What he says now, standing between the pillars, is this: "Oh Lord Yahweh, remember me, please, and give me strength, please, just this once, O God; let me be avenged on the Philistines with revenge for my two eyes" (16:28). The elements notably lacking in the earlier prayer are here now. There is not just one invocation of God in this prayer; there are two. And although the prayer is very short, just a sentence in effect, 'please' also occurs twice in it. There is a plea in it, too, of the sort that was lacking in the earlier prayer. Someone who says "please, just this once" to another person thereby conveys the power of his need or desire and his awareness of his dependence on the other to give him what he wants.

The implicit repentance in Samson's later prayer of his earlier contumely towards God is by itself a huge change for the better in Samson. At least equally importantly, the things which in the earlier prayer showed that Samson was not willing to let Delilah or God be close to him are missing in this later prayer. In this prayer, Samson's need, his vulnerability, his recognition that his own will isn't enough to save him, are all manifest; and Samson is willing to let them be evident both to himself and to God. Just as Delilah couldn't manage by herself to be close to Samson when his will was set on being distant from her, so God also is closed out when Samson is distant from him. But in this prayer, Samson is present to God, and for that reason God can also be present to him.

That in the narrative God shares this view is made evident by the fact that God grants Samson's prayer. God, who departed from him when Samson was distant from him and contumelious towards him, returns to Samson after this prayer. God fills Samson with enough strength to bring down the entire Philistine temple.

For my purposes, it is also important to see that the turn to God represented by Samson's prayer co-exists with much of Samson's old spirit. Although Samson's suffering turns him, it doesn't tame him. In addition to the absence of any explicit request for forgiveness or direction in his last prayer for strength, there is also the fact that in Samson's last plan he is still confusing his private concerns with his public role as the liberator of his people. In his prayer, he asks God for strength not in order to fulfill his mission, but in order to get personal revenge; he wants his strength back in order, as he says, to be avenged on the Philistines for his eyes. And then there is his last recorded line: "Let my soul perish with the Philistines." (16:30) This is a prayer, too, but one which is more nearly in the style of Samson's earlier prayer at Lehi. True, it is not a prayer based on a desire that God provide miraculously for him so that he might succeed in triumphing over his enemies. On the contrary, it's a prayer that God might not let him survive the general destruction of the temple's collapse. It's a complete giving up on triumphing. In this sense, the line shows the change from the old Samson. But the style of the prayer is reminiscent of the earlier prayer; and the willfulness of it, the intransigent refusal to accept life on terms other than his own, has a lot of the old Samson in it.

God returns to Samson when Samson's turning to God is far from full and finished.

Samson's death in the temple's collapse gives us the final complication of Samson's turning again to God and his mission; it is the final part of the story of Samson's life. What are we to say here? Is Samson triumphant at the end of his life or not? On the one hand, of course, the answer has to be 'no'. Samson dies, and he dies as a blinded Philistine captive among his enemies, a ruined wreck of what he himself had wanted to be. Where is the triumph in this? This is rather the culmination of the ruining of his life. On the other hand, the text says that the Philistines who died in the temple's fall were many more than those Samson killed in all his earlier battles taken together. Furthermore, it is worth noticing that Samson's family came to get his body. If his family were able to retrieve his body from a Philistine temple in Philistine territory when Samson was responsible for the destruction of that temple and the people in it, then we can reasonably assume that the collapse of the temple seriously undermined Philistine rule in that place at least for a time. And so, in his death, Samson fulfilled his mission, finally, as he had not managed to do in his life. And he did so because in his suffering he turned to God, present to God as he was not before, so that God was also present to him. Surely, this is not defeat.

This odd and complicated mix, of conversion to God coupled to the old sin-prone character, of defeat that nonetheless effects the fulfillment of a mission, of the most broken of lives which is somehow still glorious— this is what Milton also saw in Samson's story, and maybe in his own story as well. Milton sums it up this way:

> Samson hath quit himself
> Like Samson, and heroicly hath finished
> A life heroic....
> ...To Israel
> Honor hath left, and freedom...
> To himself and his father's house eternal fame;
> And, which is best and happiest yet, all this
> With God not parted from him, as was feared,
> But favoring and assisting to the end. (ll.1709–1720)

Milton's own dreadful suffering entitles him to the next lines in the play. Lines that would be intolerable coming from those at ease are a kind of testimony from the world of horrendous evil when they are written by Milton:

> "Nothing is here for tears, nothing to wail
> Or knock the breast, no weakness, no contempt,
> Dispraise, or blame; nothing but well and fair,
> And what may quiet us in a death so noble." (ll.1721–1724)

Gloriousness

The answer to the question about God's withdrawing from Samson
and the answer to the questions with which this paper began are implicit
in Milton's view.

It will help us understand this view if we reflect on the standard of
good for human lives which Milton relies on in his reading of the story of
Samson. What is the worst thing that can happen to a human being? Bone
cancer? Leprosy? These are indeed dreadful; but a person suffers the dep-
redations of disease as an innocent, and therefore even the terrible suffering of disease is not the worst that can happen to a person. What then is
the worst? Is it betraying the woman you love to save yourself, as Winston
does in *1984?* Is it standing in the dock at Nuremberg, reviled by all the
world for unspeakable crimes against a whole people? Even this is not the
worst, because it is possible to live to be broken-hearted in contrition even
for such crimes, as Franz Stangl, the commandant of Treblinka, seems to
have done.[13] On Christian doctrine, the worst thing that can happen to a
person is to die unrepentant in evil. And that is because to die unrepentant is to be at a permanent distance from a perfectly good God; it is to be
endlessly isolated from God's redemptive goodness in self-willed, self-
protective loneliness, the full-blown horror only hinted at in Samson's
sort of distance from Delilah. *This* is the worst thing that can happen to a
human being, on Christian views.

If that is the worst, then what is the best? The best, we might think, is
to have no evil to repent. But, on Christian doctrine, there are no human
beings without evil to repent. There is a moral cancer that has infected
every human will. On this view, then, the best state for human beings—
best because it wards off the worst state for human beings—is repentance.

This is not, of course, our ordinary view of the good life for human
beings. But the story of Samson prompts a more considered view of the
nature of human flourishing. What is it for a human person to flower into
glory? On Christian views, it isn't winning your battles and building
monuments to your victories. It is drawing near to God and letting him
draw near to you. The general idea here is not uniquely Christian; something roughly similar to it can be found in pagan Greece as well. It's what
Achilles was thinking about, when he sat, grieved and angry, in his tent,
refusing to join in the battles where Greek warriors got glory and died
young. There are two sorts of honor, he explains to the embassy which has
come to try to persuade him to fight again. There's honor from men, and
that's worthless; and there's honor from Zeus, which is everything—but

---

13. Gita Sereny, *Into That Darkness* (New York: Vintage Books, 1974).

that can be had even by a person who dies in obscure old age, without any battlefield glories.[14]

So although Samson may look as if his life is a great good to him when he wins at Lehi or when he toys with Delilah and disdains his Nazirite status, it isn't. Physical strength and health, political power and honor, aren't enough for a good life if they are coupled with the proud, self-protective loneliness with which Samson keeps Delilah and God at bay. On Achilles's view, on Milton's view, and on mine, Samson is most glorious not after his victory at Lehi or in his established Superman status with Delilah. His flowering comes in his worst suffering, in his praying to God as he does and in the drawing near to God that the prayer represents. He is most glorious in the expectant repentance with which he makes his prayer and waits for God to flood him with strength. His glorious flowering comes in his turning to God and God's returning to him.

But what moves Samson from the corrupt and jaded state in which he is before God departs from him, when his mission is forgotten and his divinely given gift of strength is subservient to his concubine, to this turning to God at the end? Surely, it is his suffering. What else would do it? Ethics lectures from the deity? A divine display of displeasure in thunder and lightening? If we were going to rewrite the story of Samson, to get him from the episode with Delilah to some condition in which he makes that last petitioning prayer in which he turns to God, could we credibly write scenes moving him from the first condition to the last without including serious suffering for Samson? Anything other than 'no' seems to me not a credible answer to this question.

And that is why in the narrative God leaves Samson when he does.

---

14. Homer, *Iliad*, tr. Richard Lattimore (Chicago: University of Chicago Press, 1951) Book IX, ll. 432, 600–10.

at long last Phoinix the aged horseman spoke out

…

"Listen then; do not have such a thought in your mind; let not
the spirit within you turn you that way, dear friend. It would be worse
to defend the ships after they are burning. No, with gifts promised
go forth. The Achaians will honour you as they would an immortal.
But if without gifts you go into the fighting where men perish,
your honor will no longer be as great, though you drive back the battle."
Then in answer to him spoke Achilleus of the swift feet:
"Phoinix my father, aged, illustrious, such honour is a thing
I need not. I think I am honoured already in Zeus' ordinance
which will hold me here beside my curved ships as long as life's wind
stays in my breast, as long as my knees have their spring beneath me."

Conclusion

Nothing in this reading of Samson's story diminishes one iota the horrendous suffering of Samson's life. The laments Milton writes for Samson are moving testimony to Milton's raw sensibility to the horrendous suffering of his own life as well as that of the protagonist in his poem. And yet Milton bears witness, for himself and for the Samson of the story, that it is possible for even a life of horrendous suffering to be a great good to the sufferer. On Milton's way of reading the narrative of Samson, it is possible for there to be glorious flowering for the sufferer not in spite of the suffering but because of it. The suffering is not decreased by the flourishing; it is redeemed by it. And so it would not have been better if God had let Samson die before Samson fell into contumely against God. If Samson had died earlier, say because he had no water after the battle at Lehi, or because he had a heart attack in bed, Samson would have been the poorer for it.[15] It is possible, then, for a person to be irremediably broken and glorious nonetheless.

The gloriousness of Oedipus at Colonus, as Sophocles portrays him, consists of being specially beloved of the gods; but Oedipus's relationship to the gods is manifest largely in his ability to know things ordinary mortals don't know, including the precise time and place of his death, because the gods reveal these things to him. So for Sophocles Oedipus's suffering is redeemed by some extraordinary excellence of mind. But what redeems Samson's suffering and what constitutes his gloriousness is more nearly an excellence of will than an excellence of mind. It consists in his letting go of his willed self-protective isolation, in his willingness to be open to God, in his drawing near to God. In this condition, he accepts what God gives him as a gift, and in using that gift for the purpose for which God gave it, he in effect accepts the giver with the gift. And so his suffering is redeemed in relationship with God, in his being present to God and God's being present to him. Contrary, then, to what we might have supposed at first, it is possible for even a perpetrator of horrendous evil to have a life

---

15. There are many other people whose lives are impacted by Samson's, of course, and so it will occur to someone to wonder whether or not other lives would have been better if Samson had died before the episode with Delilah. Insofar as the narrative in question is about Samson primarily, and about those others only secondarily, the story doesn't give us the information needed to evaluate the impact of Samson's story on them. But perhaps at least this much can be said. Insofar as Samson's story includes his being glorious in some sense, then all those who care about Samson or whose welfare depends on Samson are also the beneficiaries of the good that comes to Samson. I am grateful to Michael Barber for calling my attention to this point.

which is a great good for him; but the great good consists in relationship, and first and foremost in his relationship to God.

So the story of Samson is suggestive for thinking about the problem of evil. It suggests that we think about the justification for God's allowing suffering in terms of human relationship to him, and it also suggests something about methodology. The insights we gain about the problem of evil from the story of Samson came just because we are focused on a story. Among other things, the story portrays for us the intimate details of one person's life and psychology and the complexities of that person's interactions with God, and those details and complexities matter to us in evaluating whether or not God was justified in allowing Samson's suffering. Without the story and all that the story gives us, if we had had only a sort of Cliff Notes summary of the facts of Samson's life, we would have had a much harder time seeing anything that would have justified his suffering. And so, although nothing in this story gives us a full solution to the problem of evil, reflection on the story of Samson does show us something about the right direction in which to look for one, if it is to be found, and one good and helpful way in which to go about looking for it.[16]

---

16. I am grateful to William Alston, Michael Barber, Jeffrey Brower, Frank Burch Brown, Rachel Douchant, John Foley, Robert Gahl, John Kavanaugh, Scott Macdonald, Michael Murray, Paul Philibert, Alvin Plantinga, Michael Rea, William Rehg, and Theodore Vitali.

AGAINST THEOLOGY

Howard Wettstein
University of California, Berkeley

THAT ATHENS AND JERUSALEM represent dramatically different ways in the world is hardly a new idea. But there are implications that remain to be explored. Twentieth-century thinkers such as A.J. Heschel and Max Kadushin inspire my project. Their voices, though, have been dimmed by current theological orthodoxy. I don't mean denominational Orthodoxy but rather the standard modes of theological thought bequeathed by the medievals. Developments in philosophy, like the work of Wittgenstein, suggest that the time may be ripe for another pass through the terrain.

Philosophy, born in Greece, is one of the supreme achievements of that culture, a reflection of its distinctive greatness. The Hebrew Bible is a parallel reflection, another supreme achievement, but of a very different culture. Eventually, considerably later than biblical times, the two cultures met; their subsequent marriage issued in another of the world's great cultural wonders, medieval theological philosophy, or philosophical theology.

In conventional terms, the match was a great success; its offspring has had an illustrious history. The way we—theists, agnostics, and atheists— think about religious things is a tribute to the philosophical theology of the medievals. And yet....

Today's situation has analogies to that of the philosophical tradition itself, when it came upon modern times. So much of the way we—and our post-Cartesian forbears—pursue philosophy is a tribute to Descartes,

---

* Versions of this paper were presented at Brandeis University, Hendrix College, London School of Jewish Studies, and at a conference titled "Philosophers and the Bible" at the University of Maryland in 2003. I'm grateful to David Berger, Brian Copenhaver, Eli Hirsch, Menachem Kellner, Chip Manekin, Josef Stern, and Eleonore Stump for comments on earlier drafts.

often honored as the father of modern philosophy. And yet some, me included, contend that the Cartesian revolution in philosophy imposed significant costs and in some ways represented a step backward.[1] The liabilities include some of the most well-known features of Descartes' thought, such as his famous distinction between mind and body—the realm of spirit versus that of the mechanical. Something funny, one might say, happened in the early 1600s in philosophy that, for better and worse, changed its subsequent course.

My contention is that something similarly funny happened in early medieval times when the Jewish religious tradition[2] entered into a long-term flirtation with the philosophical tradition. When I say that something funny happened, I don't mean that it was all bad, and I certainly don't mean that we have nothing to learn from the new course. We have much to learn. Still, the substantial change was not without cost, or so I'll be arguing. My central concern in this paper is not the cost. It is rather the idea that we are dealing here with a major transition, a new paradigm, in Kuhn's vocabulary.[3]

Previously, mainstream Jewish tradition, having resisted the incursion of philosophical modes of reflection, was more or less philosophically innocent. The Greek-inspired style of thinking would show up here and there—in the relatively early work of Philo, for example. But it never really caught on until considerably later; by the time the Jews found themselves in the world of Sefarad, the Muslim world in which philosophy played a dominant role in intellectual culture, the philosophical mode had become central, even if still controversial.[4]

---

1. See, e.g., Richard Rorty, *Philosophy and the Mirror of Nature* (Princeton, 1979).

2. My exclusive concern in this paper is Jewish tradition, rabbinic Judaism. If my approach has merit, there likely will be wider applications. But here I'll be satisfied to navigate local waters, deep as they are.

3. Kuhn's approach to the history of science is important here. Kuhn sensitized historians of science to the existence of radical differences, discontinuities, between scientific epochs, e.g., between the eras of Newton and Einstein. Previous to Kuhn there was a tendency to see Einstein's work, e.g., as simply building on Newton's. Kuhn argued convincingly that the differences needed new emphasis and that it was more correct to see Einstein as a revolutionary, overthrowing the Newtonian approach rather than supplementing it. Einstein's view was, indeed, not only radically different from what came before, it was in some ways incommensurable with it. The term "incommensurability" cries out for clarification, but the idea is certainly highly suggestive, equally so in connection to my topic in this paper.

4. This is not to say that philosophy first caught on in Jewish tradition in Andalusia/Sefarad. Saadia Gaon, in ninth-century Babylonia, was already there. But

A philosophical interpretation of the earlier Jewish religious ways was, however, quite an ambitious undertaking: to convert an outlook not fundamentally philosophical into a philosophy. And that required taking a way of thinking and feeling native to one culture and reformulating it in very different cultural terms.

That the philosophical interpretation could be seen (broadly, certainly not universally) as revealing the real meaning of the tradition was a tribute to the stature of its main architects, most importantly Maimonides, whose honorific place in the tradition hardly depends upon his philosophical activity: the *Mishneh Torah,* Maimonides' halakhic magnum opus independently renders him a premier figure in post-talmudic times. His *Guide for the Perplexed* became at once *the* Jewish philosophical work for both those inside and outside the tradition, as well as a source of great discomfort for those traditionalists who remained suspicious of the incursions of philosophical thought.

In this paper I highlight the enormity of the medieval transformation.[5] My larger aim, in the book from which this paper derives, is twofold. First, I wish to explore the theological implications of the earlier religious ways. Premedieval theological reflection has a distinctive character, continuous with literature and the arts more than with philosophy as practiced by the medievals. What, I will be asking in the sequel, is it to take seriously that early theological reflection was not in this way philosophical? How might this change the way we think about religion and religious things?

A second larger aim pursued briefly here and at more length in the sequel is to explore the role of philosophy in illuminating religious phenomena. Philosophy is a matter of thinking hard about fundamentals. But as Wittgenstein taught, philosophy often tends toward a kind of imperialism, recreating in its own image the domains it investigates. A striking example is the philosophical idea that learning one's first language involves something like theory formation. Thus an activity that is quite primitive (and, of course, also involves breathtaking sophistication) becomes a theoretical business, somehow a matter of intellect. Religion

---

in later medieval times philosophy comes to be intellectually central in an important part of the Jewish world.

5. That some sort of major transformation occurred is not news. Below I quote Moshe Halbertal and Avishai Margalit, *Idolatry* (Cambridge, Mass., 1992), and certainly Marc Shapiro's *The Limits of Orthodox Theology* (Oxford, 2004) is relevant here. Another important contribution is Menachem Kellner's *Must a Jew Believe Anything?* (Oxford, 1999). See fn. 29 below for a brief discussion of my differences with Kellner. I expect to explore the matter in more detail in the book to which the present paper is an introduction.

also is less about the head than we have learned to suppose. My point is
not to deny philosophy a significant role in the understanding of theological matters. The trick is to illuminate religious phenomena without impe-
rialistic reconception.

I begin my story with the philosophically innocent approaches of the
Bible and the oral tradition, the latter codified in the Talmud (and other
talmudic-era works). I will then turn, for contrast, to the thought of Maimonides.

LITERARY THEOLOGY

1. Biblical Literature

It is a commonplace that the Bible is a work of literary magnificence.
Magnificence granted and aside, I want to focus on its literary character.
The Bible, in its talk of God and theological matters, generally treats these
as might a poet or a writer of literary prose. The contrast is with philosophy.

Philosophy, though, is many things to many people. Philosophers,
beginning no later than Plato, have been great literary craftsmen. But
there is an approach, beginning no later than Aristotle, notable in the Middle Ages as well as in the analytic philosophy of our times, in which the
literary gives way to the logical and analytical, even scholastic.[6] For those
of us brought up in the latter kind of philosophy, there is a tendency to
think of it simply as "philosophy."[7]

Indulging this tendency, let us begin to explore the contrast between
the philosophical and literary treatments of theological matters by asking,
How would we expect philosophers to approach theology?

- To begin with, one might expect definitions—at least clarification—of key terms, for example, "God": Is "God" a proper name?
  Is it simply a tag or pointer to its putative referent, or is the term
  associated with a descriptive concept such as "Creator of the universe"? And so on for the other names of God.[8]

---

6. To see something importantly common to those who emphasize the logical
   and analytical is not to say that they look at things in quite the same way. One
   modern variant sees a philosopher simply as an intellectual worker in a certain
   domain; an ancient variant sees a commitment to a certain way of life as definitive.

7. This is not always honorific, as in Wittgenstein's deep ambivalence about
   what he calls philosophy. In what follows, it is this genre of philosophy—the
   logical, analytical—of which I speak.

8. My aim in this bulleted list is to engender a sense of difference between theological genres. In this first item I speak of a contemporary issue (in this case, to

- One might also expect to hear from the theory of knowledge. Is it possible, for example, to *know* that there is a God? Are there proofs? If not, what makes "God exists" acceptable and intellectually respectable. And even if this can be handled, how does one establish the superiority of one religion over another?

- Another arena of epistemological inquiry concerns eschatology. What can we know and how can we know about the afterlife, about messianic times, and the like?

- Then there are the notorious theological puzzles, the problem of evil, for example: Given God's perfections, specifically his goodness, knowledge, and power, how can there be any evil at all in the world, not to speak of the unspeakable horrors visited upon so many, whether righteous, religious, or not.

- Another sort of theological puzzle, although not often formulated as a puzzle, is the matter of how we manage to speak of God. The philosophical tradition beginning with the medievals has taken such talk to be problematic. Maimonides, for example, believes we cannot speak significantly of God using concepts whose primary application is to us and our world. That is, anthropomorphic vocabulary cannot signify in its usual way, with its usual meanings. So philosophy needs to address the possibility of meaningful discourse about God.

I could go on, but it should be clear that these philosophical questions do not frame the Bible's theological approach. The Bible, of course, addresses theological matters, but in the manner of poetry or literary prose, not philosophical argument.

Having said a bit about the philosophical, let me say something about the literary, specifically the Bible's literary mode. In addition to large bod-

---

philosophers of language). The other items express concerns of the medievals as well.

I couch the issue here in terms of the English word "God." But, of course, it pertains in the first instance to the relevant Hebrew expressions, some of which seem more or less descriptive, e.g., *Elohim*, often translated as "God," and some of which seem quite clearly to be names, e.g., the Tetragrammaton, often (badly) transliterated as "Yahweh" and often translated as "the Lord." The situation with translation, especially of the Tetragrammaton, is delightfully confusing. The Hebrew word is a proper name but it is not intelligibly vocalized (voweled, as it were). Traditionally it's pronounced as if it were quite another word, the formal "Lord." So the situation is this: We have a real proper name, read as if it were quite another sort of word. Imagine the havoc this wreaks.

ies of explicit poetry—for example, Psalms, or poetic sections of other works like the book of Job—the Bible abounds with imagery and poetic prose. Think of the characterization of people as reflecting God's image, a turn of phrase that eludes literal rendering.

We often speak of the biblical *narrative*, and narrative is another aspect of the Bible's literary character. The Bible's characteristic mode of "theology" is storytelling, in stories overlaid with poetic language. Never does one find the sort of conceptually refined doctrinal propositions characteristic of a philosophical approach.

When the divine protagonist comes into view, we are not told much about his *properties*. Think about the divine perfections, the highly abstract *omni*properties (omnipotence, omniscience, and the like), so dominant in medieval and postmedieval theology. One has to work very hard—too hard—to find even hints of these in the biblical text.

Instead of properties, perfections, and the like the Bible speaks of God's *roles*—father, king, friend, lover, judge, Creator, and so on.[9] Roles, as opposed to properties; this should give one pause. And even when there is mention of God's properties, they are not philosophically central *omni*properties but ethical ones, anthropomorphically characterized: slow to anger, quick to forgive, and the like.

To further emphasize the literary side of all this and the distance from philosophical theorizing, it's important that God's multiple roles don't cohere all that well. God is, or plays the role of, parent, ruler, friend, lover, judge, and so on. This is fine in the right sort of literary context.[10] Love poetry, for example, is not diminished by sundry characterizations of one's love. Indeed, highly varied depictions often facilitate literary richness, as does the inevitable imagistic language.

If the Bible's portrayal of God, his thoughts, feelings, plans, his role in history, and the like is to count as theology—and why not call it theology?—it is of a very different sort than what, under the influence of the medievals, usually goes by that name. When I suggest in the title of this paper that I am "against theology," I mean, of course, theology of the medieval sort.

Attention to the concept of *religious belief* may help to sharpen the distinction between the philosophical and literary theological modes. When

---

9. As Halbertal and Margalit emphasize in *Idolatry*.

10. It is also theologically important. Our experience of God and derivatively our ways of thinking about God reflect not a consistent, single-track sort of experience but rather an experience of, as it were, someone who fills these quite different roles. There is a certain inchoate quality to both religious experience and conception.

we think about religion and religious commitment, the idea of *belief* is never far from view. It's striking, though, that *religious belief* is not a topic that gets any discussion in the Hebrew Bible. The Bible does speak of trusting in God, of fidelity to God, of fearing (or standing in awe)[11] of God, of believing *in* God (which concerns trust rather than belief in a thesis, doctrine, or proposition), of knowing God (where the Hebrew verb *la-da'at* suggests intimacy). But of belief that God exists we hear nothing.[12] Indeed, try to say of someone in Biblical Hebrew that she is or is not a "believer" in our sense.[13] Although the available biblical language might be stretched to this end, doing so would require an extension of the linguistic apparatus.

Still, something like our concept of belief seems implicated in the Bible.[14] After all, the Bible puts forth various truths about God, history, and the future.[15] And although it does not speak of believing these things, it certainly seems to take the putative facts for granted. Accordingly one who adheres to the Bible, one who takes it to be *his Bible*, would presumably take these things to be true, that is, believe them.

Even if, as we would put it, material about what one ought to think (about God, history, etc.) is all over the Bible, it remains important that the Bible, with all its instructions and commandments, does not command us

---

11. The Hebrew "*yirah*" connotes both fear and awe. In many of the relevant biblical concepts, though, it would seem that awe dominates, even if the relevant sort of awe involves fear.

12. The only exception that comes to mind is Psalm 14: "The fool saith in his heart, 'There is no God.'" Even putting aside how exceptional this language is, in context this too seems not about theoretical atheism but about those who ignore, turn their back upon, God.

13. A.J. Heschel, in *God in Search of Man*, emphasizes that there is no natural way in Biblical Hebrew to characterize one as a believer, as opposed say to a *yire shamayim*, one who stands in awe of heaven.

14. Perhaps it would be better to say that we can apply our concept of belief to the Bible in the way I go on to indicate.

15. The extent of this is easy to exaggerate. For one thing, the text does not tell us which of its narratives depict historical events and which are, as it were, parables. And such things are sometimes controversial within the tradition, e.g., the stories of Job and the Flood. Second, perhaps due to our tendency to see implicit theory in the text, there is a tendency to smooth out differences between biblical texts. Thus the ways of thinking about God's providence in Deuteronomy and, say, in Job make claims about the biblical view of providence quite risky. Nor in many of these cases does the rabbinic understanding in the Talmud rescue the situation.

to have the right thoughts.[16] When God is upset with humankind—in early Genesis for example, or later, say, in Exodus with the Israelites, or still later in the prophets with the people Israel—his gripe is not about their doctrinal irregularities but about how they live, about their betrayal of his trust.

Moreover, and of utmost importance for my project of distinguishing biblical from medieval theology, there is belief and there is belief. Eloquently put by Max Kadushin in his classic work *The Rabbinic Mind* the Bible's theological concepts and implicit beliefs remain *uncrystallized*. They are formulated by way of literary tropes, perfectly appropriate in context, but resistant to anything like definition. Biblical theology is poetically infused, not propositionally articulated.

Whereas the Bible's poetic character distinguishes it from much ordinary talk, its lack of strictly defined terms does not. Ordinary concepts, as Wittgenstein emphasizes, typically lack precise definition; this is one source of their great utility, their smooth and flexible functioning in actual (including intellectual) practice. One can always choose to impose strict definitions on what was a coherent (in practical terms), if theoretically ill-defined, practice. But this is not, says Wittgenstein, a matter of discovering what the real definitions are; there are none. It's rather a matter of imposing a more precise set of rules on the use of the term than were present before. Needless to say, there are all sorts of considerations that might motivate us to do this, that might recommend one definition over others. Still, the new definition is new; it's not built into the original practice with the terms, even implicitly.

The analogy of boundaries may be of use here. Imagine that two parties live separated by several miles of forest and that such has been the case for many generations. Never has the question arisen of where the property of one ends and where the other's begins. In some sense there is no fact of the matter; perhaps both families descend from original settlers and the question never arose. Now a feud arises and the question is raised. Where exactly is the boundary? What has happened is that certain practical considerations have emerged that make it important that there be a boundary. And the choice of boundaries may not be altogether arbitrary;

---

16. Not according to the medievals. Maimonides interprets, e.g., the first of the so-called Ten Commandments ("commandment" is not a biblical designation; "sayings" is closer), which appears to be a kind of introduction or preamble, as a commandment to believe in God. Similarly the second commandment (about not putting any other gods before God) appears to be quite personal. Maimonides interprets it as a command to believe in God's unity. See *Guide* 2:33 (translations below are by Shlomo Pines [Chicago, 1963]).

there may be reasons that motivate a choice or that exclude certain choices. But still, there is no preexistent fact of the matter.

Viewed in this light, one important thrust of the medieval theological tradition, trying to find conceptually refined formulations for the Bible's literary-theological tropes, is arguably not a mission of pure discovery. Doubly so: first, the poetic character of biblical theology renders at least problematic the quest for the "straight" theological, i.e., propositional, material lurking behind the imagery. And Wittgenstein adds another layer: never mind the poetry; ordinary vocabulary suffers from a lack of (or flourishes without) definition. Perhaps the Bible's literary theological ideas were fine as they stood, and the medieval philosopher is imposing boundaries, as it were.

I will highlight the contrast between biblical and philosophical theology by saying, a bit provocatively, that the Bible lacks theological doctrine. Of course, this depends upon what one counts as doctrine. My own predilection is to use this term for the sort of relatively clear, nonimagistic propositional articulation of theological truths (or candidates for theological truth), the sort of thing we do not find in the Bible. Here's an example: "The universe was created ex nihilo by a god who himself exists in a realm that is not part of the natural world."[17] As I use the term "doctrine" then, the Bible's theological remarks are typically, if not virtually always, nondoctrinal, formulated in figurative, often anthropomorphic, language, for example, "people reflect God's image."

Of course, the term "doctrine" is often used more widely than I'm suggesting, subsuming even highly imagistic theological sentences. Although I'll often use terms such as "doctrine" in my preferred manner, this really is just a matter of expressive convenience and nothing hinges upon it. If someone prefers the broader usage, I can be longer winded in making my points.[18]

2. The Oral Tradition

The Bible's literary way with theological matters might leave one unprepared for talmudic passages in which theological belief has become an official topic, for example, the famous passage in tractate *Sanhedrin*, chapter 10, in which the world-to-come is denied to those who fail to

---

17. Notice, even such refinement would hardly count as nonanthropomorphic. As Maimonides points out, our use of terms, even ones like "created" and "exists," have their home in talk about our world. And thus it's not clear what's going on in using them in connection to God.

18. For more on the notion of doctrine, see my paper "Doctrine" in *Faith and Philosophy* 14 (1997): 423–43.

accept certain theological claims.[19] Is the Talmud here going philosophical, as it were, or at least taking a step toward medieval philosophical theology?

I will return below to the passage just mentioned, with its emphasis
on belief. But notwithstanding such occasional passages, it is clear that in
general the Talmud is not going philosophical, quite the contrary. Consider anthropomorphism. The Talmud seems to revel in the anthropomorphic characterization of God, whose portrayal in the Bible is a source of
(almost) embarrassment to the medieval theological mind.[20] Maimonides
in the *Guide of the Perplexed* works (arguably too) hard to show that such
language goes only skin deep. Rabbinic texts, on the other hand, exhibit
what one might call hyperanthropomorphism, which I'll illustrate in an
excursion concerning *Eichah Rabbah,* the rabbinic *midrash* on the book of
Lamentations.[21]

Before looking at *Eichah Rabbah,* I offer an example of biblical (relatively tame) anthropomorphism as a contrast to the ensuing discussion of the
rabbis' hyperanthropomorphism: early in Genesis, at the time of the
Flood, God is angry at our antics, even regretful that he initiated the
human experiment. This is, of course, unabashedly anthropomorphic, but
the context of early Genesis imposes limits. For the God of early Genesis
is, despite the anthropomorphism, wholly other, the awesome and remote
Creator of the universe in whose hands was its annihilation.

The contrasting talmudic-era text that is my focus here has God at
considerably less distance. It has been said that the biblical narrative is the
history of God's learning that he cannot do it alone, that his plan crucially
requires partnership with his human reflections. By the time of the midrash on Lamentations, and in the perception of its authors, the lesson is
well learned. Not only can he not do it alone, the project is not going well.
And God's reaction reveals a new level of affective engagement and self-
awareness. Indeed, God has become effectively almost one of us. He suffers, weeps; he mourns. "Woe is me!" he cries in Proem 24, "What have I
done?"

---

19. See Kadushin, *The Rabbinic Mind,* 3rd ed. (New York: Bloch, 1972) chap. 7, for
other examples and an illuminating discussion.

20. This is to some extent true of the prophetic literature as well. Thus what is new
in rabbinic works is a matter of degree and sustained emphasis.

21. My discussion of *Eichah Rabbah* is adapted from my paper, "Coming to Terms
with Exile," in *Diasporas and Exiles: Varieties of Jewish Identity,* ed. H. Wettstein
(Berkeley, 2002). See that paper for more detail. I am indebted here as I am in
that paper to Alan Mintz's discussion in *Hurban: Responses to Catastrophe in
Hebrew Literature* (Syracuse, N.Y., 1996).

Sometimes the midrash sees God in maternal terms—or, more accurately, God, as the midrash has it, sees him/herself in such terms (Proem 22):

> Just as when you take away its young, a sparrow is left solitary," so spake the Holy One, blessed by he, "I burnt my house, destroyed my city, exiled my children among the nations of the world, and I sit solitary.

Sometimes the imagery is paternal: God is compared to a king who, enraged at his two sons (perhaps symbolically the people Israel just before the destruction of each of the two temples), thrashes them and drives them away. The king afterward exclaims, "The fault is with me, since I must have brought them up badly" (Proem 2). In Proem 24 God laments:

> Woe to the king who succeeds in his youth and fails in his old age...

> The Holy One, blessed be he, said to Jeremiah, "I am now like a man who had an only son for whom he prepared a marriage canopy, but he dies under it. Feelest thou no anguish for me and my children? Go summon Abraham, Isaac, and Jacob, and Moses from their sepulchres, for they know how to weep."

Not only does God mourn. He, it would seem, needs instruction in mourning from us.[22]

One aspect of this humanizing of the divine, interestingly parallel to (roughly simultaneous) Christian developments,[23] is a new emphasis on divine vulnerability. God is, as it were, exposed to the elements to a degree scarcely predictable by what we knew of him.

Closely related is what we might call divine approachability and emotional responsiveness. God, in Genesis, is available to the patriarchs, and to some extent to the matriarchs. The midrash on Lamentations (in the continuation of Proem 24) imagines the three patriarchs—Abraham, Isaac, and Jacob—and Moses pleading with God for mercy toward Israel. God, however, is unaffected; he cannot or will not comply. Eventually, he does promise to restore Israel to its place, but the promise is made not to the patriarchs or Moses. It is only mother Rachel who can move him. Rachel tells God that she had known of her father's plan concerning the marriage to Jacob, his plan to substitute Leah for her. Rachel attempted to foil the plan, but when that failed

> I relented, suppressed my desire, and had pity upon my sister that she should not be exposed to shame.... I delivered over to my sister all the signs that I had arranged with Jacob so that he should think that she was Rachel. More than that, I went beneath the bed upon which he lay with

22. As Mintz emphasizes. See ibid., 60.

23. Of course, in the Christian context new meaning is given to what I'm calling the humanizing of the Divine.

my sister; and when he spoke to her, she remained silent and I made all
the replies in order that he should not recognize my sister's voice. I did
her a kindness, was not jealous of her, and did not expose her to shame.
And if I, a creature of flesh and blood, formed of dust and ashes, was not
envious of my rival and did not expose her to shame and contempt, why
should you, a king who lives eternally and is merciful, be jealous of idolatry in which there is not reality, and exile my children and let them be
slain by the sword....

Forthwith, the mercy of the Holy One, blessed be he, was stirred, and he
said, "For your sake, Rachel, I will restore Israel to its place."

It is interesting that Rachel does not argue, as did Abraham in Genesis
18:23–33, on the grounds of what divine justice requires. Nor does she
appeal on the basis of her own merit, as do (earlier in Proem 24) the patriarchs, Abraham, Isaac, and Jacob. Hers is a more personal appeal, predicated on issues of character, God's character.

These developments are underscored and pushed to still another level
with the talmudic idea that after the Second Temple's destruction, God
himself leads only an exilic existence; the divine presence resides, as it
were, in *galut* (exile). This is no doubt in part a matter of empathy. To say
that God's presence is in *galut* is to say that he is with us, he feels for us.
But it is equally an expression of divine dislocation and a constricted existence. Here we approach discontinuity with what we know of God from
the Bible, certainly from the Pentateuch, a kind of anthropomorphic quantum leap.[24]

I've been focused on the rabbinic response to Lamentations in *Midrash
Rabbah*. But rabbinic hyperanthropomorphism is by no means limited to
contexts of mourning. The Talmud speaks in various places about God
hurting when we hurt, about God praying that his attribute of mercy/nur-
ture will overcome his demand for strict justice. It speaks of God's wear-
ing *tefillin* when he prays. The point, I hope, is made. Talmudic theologiz-
ing is hardly an intermediate phase, en route, as it were, to medieval
philosophical theology.

---

24. One might argue that there is no quantum leap here, but that the powerful
    imagery of divine exile is a mere rhetorically supercharged variation on what
    we have already seen: God in a state of mourning, weeping bitterly, feeling
    lost, even at times hopeless. But one has the sense that this is not simply a mat-
    ter of divine affect, that something more "objective" is at stake here. God's
    project for humanity, his partnership with Israel for *tikkun olam*, the repair and
    redemption of the world, has been thwarted. The universe is thus dislocated,
    thrown off course. Israel's political, social, and national catastrophe is thus
    transformed into a metaphysical cataclysm, a real cosmic jolt. The universe is
    shaken to its foundations.

Hyperanthropomorphism dramatizes the literary character of talmudic theology. But here's another way to see what I have in mind. The Talmud is renowned for its highly analytical legal (halakhic) discussions. But
interspersed are passages of a very different genre, aggadah, a literary treatment of theological and ethical issues, narratives, and parables. The almost
seamless movement between these radically different styles may reflect the
Talmud's recording of free-flowing discussions in the academies.

The shift from halakha to aggadah can seem stark, from the most
acute analysis to the most powerful religious imagery. It can also be bewildering: How can it be that the sages do not use their highly developed
conceptual acumen to analytically dissect the aggadah? Why are these
lovers of definition and distinction not tempted to inquire about what lies
behind all the impressionistic imagery? Who exactly is the protagonist?
What are his properties? Instead of raising these and other fundamental
questions, they tell more stories.

This—and here is my suggestion—makes sense on the following
assumption: perhaps there is something particularly appropriate or natural about what I'm calling the literary mode in theological, as opposed to
legal, discourse. Perhaps the apparently good questions that are so natural
to the philosophical bent of mind are, or anyway seemed to the rabbis, less
appropriate, even irrelevant.

Why should that be so? The rabbis see themselves as articulating a
way of life. What I am calling their literary theology, embedded in the
aggadic material, provides a situating environment for the *mitzvot*, specifically the edification, comfort, and meaning that, together with the practices, constitute the religious life. Their aims are thus dramatically different from those of later theologians. The questions and modes of approaching those questions that are natural to the philosopher are not theirs.

I now return to the topic with which I began this section—a possible
problem for my conception—the occasional talmudic emphasis on belief.
My picture is as follows: The Bible provides narratives such as the split-
ting of the Red Sea, the revelation on Mount Sinai, even suggestions about
the eschatological future (later in the Prophets). The rabbis remind us of
these things, occasionally even add to them, and insist that they be
believed. Still, their admonitions leave intact the uncrystallized character
of the theological concepts. The imagery and the poetically infused narratives remain philosophically undeveloped. A philosopher would find
them puzzling; and the puzzles remain unaddressed in the Talmud. So
although the rabbis not only endorse biblical theology and produce some
new theological ideas and emphases and, indeed, explicitly require certain beliefs, this is not to make the rabbis into philosophers. Their way in
theology remains literary and contrasts dramatically to the later philosophical approach.

Still, we should not suppose that rabbinic culture was hermetically sealed against the influence of Greece. Perhaps the attention to belief—albeit philosophically undeveloped belief—does represent some philosophical influence. But there is, I'm inclined to think, another and at least in some times and places a more powerful reason for this concern with belief: threat from the outside to a community's very existence. One measure of a community's defensiveness is how it defines heresy, a concept that can be viewed as a stand-in for belief.[25]

When a community's religious authority or religious identity is internally or externally threatened, one sort of defensive reaction is to draw boundaries, to say, "This is what it takes to be one of us." And so it becomes important to say what otherwise might have remained unsaid about belief and its opposite number, heresy. The heresy, after all, might comprise a strange reading of the theological imagery or narrative.

In an era of political, social, and religious tranquility, the need for doctrinal articulation may not be felt. The images, stories, and the rest do their work of supplementing and enriching religious practice; one is not pressed to sharpen the ideas, to articulate further the conditions of membership. Even radical, unorthodox interpretations of the narrative or of the commandments may be tolerated. Alternatively, such outré interpretations may be strongly criticized without the suggestion that their propounders are somehow outside the fold.

But in troubled times, things are different. In the Middle Ages, for example, the exiled Jews were a minority, living in communities that threaten them sometimes physically, sometimes culturally, and certainly theologically. This should issue in the prediction, or postdiction, that more or less sharp lines will be drawn. Who is in and who is out will be important questions.[26] Similarly in earlier, talmudic times, we see at least the seed of doctrine and the beginnings of the emphasis on belief, for the rabbis are worried about the Sadducees, the Karaites, and the emerging Christians. This tendency remains restrained for the rabbis, however, because their concern about Greek culture and its philosophy limits

---

25. Too late for inclusion in my discussion here, I have come across Daniel Boyarin's *Border Lines: The Partition of Judaeo-Christianity* (Philadelphia: U. of Pennsylvania Press, 2004), an extremely valuable discussion of the role of heresy and related matters.

26. At the same time, even in medieval times (but arguably less so in our own) one finds the phenomenon of radical critique of unorthodox ideas without hint of personal exclusion. See for example Nachmanides' commentary on Gen 18:20, where he roundly criticizes Abraham ibn Ezra for the latter's idea that God knows the world only in general terms, a radical idea then as now.

movement toward philosophically refined doctrinal explication. The medievals, by contrast, live in a time and culture in which philosophical theology is the reigning intellectual norm.

The competing religious orientations of medieval times, I'm suggesting, is a factor in the period's doctrinal orgy.[27] Needless to say, this is only part of the story. Clearly the work of the medieval giants is not driven by the need to exclude heretics; philosophical ideas have their own power. Nevertheless the times have their influence.[28]

What I am suggesting militates toward reversing the usual understanding that exclusion of heretics is grounded in their denial of previously well-known and well-articulated doctrine. A related thought concerning Judaism in our times is this: the Reform movement, in posing what was perceived as a grave threat to the tradition, prompts Orthodoxy, a new movement of those committed to the traditional ways, to a renewed and intense focus on theological doctrine and the sharpening of theological boundaries.[29]

---

27. See T. M. Rudavsky, "The Impact of Scholasticism upon Jewish Philosophy in the Fourteenth and Fifteenth Centuries," in *The Cambridge Companion to Medieval Jewish Philosophy*, ed. D. H. Frank and O. Leaman (Cambridge, 2003), 347:

> The subject of dogma and belief is revisited with even greater urgency in the fifteenth century. In large part this is due to the intense Christian persecutions experienced by Iberian Jews between 1391 and 1418. Jewish intellectual leaders were drawn into the debate not only to define who is a Jew, and who merits immortality, but also to articulate the doctrinal content of Judaism in contradistinction to Christianity. Jews were forced to respond to a Christian challenge rooted in creedal concerns, thus bringing to the fore questions concerning the nature of belief.

28. As Pierre Keller suggested, the importance of excluding heresy may be a factor in the centrality of doctrine in early Christianity.

29. Having completed my discussion of literary theology, I can now say more about my differences with Menachem Kellner's *Must a Jew Believe Anything?* (London: Littman Library of Jewish Civilization, 2004. Kellner appears to go farther than I do in denying rabbinic theological belief. Along the lines suggested by one of Kellner's critics, David Berger, I'm not at all sure that the theological-sounding passage in the Mishnah in *Sanhedrin* 10:1 does not mean what it says about denying the world-to-come to certain heretics (which is not to say that I find it appealing to make God into, as it were, a one-issue candidate). But the interpretation of the Mishnah is another matter. Moreover, as I argue above, while it's surely significant that required beliefs are never spoken of in the Bible and barely spoken of in talmudic-era literature (*Sanhedrin* 10 is an exception), still it's clear that there are things one is supposed to think. At the same time, I argue that these key "beliefs" are, in Kadushin's word, uncrystal-

PHILOSOPHICAL THEOLOGY

The literary style of theology—naïve from the vantage point of later philosophy—makes immediate contact with religious life. The narratives, parables, and the like provide the edification, comfort, and meaning that, together with religious practice, constitute the hallmark of that life. When one turns to the philosophical writings of Maimonides, *the* medieval Jewish philosopher—a philosopher's philosopher I will suggest[30]—one finds a very different and esoteric style of theology, one that is suggestive of a dramatically different religious sensibility.[31] Thinking one's way from one theological style and religious sensibility to the other, requires, in fact, a virtual switch in *Gestalt*.

Not that such is the common perception. If the contrast is as dramatic as I suggest, how is this missed? Maimonides' ideas are developed differently—in some aspects dramatically so—in his philosophical and halakhic texts.[32] It becomes tempting to harmonize the radical philosophical

---

lized. It is not only that they are not articulated in a philosophically adequate way by the rabbis; they are likely not articulable in such terms, at least not without imposition. Accordingly, rabbinic "dogmas" can be required and yet still fail to count as philosophical doctrine. Kellner asks in the "Afterword" to the new edition of his book,' Had the authors of the Mishnah really held [that the Torah is 'from heaven'—*Sanhedrin* 10:1 to be a dogma of Judaism, does it not seem odd that not one of them, or their amoraic successors, or the *ge'onim* who followed them took the trouble to define the term ['heaven'] with any specificity." It is just this question that I have tried to resolve here. Beliefs they had, but they were not philosophers and never saw those beliefs as standing in need of the sort of conceptual clarification characteristic of philosophy.

30. Maimonides' views are in some ways typical of Jewish medieval theology, in other ways not so. Some of the philosophical ideas and tendencies already mentioned as characteristic of medieval theology are Maimonidean, some not so. Nevertheless, for good reason he is often seen as the central player in medieval Jewish philosophy.

31. I am grateful here to a remark by David Hartman to the effect that Maimonides' approach reflects a different "religious sensibility" from that of the midrash. I think that the concept of religious sensibility—incorporating both cognitive and affective dimensions—is an important one for further reflection. It is (importantly) not the same idea as religious philosophy or anything similar.

32. Josef Stern in conversation points out that this distinction between the philosophical and legal works is hardly an absolute one; there are, e.g., important philosophical developments in the *Mishneh Torah*. No doubt this is correct. Indeed, high-level theoretical legal texts often have implications for, and sometimes explicit discussions of, pertinent philosophical issues; all the more

ideas with the more traditional characterizations of practice, a temptation that has a long history. And who is to say exactly how to balance these elements? What is clear is that over time, certainly in the communal perception of the overall picture, the more radical elements have been reined in. This seems at least in part a function of the fact that the largely legal characterizations in the *Mishneh Torah* are exceptionally lucid, written in a beautiful, plain Hebrew, whereas the *Guide*, originally in Arabic, is relatively tortured stylistically. Indeed, perhaps the radical philosophical material was meant to be so reined in. Certainly, as Maimonides notes, it was never meant to be publicized to the community.

In what follows I will highlight aspects of Maimonides' philosophical thought that are particularly relevant to the distinction in styles of theology in which I am interested. Even if in the end one rejects my thesis of an ancient to medieval paradigm change, the exercise of seeing these in *Gestalt* terms may be useful—this since we are so accustomed to the assimilation of the older and medieval views.

Sound bites are for politicians, not philosophers. Yet occasionally there is a turn of phrase that encapsulates something crucial about a philosophical outlook, Descartes dictum, for example, that the mind is better known than the body. Consider in this light Maimonides' idea that the intellect constitutes the bridge between man and God.

To give intellect such pride of place seems striking, even astounding, in the context of Jewish religious life. More consonant with that life is the recognition that in trying to understand God we are, to put it lightly, out of our depth. The Bible suggestively relates that Moses, God's intimate, was allowed to see only God's back.[33] Jewish religious life proceeds in the absence of theoretically adequate theological ideas.

Not that Maimonides, in the end, allows us much in the way of conceptual contact. Indeed, on his view our thinking about God has more than severe limitations. First, since God's unity does not allow even for the

---

so if the legal thinker lives, as it were, in philosophical issues, similarly for halakhically relevant remarks in the *Guide*. Nevertheless, in some plain sense one is a philosophical work, the other a legal one. And as I say, there are significant ideas that are developed quite differently in the two works.

Stern prefers another way of distinguishing the two texts, a way that I find helpful but not inconsistent with what I just said. The *Mishneh Torah*, he says, aims at articulating a way of life for the community; the *Guide*, on the other hand, is written for the exceptional individual, a manual to supplement the *Mishneh Torah*'s instructions and to give a new and different perspective on the religious life.

33. Exod 33:23.

possession of properties—this is quite a difficult idea—our attribution to him of *any* property must be mistaken. Indeed, God's essence, a property-less unity, is unknowable.[34]

Second, even were we to admit property talk about God, the property terms that we use in connection to God—goodness, unity, power, even existence—cannot mean anything like what they usually mean in the human/this-worldly context. Consider ascriptions of goodness to God. Maimonides insists that if one were careful in one's talk about God, one would not say or wish to say that God is good in something like our sense, just much better than we are or could be. That's not it at all. Such a conception of goodness is much too derivative of our own application of ethical vocabulary to people. God and his goodness are altogether other. Indeed, in connection to God we don't get so far as to attach (positive) concepts to our property terms. But this seems to leave talk of God's goodness without cognitive content.

Not quite. There is a kind of content, but not the usual kind. I allude here to Maimonides' famous doctrine of negative attribution. The intuitive idea is that there may be circumstances in which we don't know much about a thing, but in which we can circumscribe the thing by saying what it is not. To use property terms in connection to God, according to Maimonides, can at most be to circumscribe God's nature in that way, by saying what he is not.

It is often supposed, at least in more or less popular discussions, that the *via negativa* restores some measure of cognitive content to talk of God's properties. I'm not sure that this is even Maimonides' view; I'm not sure that it isn't. In any case, the content of discourse about God remains extremely thin. Indeed, given how meager it is, it becomes very difficult to wrap one's mind around Maimonides' idea that the intellect constitutes the human-divine meeting ground. If intellect is, indeed, the meeting ground, what sort of religious life might this support?

Let's reconsider the intellect-as-meeting-ground idea. Perhaps I have been too fixed on intellect as a faculty for the intellectual apprehension of God. An alternative is suggested by the famous remark of Einstein—no doubt reflecting the spirit of Spinoza as well as Maimonides—that his interest was in sharing God's thoughts, all the rest being mere commentary. In Maimonides' view the student of physics has special access to God's thoughts about the natural world.

---

34. These ideas are very difficult given our (probably Aristotle-inspired) intuitive thinking about property possession. But in the Neoplatonic tradition—one of the important influences on medieval theological thought—it's commonplace to suppose that unity of the One defies any division, even intellectual division.

Metaphysics, moreover, is for Maimonides the only tool for thinking effectively about God and God's nature, at least negatively. One can, for example, see that there is no other route to God than intellect, and that all thought about God is (at best) negative. Does this really constitute a bridge to the divine? While it is more like a bridge that ends in midair, Maimonides presumably would be quick to add that it takes one as close as one can get to the unknowable divine. And as with physics, but concerning the subject matter of God himself, the student of metaphysics shares God's thoughts.

Perhaps, to supplement these last reflections, we ought to focus not on the product, the result, of theological inquiry so much as the process. In *Guide* 3:51 Maimonides waxes poetic about "the intellectual worship of God." He writes, almost in the exhortative style of a work of moral piety (*mussar*): "When you are alone by yourself, when you are awake on your couch, be careful to meditate in such precious moments on nothing but the intellectual worship of God, viz. to approach him and to minister before him in the true manner that I have described to you—not in hollow emotions. This I consider as the highest perfection wise men can attain."

One is reminded here of the tradition's way of seeing deep involvement in talmudic study as edifying, almost cleansing. One engages in such study not only, not even mostly, for practical knowledge of halakha. Indeed, such practical knowledge requires a very different kind of study.[35] Rather, the process itself—albeit a sort of heady, unemotional business—constitutes a refined form of religious worship. With some irony Maimonides, talmudic giant *par excellence*, elevates philosophical inquiry above talmudic inquiry.[36] The philosopher on his couch approaches as close to God as is humanly possible and ministers to him in the true manner, with his mind and not with what Maimonides calls hollow emotions.[37]

---

35. Although unquestionably study of the theoretical underpinnings can enhance practice and add dimensions of meaning.

36. At the beginning of *Guide* 3.51, Maimonides presents a highly suggestive parable of the palace in which various categories of people are envisioned as occupying various stages of proximity to the ruler in his palace. Talmudists are thought of as having "come up to the habitation and walked around it," but having never even entered the antechamber, the latter requiring that one explore the fundamental principles of religion. Sarah Pessin suggested to me that for Maimonides the philosopher's study *becomes*—replaces—the traditional study hall, or *beit ha-midrash*, as the primary locus of the intellectual worship of God.

37. However especially in *Mishneh Torah* he sometimes speaks in a very different religious voice. In *Mishneh Torah*, "Hilchot Teshuvah," chap. 10, he sings the

Another corollary of the Maimonidean elevation of intellect is the role given to philosophy. Just imagine announcing in one of the amoraic academies—or, indeed, nowadays in a yeshiva—that philosophy is the *sine qua non* for understanding the Bible. Yet this is Maimonides' thesis. Only philosophy equips us to know which of the things the Bible says about God are literally true, which are metaphorical. It is only on the basis of philosophy that we know that, for example, the Bible's talk of God's right arm must be figurative. We know this because divine corporeality is incompatible with established philosophical truth.

The demonstrations of philosophy are, moreover, final; they need no sanction from religion. Indeed, if, contrary to fact according to Maimonides, the Aristotelian attempts succeeded in demonstrating the eternity of the world, we would be forced to read the Genesis creation story in a figurative way.[38]

Maimonides' position that philosophy is essential to the proper reading of the Bible and, in effect, the final arbiter of the facts is quite extreme even among medieval philosophers. He is, one might say, a philosopher's philosopher. But this makes him a perfect example for my purposes, perfect in representing the philosophical tendency in a particularly pure form.

---

praises of a passionate, boundless love of God, one he compares to a man's lovesickness for a woman—the latter being apparently less passionate in his view than what one might feel for God. It is striking that Maimonides takes as a kind of model for our love of God such passionate, first-moments-of-love episodes, rather than the sustained love of a long-term relationship. If one is thinking about the love between God and Israel—their extended relationship—one would presumably emphasize the latter. It's also worth noting Maimonides' individualistic emphasis in his chap. 10 discussion of love, a topic to which I return below.

I've been struggling with Maimonides' conception of the intellect as meeting ground. In addition to the considerations I have mentioned, his view may reflect his distinctive philosophical framework, very different from our own, specifically Aristotelian ideas about Active Intellect and the like, material beyond the scope of this paper.

38. The implications of this are radical. I spoke above about the fact that there are beliefs that are crucial to the tradition, even if in Kadushin's expression they remain uncrystallized. Maimonides' remark about the failed Aristotelian attempt to demonstrate eternity of matter in effect tells us that if one of these *prima facie* crucial religious beliefs conflicts with the dictates of the highest standards of human knowledge—philosophy, science, etc.—then one should reinterpret the traditional idea. Maimonides here anticipates a not uncommon liberal religious idea that there cannot be a conflict between science/philosophy and religion, for the former is authoritative in the realm of the factual.

The idea that the intellectual realm is the meeting place of man and God has not become commonplace, the accepted wisdom. But along with that idea came something that did become commonplace, something that seems to us to go without saying: the centrality of belief and doctrine.[39] We speak of religious people as believers, of the irreligious as nonbelievers.[40] And this despite the oddness of this characterization, given the way the Bible and the rabbis address the religious stance.

The Maimonidean elevation of the cognitive dimension to a pivotal position is occasionally evident even in the halakhic realm. Consider religious conversion. When one wants to convert to Judaism, one is told what he is, as it were, getting into. Maimonides' elaboration gives pride of place in the conversion process to articulating for the convert the "fundamentals of the faith, i.e., the unity of God...."[41] The talmudic discussion mentions no such thing![42] For the rabbis of the Talmud it was a matter of the person's sincere commitment to the Jewish people and the difficult life of Jewish religious observance.

Let's turn to the implications for religious practice. When Maimonides reflects (still in *Guide* 3.51) on a point of religious ritual, he gives it relatively short shrift. One of its central purposes is to separate people from the everyday worldly encounters that divert a person from deep thought about God. The practices—his examples are reading the Torah, prayer, performing the other commandments—constitute training to be

---

39. Strictly speaking, Maimonides in the *Guide* is concerned with knowledge of God rather than belief. Not only that, but he, in effect, denies that we can have knowledge of God. Still, it is the elevation of the epistemic dimension by him and other medieval philosophers that is responsible for the tendency in question.

40. This tendency to put belief at the center is restrained in the context of Judaism, as opposed say to certain strains in Christianity, by the tremendous role of practice. It's difficult to even imagine one who wholeheartedly believes but does not at least minimally observe the practices. Nevertheless, the idiom of "believer" is one that has caught on, and this testifies to the centrality of belief. If one claims to be Orthodox but does not adhere to the Maimonidean thirteen principles of faith, one's claim will in many, most, circles be thought to be tenuous at best. But see Marc B. Shapiro, *The Limits of Orthodox Theology: Maimonides' Thirteen Principles Reappraised* (Oxford: Littman Library of Jewish Civilization, 2004), for a scholarly argument that these principles are, every one of them, controversial from a traditional point of view, that is, in traditional Jewish sources.

41. In *Mishneh Torah, Hilhot Issurei Bi'ah*, chap. 14, trans. Rabbi Eliyahu Touger (New York, 2002).

42. Babylonian Talmud, *Tractate Yevamot* 47a.

involved with God's commandments rather than with, say, your check-
book, this toward the ultimate end of freedom from worldly things so
important for philosophical contemplation. And it's the latter that constitutes the real religious encounter. Prayer then, like the other practices, is
of instrumental value, not the religious moment.

It would be one thing to complain that much of ordinary religious
practice is insufficiently focused, and Maimonides also comments upon
that in chapter 51. But, our limited success aside, prayer, for us and the
rabbis of the Talmud, is all about communication with God. This is no
stretching exercise in the service of detached philosophical contemplation. It is an important religious moment, one of the central ones. And
when it works, when we are able to focus, to succeed in overcoming dis-
traction, prayer can represent a religious intimacy that stands at great distance from detached contemplation.[43] Not that there is only one way that
prayer works or, indeed, one sort of religious moment. Perhaps there are
times that prayer succeeds just because one is contemplative, even
detached. Nevertheless, all this remains a far cry from the religious sensibility of chapter 51.

Another thing that's striking about this side of Maimonides' thought
is its stark individualism. The Maimonidean philosophical/religious
moment is a solitary one. Of course, there are genuinely solitary religious
experiences. But it seems hasty to suppose, in the context of Jewish religious life, that the essential moment is either solitary or communal. Surely
there is a place for each. Think about the encounter at Sinai, which has
aspects of both the individual and the communal. And in the *Amidah,* the
heart of every prayer service, one speaks in the midst of a sometimes very
personal encounter, not of "I," but of "we."

Let me turn to the conception of the religious giant,[44] of religious
greatness. When we think of people who exhibit such greatness, they may

---

43. There are talmudic stories of Rabbi Akiva's praying, beginning the *Amidah*—a
standing prayer during which one does not move one's feet—in one location
and somehow ending up across the room. Or think of our sometimes profound
sense of God's presence at the end of the *N'eilah* prayer, at the end of a 25-hour
fast on Yom Kippur.

One thing that makes all this quite confusing is the thought that surely
Maimonides not only knew stories like that of Rabbi Akiva, but he must have,
one supposes, himself known the intimacy of prayer.

44. The word "giant" seems not quite apt here. But it translates a wonderful
expression in Hebrew. We speak of a *gadol* and of a *gadol b'dor*—a giant (great
person) and a giant of a particular generation. One could use the word
"leader," but even if a giant is almost necessarily a leader, the term *gadol* means
"giant," not leader.

or may not be philosophers. They are typically talmudic masters whose intellectual mastery is integrated with, and perhaps partly responsible for, a kind of heightened ethical and spiritual sense. To put it as Heschel might have, such a person lives with one eye on God, in a kind of intimacy with God. While awe and love toward God are for us sometime affairs, the *gadol* lives in God's presence.

Maimonides, again by stark contrast, sees religious greatness in terms of philosophical profundity. I don't mean that he would grant such greatness to a philosophically profound scoundrel, if on his view this were possible. But there cannot be religious greatness—dwelling with the king in the inner courtyard—in the absence of philosophical profundity. The prophets, according to Maimonides, were philosophers, from Abraham on.

CONCLUSION

Since medieval times—and this is a tribute to the power of medieval theological philosophy—it has seemed natural to suppose that religion and philosophy are natural bedfellows. Indeed, the word "theology," not unlike "doctrine," rings with the marriage of religion and philosophy. Still, "theology," as I've noted, can have a more neutral resonance, as it does when we consider premedieval Jewish theological reflection.

My larger project is to shift focus back to the literary expression of theological themes. Indeed, the arts more generally deserve attention here, as a glance at the history of western religion suggests: the role of music, for example, in the ancient temple service or in the Christian liturgical tradition, or in the liturgical practice of certain sects of Hasidism, as well as in much contemporary synagogue practice that derives from Hasidism; or the role of art in Christianity; or the role of dance and bodily movement in certain traditional rituals (prostration, for example) or in Hasidic dance.

But medieval philosophical theology stands as a formidable counterpart to literary expression. And this is so even where the philosophical approach has failed to win the hearts and minds of religious practitioners, as in contemporary traditional Jewish religious life, where other approaches dominate: various strains and forms of mysticism—Kabbalah, including the powerful Hasidic tradition—as well as *mussar*, a nineteenth-century ethical revival. These have considerably more influence on actual religious life and thought than medievally inspired Jewish philosophy. And yet the power of the latter somehow remains.

Example: anthropomorphism. Notwithstanding the inestimable power of anthropomorphic ways of thinking of God in actual religious life—as loving, caring, and so on—still one constantly hears the comment that, of course, as Maimonides taught, such anthropomorphic characterizations are literally incorrect.[45] Second example: God's perfections. Ask almost anyone—theist, agnostic, or atheist—about his or her concept of God and typically you will receive the same (medievally inspired) answer: God as a constellation of perfections, omnipotent, omniscient, perfectly good, etc.

These examples of the power of medieval theological thought are striking, in part because neither is in any obvious way true of the tradition in its premedieval incarnation. To begin with anthropomorphism, one does find among the rabbis considerable discomfort with anthropomorphism. But, as Kadushin points out, this is not the medieval philosophers' theoretical discomfort with the very idea of anthropomorphic characterization of God. The rabbis' hesitation has, one might say, religious rather than philosophical/theoretical motivation. God, in the rabbinic experience and imagination, is both like us (thus anthropomorphic talk) and wholly other. One has two sorts of intuitions and is not prepared to deny either, on pain of falsifying the experience. The problem for the rabbis is that anthropomorphic talk, crucial as it is, brings us to the edge of presumption, of reducing God to our terms. And this is something about which the rabbis are especially sensitive. A second and related reason for rabbinic anxiety about such talk concerns the religious intuition that when we speak of God we are in deep water, over our heads. In some quite strong sense, we don't know what we are talking about. Anthropomorphic talk, true as it is to our experience, threatens on this front as well.

The second example I gave of the power of medieval thought, the persistence of the idea that God is a constellation of perfections, requires much more discussion than I can give it here. Certainly the perfections picture, even if it awaits medieval times to become the received view, has early antecedents. Still, it is very striking how much of Bible is, in its plain meaning, at odds with the perfections picture.

There are countless biblical texts, passages in which God fails to know something, in which he changes his mind, regrets what he has done, suffers from rage and frustration. Think of the Garden of Eden and God's

---

45. When we characterize God in terms of such imagery, so the comment will often continue, we adopt the Torah's practice of "speaking in the common language," in *lashon b'nei adam* (literally, the language or vocabulary of people, "human talk"). This is a medieval analog to Bishop Berkeley's remark (on another topic) that the philosopher should speak with the vulgar, but think with the learned. The thought that in all these contexts the Bible and the rabbis are speaking "with the vulgar" is itself a medieval idea, as Halbertal and Margalit point out in Chapter 2, "Idolatry and Representation" of *Idolatry*. While we do find in the Talmud the idea that the Torah "speaks in the common language," the talmudic context is, as Halbertal and Margalit emphasize, very different and has nothing to do with anthropomorphism.

question to Adam, "Where are you?" Or God's taking moral instruction from Abraham in Genesis 17. Of course, we know how to read those passages to preserve the medieval perfections picture; we have, indeed, learned our lessons quite well. But the plain meaning of the biblical text is so often otherwise.

Not that the Bible always talks in ways that are at odds with the perfections picture: the Bible sings God's praises as, for example, being flawless. But this is poetry, a profound expression of love, awe, and gratitude, hardly a theoretical pronouncement, no more than in love poetry in which the poet declares that his lover is flawless. Clearly, according to the biblical text, God is amazingly—supremely if you like—powerful, similarly outstanding in his knowledge, character, and the rest. But this is hardly to endorse the philosophers' conception of absolute perfection. To be supreme in power is not necessarily to be theoretically unlimited in power, similarly for the other traits.

I have emphasized the lingering power of medieval philosophical theology. Indeed, one sees its influence not only in popular religious thinking, but even in Hasidism and *mussar*, which can hardly be accused of rationalism. We are dealing here, or so I want to suggest, with a phenomenon highlighted by Alasdair MacIntyre in his seminal work, *After Virtue*. MacIntyre advances his idea in connection to ethics, but I believe it to have widespread application. Our ethical thinking, he points out, is influenced by the diverse ethical approaches of our ancestors, representing many different epochs and cultures. Greek philosophy and the culture from which it emerged emphasized the social dimension of the ethical life and the virtues. A very different and more individualistic direction was pursued by Kant, who gave less play to character and virtue and more to the individual's moral duty. Later utilitarianism emphasized not the intrinsically obligatory character of an act, *à la* Kant, but the desirability of its consequences. And so on. Our own ethical thought, maintains MacIntyre, is often a kind of admixture of considerations, each having its home in some one of these approaches. An important consequence is that our thinking shows signs of incoherence bred of its sundry antecedents.

MacIntyre's remarks are suggestive with regard to many areas of philosophy, indeed, many arenas of reflective life.[46] In the present context the idea is that medieval Jewish philosophy figures as a key ingredient— admixed with others—in a not necessarily coherent overall approach.

---

46. In recent work of mine in the philosophy of language (*The Magic Prism: An Essay in the Philosophy of Language* (Oxford, 2004), I saw the MacIntyre phenomenon at work in philosophers' treatments of Frege's famous puzzle concerning the informativeness of identity statements.

Observe our religious lives, the things we find religiously moving, and comforting, the sorts of things we turn to in dark or happy times, and one finds the religious world of the Bible, midrash, aggadah. The God that is, as it were, relevant is the anthropomorphic God who feels for us, who is with us in troubled and wonderful times, with whom we share our sorrows and joys and wishes. But then ask us about our conception of God and one hears the echoes of medieval philosophy.

Perhaps it will seem as if my aim in this paper has been antiphilosophical, a plea for a return to prephilosophical theological innocence. Compare: Wittgenstein himself is often accused of being antiphilosophical. But Wittgenstein, in his critique of philosophical theorizing, evinces great respect for the illumination that philosophical reflection can provide. The problem is that philosophy is just so hard to get right; in an all-too-human way philosophers fall into characteristic traps.[47] They tend, for example, to recreate the subject matter under scrutiny in their own image, to overintellectualize the object of study. "Don't think; look" is one of Wittgenstein's characteristic exhortations. Don't think about what our practices must be like if they are to make sense (by one's philosophical lights). Instead observe; for it is actual practice that is our intellectual quarry. And this is so whether one is exploring the character of linguistic practice or the character of religious practice and religious life.

My gripe has not been that philosophers have subjected Jewish religious life—its practices and integrated structure of meanings—to philosophical scrutiny. Perhaps one could lodge such a complaint, beginning as I did with the dramatic differences between Israelite and Athenian cultures. My own complaint was different. It concerned a certain indelicacy in thinking about one culture from the point of view of another, an indelicacy that issued in a denial of the relevant differences. Maimonides' view that the prophets and even the patriarchs were philosophers is more than a perfect example.

It would be one thing to self-consciously explore and explicate the "uncrystallized" theological ideas that are so integral to Jewish religious life, bringing to bear one's favored philosophical outlook. One could appeal to aid from the neo-Kantians, or Wittgenstein, or Levinas, or for that matter Aristotle. One would then need to face a crucial question: How much and in what ways does one's favored way of thinking map on to that of the rabbis? It's quite another to claim, as is the thrust of much medieval philosophical theology, that biblical and rabbinic theological ideas are captured, virtually without remainder, by some favored philosophical explication. If one sympathetic to the medieval project were to

---

47. I hear Larry Wright's voice here.

forego this latter claim, there would remain the other problem to which I've directed attention, that Maimonidean philosophical theology substantially alters the religious sensibility of biblical/rabbinic tradition.

Here I am of two minds. On one side is the methodological idea that philosophy would do better to give up its imperialism. In my preferred picture it is the tradition itself and not philosophical criticism that dictates the character of religious life, of the religious moment. To substantially alter the traditional religious sensibility is thus to violate what might well be considered to be a condition of adequacy for a nonimperialistic philosophical account.

On the other side is the thought that drawing lines between us and them, particularly when the "them" are giants of talmudic scholarship (and, of course, full participants in the practices of the community), needs to be tempered by a welcoming of differences and new ideas. It is plausible that one of the factors in the survival of the tradition is the extreme flexibility at the interpretive level, this against the background of shared practice.[48] Not that this flexibility always comes easy, as with the case of the difficult beginnings of early Hasidism. In this spirit it is better to welcome our interpretive opponents, Maimonidean or other, as sharing an interpretive *Beit Midrash*.[49]

---

48. It is not bare practice that we share but some sort of basic understanding. What I have in mind is the sense in which right-thinking Americans agree that "all men are created equal," without any agreement about what this comes to. Similarly, it is not only bare practice that different interpretive approaches to Jewish tradition share, it is also basic (and uncrystallized) thoughts about God and Torah.

409. Thanks to Avi Ravitsky for pointing out the "with us or against us" exclusivity of an earlier draft.

STUDIES AND TEXTS IN JEWISH HISTORY AND CULTURE

The Joseph and Rebecca Meyerhoff Center for Jewish Studies
University of Maryland

General Editor: Bernard D. Cooperman

Pauline Wengeroff; translated by Henny Wenkart, edited with afterword by Bernard D. Cooperman.
ISBN: 1883053-587 (hard.), ISBN: 1883053617 (soft.); xvi + 306 pp.; 2000.